UNLOCK

Second Edition

5

Reading, Writing & Critical Thinking

STUDENT'S BOOK

Jessica Williams and Sabina Ostrowska
with Chris Sowton, Jennifer Farmer,
Christina Cavage and Wendy Asplin

CAMBRIDGE
UNIVERSITY PRESS

CAMBRIDGE
UNIVERSITY PRESS

University Printing House, Cambridge CB2 8BS, United Kingdom

One Liberty Plaza, 20th Floor, New York, NY 10006, USA

477 Williamstown Road, Port Melbourne, VIC 3207, Australia

314–321, 3rd Floor, Plot 3, Splendor Forum, Jasola District Centre, New Delhi – 110025, India

79 Anson Road, #06–04/06, Singapore 079906

Cambridge University Press is part of the University of Cambridge.

It furthers the University's mission by disseminating knowledge in the pursuit of education, learning and research at the highest international levels of excellence.

www.cambridge.org
Information on this title: www.cambridge.org/9781108593519

First published 2019

20 19 18 17 16 15 14 13 12 11 10 9 8 7 6 5 4 3 2 1

Printed in Dubai by Oriental Press

A catalogue record for this publication is available from the British Library

ISBN 978-1-108-59351-9 Reading, Writing and Critical Thinking Student's Book, Mobile App & Online Workbook 5 with Downloadable Video

CONTENTS

MAP OF THE BOOK

UNIT	VIDEO	READING	VOCABULARY	
1 CONSERVATION Reading 1: Are we living in the digital dark ages? (Information technology) Reading 2: Preserving our heritage (Urban planning)	Preserving CDs at the Library of Congress	**Key reading skills:** Identifying an argument Distinguishing fact from opinion Using your knowledge Previewing Understanding key vocabulary Reading for main ideas Reading for detail Making inferences Predicting content using visuals Synthesizing	Time expressions Compound adjectives	
2 DESIGN Reading 1: What makes a successful logo? (Marketing) Reading 2: Rebranding and logos (Marketing)	The role of Helvetica font in graphic design	**Key reading skills:** Taking notes in outline form Challenging ideas in a text Previewing Understanding key vocabulary Reading for main ideas Reading for detail Making inferences Synthesizing	Describing emotional responses	
3 PRIVACY Reading 1: Cyber harassment (Ethics/Law) Reading 2: Combatting cyber harassment (Ethics/Law)	The Safer Internet campaign	**Key reading skills:** Previewing a text Identifying perspective and purpose Using your knowledge Understanding key vocabulary Previewing Reading for main ideas Reading for detail Identifying purpose Synthesizing	Collocations for behaviour Problem–solution collocations	
4 BUSINESS Reading 1: Starting out mobile (Business management) Reading 2: Keeping your customers (Marketing)	Small Business Saturday	**Key reading skills:** Working out meaning from context Using your knowledge Understanding key vocabulary Previewing Reading for main ideas Working out meaning from context Summarizing Making inferences Synthesizing	Business and marketing vocabulary	
5 PSYCHOLOGY Reading 1: The creative mind (Psychology) Reading 2: Can we learn to be more creative? (Psychology)	Lego artist Nathan Sawaya	**Key reading skills:** Annotating a text Interpreting quotes Understanding key vocabulary Previewing Reading for main ideas Annotating Making inferences Predicting content using visuals Using your knowledge Summarizing Synthesizing	Experimental science terminology	

GRAMMAR	CRITICAL THINKING	WRITING
Grammar for writing: First and second conditionals	Evaluating facts to build support for an argument	*Academic writing skills:* Paragraph structure and unity Impersonal statements *Writing task type:* Write an argumentative essay *Writing task:* Make and support an argument for what to do with an ageing but culturally or historically significant area or neighbourhood in your city or country.
Paraphrasing *Grammar for writing:* Non-defining relative clauses Appositives	Determining and applying criteria	*Academic writing skills:* Structuring a summary–response essay Writing a conclusion *Writing task type:* Write a summary–response essay *Writing task:* Summarize criteria and then analyze a logo in terms of those criteria.
Grammar for writing: Impersonal passive constructions Passive for continuity	Analyzing problems and solutions	*Academic writing skills:* Writing about problems Writing about solutions *Writing task type:* Write a problem–solution essay *Writing task:* Describe an online behaviour that you think is problematic and explain what you think should be done to prevent or eliminate it.
Expressing contrast *Grammar for writing:* Reductions of subordinate clauses	Analyzing advantages and disadvantages	*Academic writing skills:* Writing about similarities and differences *Writing task type:* Write a compare and contrast essay *Writing task:* Compare and contrast two products or services regarding their potential as a mobile business.
Grammar for writing: Complex noun phrases with *what*	Synthesizing information from more than one text	*Academic writing skills:* Citing quoted material Writing an expository essay *Writing task type:* Write an expository essay *Writing task:* What is creative thinking? Explain the current understanding of this concept, synthesizing information from different sources.

UNIT	VIDEO	READING	VOCABULARY	
6 CAREERS Reading 1: The skills gap (Education) Reading 2: What is the value of a university education? (Education/Business)	Vocational training	*Key reading skills:* Interpreting graphical information Predicting content using visuals Previewing Understanding key vocabulary Reading for main ideas Reading for detail Identifying purpose Making inferences Synthesizing	Compound nouns	
7 HEALTH SCIENCES Reading 1: Superbugs (Medicine) Reading 2: The globalization of infection (Medicine)	Growing concerns over antibiotic usage and resistance	*Key reading skills:* Recognizing discourse organization Using your knowledge Understanding key vocabulary Reading for main ideas Understanding discourse Reading for detail Scanning to predict content Making inferences Synthesizing	Verbs and verb phrases for causation Word families	
8 COLLABORATION Reading 1: The value of talent (Business / Sports management) Reading 2: The perfect work team (Business)	Behind the scenes look at the RAF Red Arrows	*Key reading skills:* Using context clues to understand terminology Using context clues to understand fixed expressions Previewing Understanding key vocabulary Reading for main ideas Summarizing Reading for detail Working out meaning from context Using your knowledge Synthesizing	Language for hedging	
9 TECHNOLOGY Reading 1: AR: Changing the world around us (Design / Technology) Reading 2: AR in education – A positive or negative development? (Education)	Phone hacking	*Key reading skills:* Drawing out common themes Predicting content using visuals Understanding key vocabulary Reading for main ideas Summarizing Distinguishing fact from opinion Using your knowledge Working out meaning from context Synthesizing	Reporting expert opinions	
10 LANGUAGE Reading 1: Loanwords in English (Linguistics) Reading 2: Linguistic purism and English as a global language (Linguistics/Sociology)	Irish	*Key reading skills:* Using background knowledge to annotate a text Understanding key vocabulary Using your knowledge Reading for main ideas Reading for detail Making inferences Working out meaning from context Synthesizing	Latin prefixes in academic English	

GRAMMAR	CRITICAL THINKING	WRITING
Grammar for writing: Active vs. passive voice to discuss figures	Analyzing information in graphs and other figures	*Academic writing skills:* Making a claim *Writing task type:* Write an argumentative essay with graphical support *Writing task:* What is a good choice for a career path with a secure future?
Grammar for writing: Cause and effect: logical connectors	Analyzing causes and effects	*Academic writing skills:* Writing about causes and effects *Writing task type:* Write a cause-and-effect essay *Writing task:* Choose one infectious disease and discuss the factors that may have contributed to its development and spread or could do so in the future.
Grammar for writing: Concession and refutation	Understanding audience and purpose	*Academic writing skills:* Anticipating counter-arguments *Writing task type:* Write a report giving recommendations *Writing task:* Present your recommendations for assembling and organizing an effective and satisfied team for a start-up company.
It clefts *Grammar for writing:* Parenthetical phrases Using the semicolon	Constructing an argument using a premise	*Academic writing skills:* Formal style in academic writing *Writing task type:* Write an argumentative essay *Writing task:* Make and support an argument as to whether the use of a particular technology in education will have a positive or negative impact on learning outcomes.
Highlighting supporting examples *Grammar for writing:* Hedging predictions	Evaluating and synthesizing arguments	*Academic writing skills:* Avoiding overgeneralizations Refuting counter-arguments *Writing task type:* Write a pros and cons essay *Writing task:* Write an essay on the pros and cons of English-medium university education in your country or another country that you know well.

YOUR GUIDE TO
UNLOCK

Unlock your academic potential

Unlock Second Edition is a six-level, academic-light English course created to build the skills and language students need for their studies (CEFR Pre-A1 to C1). It develops students' ability to think critically in an academic context right from the start of their language learning. Every level has 100% new inspiring video on a range of academic topics.

Confidence in teaching.
Joy in learning.

Better Learning WITH UNLOCK SECOND EDITION

Better Learning is our simple approach where insights we've gained from research have helped shape content that drives results. We've listened to teachers all around the world and made changes so that *Unlock* Second Edition better supports students along the way to academic success.

CRITICAL THINKING

Critical thinking in *Unlock* Second Edition ...

- is **informed** by a range of academic research from Bloom in the 1950s, to Krathwohl and Anderson in the 2000s, to more recent considerations relating to 21st Century Skills
- has a **refined** syllabus with a better mix of higher- and lower-order critical thinking skills
- is **measurable**, with objectives and self-evaluation so students can track their critical thinking progress
- is **transparent** so teachers and students know when and why they're developing critical thinking skills
- is **supported** with professional development material for teachers so teachers can teach with confidence

... so that students have the best possible chance of **academic success.**

INSIGHT

Most classroom time is currently spent on developing lower-order critical thinking skills. Students need to be able to use higher-order critical thinking skills too.

CONTENT

Unlock Second Edition includes the right mix of lower- and higher-order thinking skills development in every unit, with clear learning objectives.

RESULTS

Students are better prepared for their academic studies and have the confidence to apply the critical thinking skills they have developed.

CLASSROOM APP

The *Unlock* Second Edition Classroom App ...

- offers extra, **motivating** practice in speaking, critical thinking and language
- provides a **convenient** bank of language and skills reference informed by our exclusive Corpus research
- is easily **accessible** and **navigable** from students' mobile phones
- is fully **integrated** into every unit
- provides Unlock-**specific** activities to extend the lesson whenever you see this symbol 📱PLUS

... so that students can easily get the right, extra practice they need, when they need it.

INSIGHT

The learning material on a Classroom app is most effective when it's an integral, well-timed part of a lesson.

CONTENT

Every unit of *Unlock* Second Edition is enhanced with bespoke Classroom app material to extend the skills and language students are learning in the book. The symbol 📱PLUS shows when to use the app.

RESULTS

Students are motivated by having relevant extension material on their mobile phones to maximize their language learning. Teachers are reassured that the Classroom App adds real language-learning value to their lessons.

RESEARCH

We have gained deeper insights to inform *Unlock* Second Edition by ...

- carrying out **extensive market research** with teachers and students to fully understand their needs throughout the course's development
- consulting **academic research** into critical thinking
- refining our vocabulary syllabus using our **exclusive Corpus research** ◉

... so that you can be assured of the quality of *Unlock* Second Edition.

INSIGHT

- Consultation with global Advisory Panel
- Comprehensive reviews of material
- Face-to-face interviews and Skype™ calls
- Classroom observations

CONTENT

- Improved critical thinking
- 100% new video and video lessons
- Clearer contexts for language presentation and practice
- Text-by-text glossaries
- More supportive writing sections
- Online Workbooks with more robust content
- Comprehensive teacher support

RESULTS

"Thank you for all the effort you've put into developing Unlock Second Edition. As far as I can see, I think the new edition is more academic and more appealing to young adults."

Burçin Gönülsen,
Işık Üniversity, Turkey

Unlock your knowledge

Encourages discussion around the themes of the unit with inspiration from interesting questions and striking images.

UNLOCK YOUR KNOWLEDGE

Work with a partner. Discuss the questions.

1 Which of the languages in the box are global languages? Which ones may become even more important in the future? Why?

> Hindi   Russian   Chinese   Spanish   Arabic

2 What are the benefits of knowing a number of languages?
3 In your opinion, are some languages easier to learn than others? Give examples.
4 What problems would somebody face when learning your language?

Watch and listen

Features an engaging and motivating video which generates interest in the topic and develops listening skills.

WATCH AND LISTEN

ACTIVATING YOUR KNOWLEDGE

PREPARING TO WATCH

1 You are going to watch a video about the Irish language. Before you watch, work with a partner. Discuss the questions.

1 Where is Ireland?
2 What do you know about the history of the relationship between

READING

Reading 1

The first text offers students the opportunity to develop the reading skills required to process academic texts, and presents and practises the vocabulary needed to comprehend the text itself.

READING

READING 1

UNDERSTANDING KEY VOCABULARY

PREPARING TO READ

1 You are going to read the introduction to a linguistics textbook about loanwords. Read the words and their definitions. Use the correct form of the words in bold to complete the sentences below.

be derived from (phr v) to come from a particular origin
commodity (n) product you can buy or sell
commonly (adj) frequently, usually
conquer (v) to take control of a country or people, or defeat by war
dialect (n) a local, usually spoken, form of a language

Reading 2

Presents a second text which provides a different angle on the topic and serves as a model text for the writing task.

READING 2

UNDERSTANDING KEY VOCABULARY

PREPARING TO READ

1 You are going to read an essay about English loanwords entering other languages. Read the sentences. Write the correct form of the words in bold next to their definitions below.

1 Many people believe that our leaders should take a stronger **stance** on maintaining standards for our language.
2 I fully **endorse** the necessary steps that the government is taking to simplify our spelling rules.
3 The book we read about the history of English **distorted** the facts. What really happened was very different.

Language development

Consolidates and expands on the language presented in preparation for the writing task.

◎ LANGUAGE DEVELOPMENT

LATIN PREFIXES IN ACADEMIC ENGLISH

Understanding the meaning of some common prefixes can help you with the meaning of new words.

prefix	meaning	examples
inter-	between, among	interaction (n), intervene (v), intercontinental (adj), interpretation (n), interface (n)

WRITING

Critical thinking

Develops the lower- and higher-order thinking skills required for the writing task.

WRITING

CRITICAL THINKING

At the end of this unit, you will write a pros and cons essay. Look at this unit's writing task in the box below.

> In the last century, English has become a global language, the lingua franca of science, technology, business and education. Its global dominance has affected other cultures and languages in various ways.

Grammar for writing

Presents and practises grammatical structures and features needed for the writing task.

GRAMMAR FOR WRITING

HEDGING PREDICTIONS

Predictions about the future will always require supporting evidence. However, even when you do provide such evidence, it is usually a good idea to avoid making claims which are too bold or overly general. To hedge claims about the future, use these modal verbs and other expressions of probability to hedge your predictions:

| tentative certainty | should / may well / be (highly) likely to / be (highly) unlikely to |
| possibility | could / might / have the potential to |

French scientists and IT experts had already begun using the technology and the accompanying English term. It is likely that many will continue to do so.

Academic writing skills

Practises all the writing skills needed for the writing task.

ACADEMIC WRITING SKILLS

AVOIDING OVERGENERALIZATIONS

To avoid overgeneralization in academic writing, make sure that your statements are true in all cases. If not, you may need to modify your claims or provide evidence to prove them.
Students don't know enough English to understand the material.
All cutting-edge research is published in English.
These statements are too general. You can modify them by being more specific.
Most of the students don't know enough English to understand.

Writing task

Uses the skills and language learned throughout the unit to support students in drafting, producing and editing a piece of academic writing. This is the unit's main learning objective.

WRITING TASK

> In the last century, English has become a global language, the lingua franca of science, technology, business and education. Its global dominance has affected other cultures and languages in various ways. One outcome has been an increase in the use of English as the language of instruction in universities that had previously used the local or national language. Write an essay on the pros and cons of English-medium university education in your country or another country that you know well.

PLAN

1 In a pros and cons essay you must present a balanced view. Review your notes in the Critical thinking section on page 246. Choose the three strongest arguments related to EMI in your country. Write each of them as a topic sentence in the table.

| Argument 1 |
| Topic sentence: |

Objectives review

Allows students to evaluate how well they have mastered the skills covered in the unit.

OBJECTIVES REVIEW

1 Check your learning objectives for this unit. Write 3, 2 or 1 for each objective.

3 = very well   2 = well   1 = not so well

I can ...

watch and understand a video about languages in Ireland.   ____

use background knowledge to annotate a text.   ____

evaluate and synthesize arguments.   ____

hedge predictions.   ____

2 Go to the *Unlock* Online Workbook for more practice with this unit's learning objectives.

Wordlist

Lists the key vocabulary from the unit. The most frequent words used at this level in an academic context are highlighted. ⊙

WORDLIST

be derived from (phr v)	displace (v)	it follows that (phr)
coexist (v)	disproportionate (adj)	misguided (adj)
cofounder (n)	distasteful (adj)	namely (adv) ⊙
coincide (v) ⊙	distort (v)	postdate (v)
collaborate (v)	endorse (v)	postgraduate (adj)
commodity (n) ⊙	enforce (v) ⊙	postpone (v)
commonly (adj) ⊙	equivalent (n) ⊙	postwar (adj) ⊙
conquer (v)	futile (adj)	precede (v)
cooperation (n) ⊙	incorporate (v) ⊙	preliminary (adj) ⊙
dialect (n) ⊙	interact (v) ⊙	presume (v)
dilution (n) ⊙	interaction (n) ⊙	stance (n) ⊙
disambiguation (n)	intercontinental (adj)	terminology (n) ⊙
discourage (v)	interface (n) ⊙	

COMPONENTS

Unlock offers 56 hours per Student's Book, which is extendable to 90 hours with the Classroom App, Online Workbook and other additional activities in the Teacher's Manual and Development Pack.

Unlock is a paired-skills course with two separate Student's Books per level. For levels 1–5 (CEFR A1 – C1), these are **Reading, Writing and Critical Thinking** and **Listening, Speaking and Critical Thinking**. They share the same unit topics so you have access to a wide range of material at each level. Each Student's Book provides access to the Classroom App and Online Workbook.

Unlock Basic has been developed for pre-A1 learners. **Unlock Basic Skills** integrates reading, writing, listening, speaking and critical thinking in one book to provide students with an effective and manageable learning experience. **Unlock Basic Literacy** develops and builds confidence in literacy. The *Basic* books also share the same unit topics and so can be used together or separately, and **Unlock Basic Literacy** can be used for self-study.

Student components

Resource	Description	Access

Student's Books	• Levels 1–5 come with Classroom App, Online Workbook, and downloadable audio and video
	  – Levels 1–4 (8 units)
	  – Level 5 (10 units)
	• *Unlock Basic Skills* comes with downloadable audio and video (11 units)
	• *Unlock Basic Literacy* comes with downloadable audio (11 units)
		• The Classroom App and Online Workbook are on the **CLMS** and are accessed via the unique code inside the front cover of the Student's Book
		• The audio and video are downloadable from the Resources tab on the **CLMS**

Online Workbook	• Levels 1–5 only • Extension activities to further practise the language and skills learned • All-new vocabulary activities in the Online Workbooks practise the target vocabulary in new contexts	• The Online Workbook is on the **CLMS** and is accessed via the unique code inside the front cover of the Student's Book
Classroom App	• Levels 1–5 only • Extra practice in speaking, critical thinking and language	• The app is downloadable from the **Apple App Store** or **Google Play** • Students use the same login details as for the **CLMS**, and then they are logged in for a year
Video	• Levels 1–5 and *Unlock Basic Skills* only • All the video from the course	• The video is downloadable from the Resources tab on the **CLMS**
Audio	• All the audio from the course	• The audio is downloadable from the Resources tab on the **CLMS** and from **cambridge.org/unlock**

Teacher components

Resource	Description	Access
Teacher's Manual and Development Pack	• One manual covers Levels 1–5 • It contains flexible lesson plans, lesson objectives, additional activities and common learner errors as well as professional development for teachers, *Developing critical thinking skills in your students* • It comes with downloadable audio and video, vocabulary worksheets and peer-to-peer teacher training worksheets	• The audio, video and worksheets are downloadable from the Resources tab on the **CLMS** and from **eSource** via the code inside the front cover of the manual
Presentation Plus	• Software for interactive whiteboards so you can present the pages of the Student's Books and easily play audio and video, and check answers	• Please contact your sales rep for codes to download Presentation Plus from **eSource**

   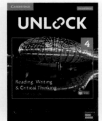 

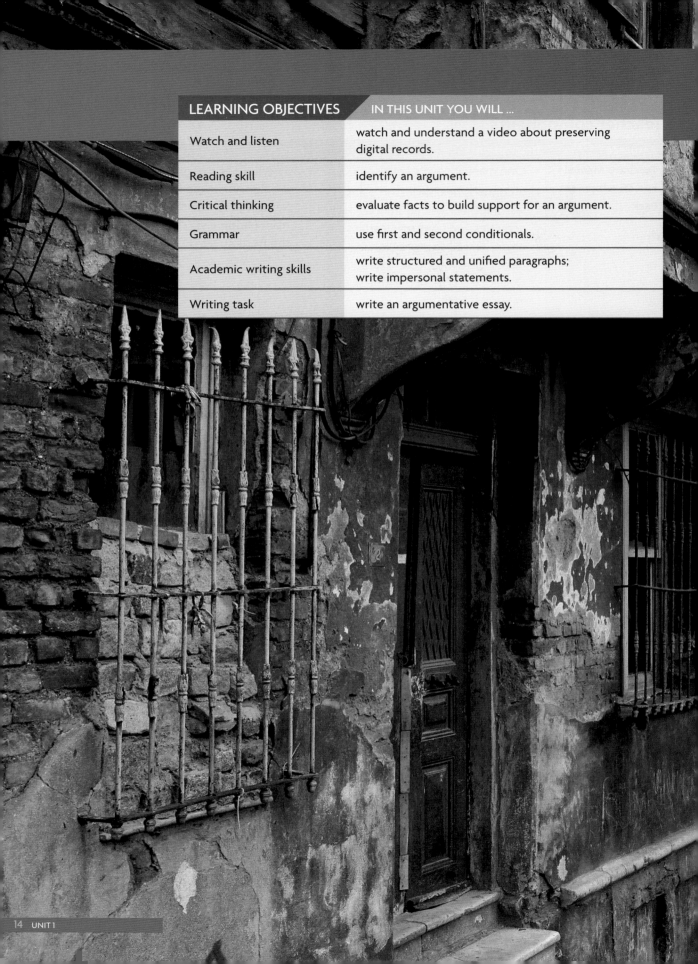

LEARNING OBJECTIVES	IN THIS UNIT YOU WILL ...
Watch and listen	watch and understand a video about preserving digital records.
Reading skill	identify an argument.
Critical thinking	evaluate facts to build support for an argument.
Grammar	use first and second conditionals.
Academic writing skills	write structured and unified paragraphs; write impersonal statements.
Writing task	write an argumentative essay.

CONSERVATION

UNLOCK YOUR KNOWLEDGE

Work with a partner. Discuss the questions.

1 Do you like to visit old buildings or museums that show something about our past? Why / Why not?

2 How important is it to preserve things from the past, such as buildings, records and art? Is preserving the past more important than creating new things?

3 What kind of things do you have in your family home that you would like to share with future generations of your family?

PLUS

PREPARING TO WATCH

ACTIVATING YOUR KNOWLEDGE

1 Work with a partner. Discuss the questions.

    1 Do you own a collection of music or films? If so, is it stored on discs in your home, in a digital download folder on your computer or in the cloud?

    2 Do you still have any CDs or DVDs? How long do you think they will last?

    3 What could you do to preserve your CDs and DVDs? What other belongings do you have that might need to be preserved?

PREDICTING CONTENT USING VISUALS

2 You are going to watch a video about preservation work in the US Library of Congress. Look at the photos and discuss the questions with a partner.

    1 What problem do you think the woman is investigating?

    2 Why do you think it is a problem?

    3 What do you think will be learned from the research the woman is doing?

GLOSSARY

Library of Congress (n) the national library of the United States

posterity (n) the people who exist in the future

figure out (US phr v) work out

degrade (v) to reduce the quality of something

longevity (n) how long a person or group of people lives, or how long a physical thing generally lasts; lifespan

fancy (adj) special, elaborate

Sharpie (n) a brand of permanent marker pen

WHILE WATCHING

3 ▶ Watch the video and check your predictions from Exercise 2. Which sentence best expresses the main idea of the video?

UNDERSTANDING MAIN IDEAS

1 The Library of Congress is testing the longevity of CDs every three to five years.

2 CDs are being aged to help learn which type of manufacturing is best for CD development.

3 How a CD is manufactured, how it has been handled and how it has been stored all affect its longevity.

4 ▶ Watch the video again. Write a detail for each main idea.

UNDERSTANDING DETAIL

1 Fenella France and her colleagues are studying the preservation of CDs.

_____

2 To test CD durability, the Library of Congress is accelerating ageing.

_____

3 There are several things people can do to preserve their CDs at home.

_____

5 Work with a partner. Discuss the questions.

MAKING INFERENCES

1 Why is it important for the Library of Congress to understand CD preservation?

2 What other items might the Preservation Research and Testing Division of the Library of Congress be researching and testing?

3 What kinds of conditions might negatively affect old books, CDs, films, etc.? How might researchers go about testing these items under different conditions?

4 What is the general importance of preserving items for posterity?

DISCUSSION

6 Work with a partner. Discuss the questions.

1 France offered suggestions on ways to preserve CDs. Will you pass the advice along to anybody? If so, who?

2 What are some other items that are being preserved in national libraries or museums?

3 Is there a value in preserving items in their original format? Why not transfer the information to a new form of technology and discard the original thing?

4 Can we really learn from the past? Or do we learn just as much when we focus on the present and the future?

READING

READING 1

PREPARING TO READ

USING YOUR
KNOWLEDGE

1 You are going to read an article about storing records. Look at the list of types of record in the left-hand column of the table below. Add six more examples of your own. Then tick (✔) where you store each type of thing. Compare your answers with a partner.

type of record	in a box or drawer	on my phone/ tablet	in the cloud	I throw them away / delete them.
old school records				
family photos				
bank statements				
holiday selfies				
medical records				
receipts from major purchases				
playlists of music				

2 Work with a partner. Discuss the questions.

1 Think about items in the table in Exercise 1. How long do you think these records will last? Do you think your grandchildren will be able to access them? Your great-grandchildren? Why / Why not?

2 Look at the title of the article on page 20. What does the word *digital* mean there? Give some examples of digital devices that you use. What are some digital devices that are no longer widely used – perhaps devices that your parents used?

3 *The Dark Ages* is the term used to refer to Europe from about the fifth to the tenth century. We have very few records from this time, so it is difficult to find out about how people lived then. How do you think *digital* could be related to *the Dark Ages*? What do you think the title means?

3 Read the sentences. Write the correct form of the words in bold (1–8) next to their definitions below (a–h).

1 The internet is not working so I have been unable to **retrieve** the files I uploaded yesterday.

2 Many employees have still not adopted the **practice** of saving their work regularly.

3 The company has been in business for almost 200 years. Its **longevity** is a result of the quality of its products and service.

4 You need to use the same document format as the rest of us. The one you are using is not **compatible**.

5 Your computer files are **vulnerable** if you do not protect them by using a strong password.

6 We are working on two different possible **scenarios**: one, if our business grows slowly, and the other, if success comes more quickly.

7 Problems with security **prompted** software designers to make major changes to the new version of the program.

8 The cupboard was filled with boxes of **memorabilia** from my childhood and the early years of my parents' marriage.

a _____ (adj) not well protected; able to be harmed

b _____ (n) something that is usually or regularly done

c _____ (v) to make someone decide to do something

d _____ (n) how long something lasts

e _____ (n) a description of a current or future situation

f _____ (v) to find and bring something back

g _____ (n) a collection of items connected to a person or event

h _____ (adj) able to work successfully with something else

ARE WE LIVING IN THE DIGITAL DARK AGES?

1 Imagine these **scenarios**: (1) 2040: A box of **memorabilia**, including floppy disks and VHS tapes[1], is found in the attic of an old house with a label that says, 'Records and early videos of Bill Gates (1975–1985)'. (2) 2050: You find an envelope labelled 'bank records' in your grandmother's desk. Inside the envelope, there is an old CD marked with the date 1998, your great-grandfather's name, and the words 'all overseas bank accounts'.

2 If these stories were really to happen, the people who found these items would be very excited – at least at first. Their excitement would be quickly followed by frustration because it would be difficult for them to **retrieve** the information on the disks and tapes. Even if the records were still in good condition, it would be hard to find a device that could read them. Compare these discoveries to one that might have occurred around the turn of the twentieth century: a box of old letters and photographs on a high shelf at the back of a cupboard. The information these items contain would be immediately accessible because you would only need your eyes.

3 Computers and digital technology have vastly expanded our capacity to store all kinds of information, but how long will our access to this stored information last? In fact, the people who found the disks and tapes in our scenarios would be lucky because disks and tapes are physically real. Although those technologies are long out of date, it's information on the web that is much more **vulnerable**; it is completely digital and can disappear in a flash. This is a problem that began to worry technology experts in the early twenty-first century. They became concerned that, without better ways of preserving information, future generations might look back on our times as the 'digital dark ages'. If current **practice** continues, future generations may not have access to the digital record of our lives and our world.

4 Vint Cerf, a vice president at Google, argues that this could happen if we do not quickly take steps to address the issue. He uses the term 'bit rot' to describe how our digital records may slowly but surely become inaccessible. In our scenarios, for example, it is not the **longevity** of the records themselves that is the concern; it is that we may no longer have **compatible** devices, such as video cassette and CD players, to access them. Most software and apps that were used to create documents and websites ten or twenty years ago are already out of date, and in another sixty years they may not even be available. The problem is particularly challenging with interactive apps and websites. We can read letters from long ago, but will we be able to read a Twitter feed or access a Snapchat exchange a hundred years from now?

5 This problem has **prompted** technology experts like computer scientist Mahadev Satyanarayanan of Carnegie Mellon University to take action. He has found a way to store everything that is needed to interpret a record – the record itself, as well as the original operating system and the application it used – all together in the cloud. Using his state-of-the-art approach, Satyanarayanan has been able to recover and preserve digital records that might otherwise have been lost forever.

6 Both Cerf and Satyanarayanan stress the importance of deliberate preservation. In the past, you could throw your old photos into a box without having to decide what to save and what to throw away. With digital records, however, you need to make an active decision about what to keep. Satyanarayanan says it is likely that important records – government documents, big news stories, etc. – will be transferred to new forms of storage technology as they emerge. It is the records of everyday life, the ones we do not yet know the value of, that may disappear into the digital dark ages.

[1]**floppy disks and VHS tapes** (n) early forms of electronic media storage

WHILE READING

Identifying an argument

Most academic texts put forward a *claim*. It is important to be able to identify the central claim in a text because this is the most important thing the writer is trying to express. Once you have identified the claim, the next step is to understand the ways that the author supports that argument. This will help you evaluate the strength and quality of the claim. Three common ways to support an argument are to (1) appeal to the reader's **emotions**, (2) rely on the words of an **expert** and, perhaps most common, (3) present **facts**.

4 Read the article. Complete the tasks.

READING FOR MAIN IDEAS

1 Which sentence best captures the writer's central claim?
   a Digital technology is not keeping up with the need to save records.
   b It would be easier to keep records if we made a physical copy of everything.
   c We are not preserving our digital records, so our history may be lost.
   d As our capacity to store records increases, we have to throw more things away.

2 Underline the sentence in the article that expresses this claim.

5 Read the article again. Complete the tasks.

READING FOR DETAIL

1 The writer begins with two examples to illustrate the central claim. What are they? Underline them in the article.

2 Read the extracts from the article below. What kind of support do they provide for the claim: emotional appeal (EA), expertise (E) or facts (F)?
   a If common practice continues, future generations may not have access to the digital record of our lives and our world. _____
   b Vint Cerf, a vice president at Google, argues that this could happen if we do not quickly take steps to address the issue. He uses the term 'bit rot' to describe how our digital records may slowly but surely become inaccessible. _____
   c Most software and apps that were used to create documents and websites ten or twenty years ago are already out of date. _____
   d Satyanarayanan says it is likely that important records – government documents, big news stories, etc. – will be transferred to new forms of storage technology as they emerge. _____
   e It is the records of everyday life, the ones we do not yet know the value of, that may disappear into the digital dark ages. _____

6 Reread Paragraph 4. Circle two problems with our current practices that Vint Cerf points out.

1 Physical records take up much more space than digital records.
2 The devices necessary to read our records will not be available.
3 Software used to create applications goes out of date quickly.
4 We may not have access to the cloud in the future.
5 It is not possible to preserve interactive applications such as Snapchat and Twitter.

7 Read the article again. Write *T* (true), *F* (false) or *DNS* (does not say) next to the statements below. Then correct the false statements.

_____ 1 Some early records of Bill Gates were recently found.
_____ 2 The capacity to store a lot of digital records does not guarantee future access to them.
_____ 3 Maintaining access to out-of-date interactive applications is particularly difficult.
_____ 4 Google is working on this problem and will reveal their solution soon.
_____ 5 Satyanarayanan has been working on this problem, but has not been able to solve it.
_____ 6 All government records are currently stored in the cloud.

READING BETWEEN THE LINES

MAKING INFERENCES

8 Work with a partner. Discuss the questions.

1 In Paragraph 2, the writer states, 'the people who found these items would be very excited – at least at first.' Why would they be excited?
2 Why does the writer make a comparison to *the Dark Ages*?
3 What do you think the term *bit rot* means? Think about the meaning of a *bit* in the digital world.
4 Why is it more difficult to preserve a conversation thread on Twitter than a letter?

DISCUSSION

9 Work with a partner. Discuss the questions.

1 Have you ever found a box of memorabilia? If so, describe what you found. How did you feel as you looked through it?
2 The article talks about the need to make deliberate decisions about the kinds of records to save for future generations. What would you pick from your own life? From your family? From your community?

PREPARING TO READ

1 Read the title of the text on page 24 and look at the photos. Read the definition of the word *heritage* at the bottom of page 24 and answer the questions below.

1 How do you think the text will address the issue of heritage?
2 How do you think heritage can or should be preserved?
3 What are some of the most important aspects of your heritage?

2 Read the sentences and choose the best definition for the words in bold.

1 He lived in an **anonymous** apartment, just like all the other ones around it.
   a having no unusual or interesting features
   b without a name
   c far from the centre of life and activity
2 Many old buildings have the potential for **adaptive** reuse, for example as hotels, restaurants or shops.
   a having the potential to survive in difficult conditions
   b having the best solution to many possible problems
   c having the ability to change when conditions change
3 We couldn't decide whether to live in a house or apartment, but in the end, **opted for** the convenience of apartment living.
   a chose   b preferred   c considered carefully
4 Having considered the age and condition of the building, the owners have decided that **demolition** of the building is the only option.
   a destruction   b painting   c sale
5 The **renovation** of the old building to keep it as it once was is going to be very expensive.
   a the replacement of an old building with a new one
   b the repair of a building to bring it into good condition
   c investment of money in an old building
6 This is a very **affluent** neighbourhood, where most residents have an income that is double the national average.
   a developing quickly   b protected by the government   c rich
7 Thanks to the enthusiasm of the locals, this remains a **vibrant** community despite the challenges that it has faced over the years.
   a lively and energetic   b fortunate   c diverse
8 Chemicals from the power plant have caused **irreversible** damage to the lake. There's nothing we can do to save the animals that live there.
   a very serious
   b very unattractive
   c impossible to change back

PLUS

Preserving our heritage[1]

a *mashrabiya* window

1 Everywhere I look, there are new buildings under construction. The neighbourhoods that I knew as a boy, filled with beautiful old buildings, have mostly disappeared, and in their place, **anonymous**, modern, high-rise buildings have appeared. If we continue in this way, nothing will remain of our heritage; soon I will no longer recognize my city. What is left of the city's traditional buildings and neighbourhoods must be preserved and it is imperative that this process begins now.

2 Historic preservation has become popular all over the world in recent years, but many countries in the Middle East, with a few important exceptions, have **opted for demolition** and new construction over preservation. There is good reason for this; as the population has become more **affluent**, residents want all the conveniences of modern living. However, the built environment[2] should be more than shiny new buildings with air conditioning and washing machines; it should also reflect the beauty of our culture and heritage. How can our children understand and maintain their cultural identity if we erase so much of the physical evidence of it? Will they recognize a *barjeel*, the wind towers that once provided natural air conditioning for buildings all over the region? Will they understand the significance of *mashrabiyas*, the delicately carved wooden windows that provide a screen against the outside world? Not if they have all disappeared.

3 The arguments for preserving historic buildings are not simply about an emotional attachment to the past. There are also good economic arguments in favour of preservation. The **renovation** and preservation of historic districts can become an economic engine, drawing tourists and small businesses to the area. There are several good examples of this in the Middle East. In Dubai, the historic *Al Bastikiya* district draws thousands of tourists every year from all over the world. It also attracts local residents, eager to learn about their city's past. In Bahrain, the hundred-year-old *Beit al Jasra* was at one time the summer home of a sheikh[3]. It has been beautifully restored and is now a centre for traditional crafts, such as rug weaving and basket making. International visitors are not only interested in shopping centres; they also want to learn about our culture and traditions like these.

4 *Al Bastikiya* and *Beit al Jasra* are successful tourist attractions with exhibits, galleries and boutiques. Renovated for this purpose, they are not intended to be functioning communities for local residents. However, it is also possible to preserve old buildings and adapt them for reuse by the local community. In Bahrain, buildings in a historic district of the city of Muharraq have been restored, and today they are part of a **vibrant** neighbourhood of homes, small shops and businesses contributing to the nation's economy.

a *barjeel* tower

5 Some opponents of historic preservation have argued that it is too expensive, but many recent projects all over the world have demonstrated that this is not necessarily the case. In fact, renovation of an existing structure for **adaptive** reuse can cost about £40 per square metre less than even the most basic new construction, while preserving the beauty of the original building. And, although it is often claimed that old buildings have a more significant environmental footprint[4] than new construction because they aren't very energy efficient, architects and environmental experts maintain that the greenest building is the one that is already built. New construction almost always has a more serious environmental impact because it requires the use of all-new materials that must be transported, often over long distances, instead of recycled materials that are already on site. We recycle so many other things. We can and should recycle buildings, too.

6 Historic preservation is an option that opens many possibilities; demolition, in contrast, is **irreversible**. Once these treasures are lost, they are lost forever, an important link in our heritage that can never be recovered.

---

[1]heritage (n) features belonging to the culture of a particular society, such as traditions, languages or buildings, that were created in the past and still have historical importance
[2]built environment (n phr) man-made setting for human activity, including buildings, parks and roads
[3]sheikh (n) an Arab ruler or head of a group of people
[4]environmental footprint (n phr) the impact something or someone has on the environment

WHILE READING

3 Read the article. Then complete the tasks.

READING FOR MAIN IDEAS

1 What is the author trying to persuade his readers to do?
   a provide money to renovate important old buildings
   b support the preservation of historic buildings in the city
   c help him to stop all the new construction in the city
2 Highlight a sentence in the article that expresses the author's argument.
3 According to the author, what are the consequences of not accepting his argument?
4 Highlight a sentence in the article that expresses these consequences.

4 Read the article again. Then complete the tasks.

READING FOR DETAIL

1 What kind of support does the author provide for his argument? Underline facts and circle support that includes expertise.
2 What emotional appeals does the author use to support his argument? Summarize the emotional appeal in one or two sentences.

   _____

   _____

3 Why does the author use the examples of the *barjeel* and *mashrabiya*?

   _____

   _____

4 What reasons does the author give for the value of historic preservation? Circle all of the answers that are correct.
   a Preservation makes economic sense.
   b Renovated buildings can provide much needed housing.
   c Preserving buildings creates less environmental damage than building new ones.
   d Preservation provides employment.
   e Preservation of historic buildings promotes tourism.
   f If we lose all our old buildings, we may also lose our identity.
   g Historic buildings are more beautiful than new ones.
   h It is often less expensive to renovate old buildings than to build new ones.
   i Adapting old buildings for new uses connects us to our history and culture.
5 Find sentences in the article that express each of the reasons you circled in 4. Compare your work with a partner's.

READING BETWEEN THE LINES

Distinguishing fact from opinion

Writers often present their arguments as a combination of facts and opinions. It is important to be able to distinguish them. Opinions often contain first person references (*I, we*), modal verbs (*must, should, need*), and verbs of belief (*think, believe*). Writers may also ask questions in an effort to persuade readers to accept their arguments.

DISTINGUISHING FACT FROM OPINION

5 Work with a partner. Answer the questions.

1 Review the list of reasons you chose in Exercise 4, question 4. Which of these reasons is supported by facts? Which ones represent the author's opinion?
2 Which of the signposts of opinion occur in the article?
   a first person references **c** verbs of belief
   b modal verbs **d** questions

MAKING INFERENCES

6 Work with a partner. Discuss the questions.

1 Why does the author object to 'anonymous, modern, high-rise buildings'?
2 What does the author mean when he says *Al Bastikiya* and *Beit al Jasra* were 'not intended to be functioning communities for local residents'?
3 Do you think the author prefers the approach to preservation in *Al Bastikiya,* or the adaptive reuse of buildings in Muharraq? What makes you think so? Do you agree with him?
4 What does the statement 'the greenest building is the one that is already built' mean?
5 How does the author see the relationship between buildings and culture? Do you agree with him?

DISCUSSION

SYNTHESIZING

7 Work with a partner. Use ideas from Reading 1 and Reading 2 to answer the following questions.

1 Do you think it is better to try to preserve old buildings or tear them down to make way for new ones? Would you give a different answer if the buildings were particularly beautiful or historically important?
2 Apart from the thing itself, what do you think is lost when something from the past disappears?
3 In the future, do you think we are more likely to lose physical or digital things? Why?
4 What makes an object, a building or a record worth preserving? Make a list of criteria and rank them in order of importance.

TIME EXPRESSIONS

There are many different phrases that can tell the reader when or how something happens. There are also phrases that describe things and events as they relate to a stated or implied timeframe.

when	how	in relation to a timeframe
at the turn of the century / in recent years	*slowly but surely*	*up to date*
over the past / last week/month/year	*in a flash*	*out of date*
at one time	*in the blink of an eye*	*it is about time for*
for the time being		

1 Complete the sentences with an appropriate expression. In some items, more than one answer is possible.

1 The clothes she wears are really _____ . People have not worn jackets like that since the 1980s.

2 _____ them to think about the long-term future of the library – it is almost falling down.

3 After a two-year downturn, _____ the economy is showing signs of recovery.

4 Twenty years ago, _____ , Twitter, Instagram and Snapchat did not yet exist.

5 _____ this was the most popular restaurant in the city. Today, however, it is hardly ever full, even on Saturday nights.

6 I downloaded those files _____ . Your new computer is extremely fast.

7 If my company keeps doing well, we should be able to buy a house in the next couple of years, but _____ , we are renting a flat.

8 _____ five years, more than ten historic buildings have been torn down in the city.

9 The owners have kept the building _____ , with new lighting and an efficient heating system.

PLUS

2 Complete the sentences using your own ideas.

1 For the time being, I am _____
_____.

2 Slowly but surely, the world/country/city _____
_____.

3 In order to stay up to date with technology, I _____
_____.

4 In the blink of an eye, _____
_____.

5 It is about time for me to _____
_____.

6 At one time, this _____
_____.

COMPOUND ADJECTIVES

A compound adjective is a phrase which acts as a single adjective.

When a compound adjective comes before a noun, the phrase should be hyphenated.
Using his **state-of-the-art** approach, Satyanarayanan has been able to recover and preserve digital records.
The **out-of-date** computer systems will be replaced next month.

When the same phrase appears in other contexts, no hyphenation is necessary.

Although those technologies are long **out of date**, it's information on the web that is much more vulnerable.
This software was **state of the art** about ten years ago!

When a compound adjective before a noun includes a number, it is always singular.

The **hundred-year-old** Beit al Jasra was at one time the summer home of a sheikh.
This building is more than **a hundred years old**.

3 Choose the correct option to complete the sentences.

1 We need a more *long term / long-term* solution to this problem.
2 The committee produced a *sixty pages / sixty-page* plan for historic preservation.
3 These homes were built at the *turn of the century / turn-of-the-century,* but they already need a lot of repairs.
4 The neighbourhood has implemented a system of *one way / one-way* streets to ease the increasing volume of traffic.
5 The artists who used to live and work in this area later became quite *well known / well-known*.
6 The building has been renovated. Where there once were offices, there are now around fifty *one bedroom / one-bedroom* flats.

7 The appliances installed must be *energy efficient / energy-efficient* and meet strict government standards.

8 As in any *fast growing / fast-growing* community, we face a number of challenges.

4 Read the sentences below. Write a new sentence using the underlined phrase as a compound adjective to modify the noun in bold, as in the example below.

1 A multinational company is planning an **office building** with <u>twenty storeys</u>. It will be on the busiest corner in the city.

_____

2 Starting next year I would like to find a **job** where I can work <u>full time</u>.

_____

3 We are trying to determine which the best **plan** is for the <u>long term</u>.

_____

4 The **construction** in the new development will be <u>wind powered</u> and reduce energy costs.

_____

5 The demolition will take place in an **area** that covers <u>four square kilometres</u>.

_____

5 Write five sentences. Use the compound adjectives and choose one noun from the nouns column to modify. Compare your sentences with a partner.

compound adjectives	nouns
1 well-known	author / song / story
2 money-saving	proposal / plan / idea
3 energy-efficient	homes / windows / light bulb
4 fast-growing	industry / city / business
5 million-dollar	home / development / plan

1 _____

_____

2 _____

_____

3 _____

_____

4 _____

_____

5 _____

_____

WRITING

CRITICAL THINKING

At the end of this unit, you will write an argumentative essay. Look at this unit's writing task in the box below.

> Do some research to find an old, but culturally or historically important area or neighbourhood in your city or country. What do you think should be done with it and why?

Evaluating facts to build support for an argument

When you make an argument, you need to decide which facts will support it. You can do this by looking at the facts you have researched and deciding which are the most interesting, contain the most relevant information and are most likely to persuade your reader. Think about why the facts support your argument and the implications of using each particular fact. It is better to use relevant facts than to overwhelm your reader with too many facts – this shows that you are able to analyze information. Choosing the right facts will make your argument strong and appealing to the reader.

 ANALYZE

1 Read these facts about preservation and new construction. Which support preservation (P) and which support new construction (NC)?

1 More than 400 million tons of materials get delivered to new construction sites in the UK each year. Of these, 60 million tons are wasted. _____

2 Renovating old buildings often releases toxic materials that can be dangerous to future occupants. Removing these materials is expensive – more than £15,000 per 100 square metres. _____

3 Some research studies estimate that a new, energy-efficient building can make up for the environmental impact of tearing down an old building in as little as ten years. _____

4 Heritage tourism sites, like the old city in Fez, Morocco, bring in millions of tourists and millions of dollars every year. _____

5 A recent study suggests that it takes 35 to 50 years for a new building to save the amount of energy that is used when an existing building is torn down and a new one is built. _____

6 Traditionally, many local families lived in villas, which allowed several generations to live together. With the move towards apartments, there is less space and fewer opportunities for extended families to live together under one roof. _____

7 A study in the USA demonstrated that an average of 14.6 jobs were created per million dollars spent on renovation, compared with 11.2 jobs per million dollars spent on new construction. _____

8 When restoring old buildings, there are often surprises which can cause a project to take twice as long as new construction projects, resulting in increased costs. _____

9 On a cost per square metre basis, renovation is usually slightly more expensive than new construction. _____

10 New construction near the waterfront will allow 2,000 families to move from residences without electricity or running water to modern housing. _____

2 Work in a small group. Look at the facts from Exercise 1 and discuss the following questions.

1 How do the facts support preservation or new construction?
2 What kind of reader would find each fact interesting or persuasive? Why?
3 Which facts are the most relevant for buildings in your city or country? Why?

3 Choose the neighbourhood or area that you would like to research and write about. Try to choose an area you know well. Will you recommend that the buildings be demolished to make way for new construction or that the built environment be preserved? Research facts that support your argument.

EVALUATE

4 Work with a partner. Look at the facts you have researched and answer the questions.

1 Who will the reader be?
2 What kinds of facts and information would your reader find interesting? Which are the most interesting?
3 Are the facts relevant to your argument? Which are the most relevant?
4 Have you included information that may appeal to your reader's emotions?
5 Have you included any statements by experts?
6 Are any of the facts in Exercise 1 relevant to your argument? Which could you use in your essay?

GRAMMAR FOR WRITING

FIRST AND SECOND CONDITIONALS

Both first and second conditionals can be used to make proposals about the future and to describe their consequences.

The first conditional implies a future event is possible or likely. Use these conditionals to present your own arguments in a positive way. You can also use them to make a threat sound more immediate and serious.

If we **preserve** our heritage, our children **will grow up** with a sense of cultural identity.

If we **continue** in this way, nothing **will remain** of our heritage.

The second conditional implies a future event is unlikely, hypothetical or impossible. Use these conditionals to present alternative positions.

If the developers **were** allowed to demolish the building, the city centre **would lose** an important part of its character.

If the old building **were to be kept**, we **would waste** an opportunity to develop the local infrastructure. (formal)

1 Decide which statement (a or b) describes an event that is more likely.

1 a If we spend much more time on the plans, we will not have time for the public meeting.
  b If we were to start the plans all over again, we would choose a different layout.

2 a If we built the new office next year, the staff and the budget would be considerably smaller.
  b If we build the new office building next year, our staff numbers will be retained.

3 a If they hold the meeting in the community centre, there won't be enough room for everyone to sit.
  b If we were to hold the meeting today, not very many people would attend.

4 a If we started renovating the library now, we might be able to save it.
  b If we start renovating the library now, we might be able to save it.

2 Write three sentences about the area you have chosen to discuss, using the forms of the conditional in the Explanation box. Write two sentences that address the consequences of *not* following your recommendation using the second conditional.

1 (first conditional) _____

_____

2 (second conditional) _____

_____

3 (second conditional) _____

_____

ACADEMIC WRITING SKILLS

PARAGRAPH STRUCTURE AND UNITY

Academic essays are divided into unified paragraphs. Each paragraph should have a main idea expressed in the first sentence – the topic sentence. Paragraph unity means that the entire paragraph focuses on the main idea. All the other sentences in the paragraph provide background information or support for the main idea.

1 Decide whether each paragraph is unified. If the paragraph is not unified, delete the information that does not belong.

1 unified ☐   not unified ☐

The creation of historic conservation areas generally increases property values. Because their homes are protected, owners are willing to invest in them. Owners do not have to worry about future changes in the character and quality of their neighbourhood. As a result, these areas tend to attract wealthier families who can afford to pay for the unique character that historic conservation areas provide.

2 unified ☐   not unified ☐

People are often unaware that there are financial advantages to living in a historic conservation area. Local authorities may offer grants for repairs and renovations. Homeowners cannot make major changes that affect the appearance of their home or the surrounding gardens and trees without planning permission. Funding may also be available from other organizations, such as charities with an interest in preserving our architectural heritage.

3 unified ☐   not unified ☐

Farmers' markets are becoming increasingly popular in UK cities. In the past twenty years, their number has increased from just one or two to over five hundred. Their popularity has been driven by the public's desire for locally grown food and also by an increasing awareness of the impact on the environment of food that comes from far away. Experts predict that the demand for locally grown food will continue to increase.

4 unified ☐   not unified ☐

English Heritage (the English Heritage Trust) is a charity that manages historic buildings, such as palaces, stately homes and castles. It also protects ancient sites such as Stonehenge. Stonehenge is visited by thousands of people on the longest and shortest days of the year, which often causes significant damage to the site. More than 5,000 years of history are preserved by the charity. Donations and entrance fees fund the conservation work done by the charity across the country.

PLUS

IMPERSONAL STATEMENTS

SKILLS

When you state a position, there is no need to use phrases that mark it as your personal opinion such as *I think* or *in my opinion*. The reader understands that you are making a case based on your view of the subject.

Avoid writing a personal statement, such as:
I think we should start preserving traditional neighbourhoods.

Express the same idea with an impersonal statement:
What is left of the city's traditional buildings and neighbourhoods must be preserved and it is imperative that this process begins now.

2 Rewrite the sentences as impersonal statements. Compare your sentences with a partner.

1 It is only my opinion, but I believe that restoring the old fishing district was a huge waste of money.

_____

_____

2 As far as I am concerned, it is always better to reuse and recycle the resources that we have, instead of using up additional resources.

_____

_____

3 As I see it, a new convention centre would be an incredible benefit for this city and its citizens, as it would provide both jobs and revenue. It would be foolish to pass up this opportunity.

_____

_____

_____

4 It seems to me that by tearing down all the old buildings and building new ones, our city will lose its character and begin to look like any other large city.

_____

_____

_____

5 From my point of view, placing this building on the register of historic places is a step in the right direction because it has the potential to draw tourists who are interested in architectural and cultural history.

_____

_____

_____

WRITING TASK

▸ Do some research to find an old but culturally or historically important area or neighbourhood in your city or country. What do you think should be done with it and why?

PLAN

1 Make brief notes about the history, physical condition and location of the area you have chosen to write about. This information will be used in your introductory paragraph.

_____

_____

2 Do you think the buildings in the area should be renovated or torn down? Why? Write one or two sentences. This statement of your position will also be used in your introductory paragraph. This will be your *thesis statement*.

_____

_____

3 Review your notes in Critical thinking, Exercises 3 and 4 on page 31. What are the main ideas of your essay? Write two or three ideas in a table like the one below. These will be the basis of your body paragraphs. Make notes that support your ideas.

	main idea	notes
body paragraph 1		
body paragraph 2		
body paragraph 3		

4 What are some of the main alternative positions? What would be the consequences of each? Use these points in your concluding paragraph.

_____

_____

5 Make notes on ways to restate your position to show that it is the best option. This is how you will end your essay.

_____

_____

6 Refer to the Task checklist on page 36 as you prepare your essay.

WRITE A FIRST DRAFT

7 Write your essay. Use your essay plan to help you structure your ideas. Write 400–450 words.

REVISE

8 Use the Task checklist to review your essay for content and structure.

TASK CHECKLIST	✔
Does the introductory paragraph provide a good description of the area?	
Is your position definitely and clearly stated in your introduction?	
Do the body paragraphs offer support for your position from different angles (factors)?	
Do the body paragraphs state a proposal and its consequences?	
Does the concluding paragraph state the negative consequences of the alternative position?	
Is each paragraph unified?	
Does each paragraph include a topic sentence?	

EDIT

9 Use the Language checklist to edit your essay for language errors.

LANGUAGE CHECKLIST	✔
Have you used time expressions correctly?	
Have you stated your proposal and its consequences with first-conditional statements?	
Have you presented and dismissed alternative positions with second-conditional statements?	
Have you expressed your opinions as impersonal statements, avoiding *I think*, etc.?	

10 Make any necessary changes to your essay.

OBJECTIVES REVIEW

1 Check your learning objectives for this unit. Write *3, 2* or *1* for each objective.

3 = very well   2 = well   1 = not so well

I can ...

watch and understand a video about preserving digital records.   _____

identify an argument.   _____

distinguish fact from opinion.   _____

evaluate facts to build support for an argument.   _____

use first and second conditionals.   _____

write structured and unified paragraphs.   _____

write impersonal statements.   _____

write an argumentative essay.   _____

2 Go to the *Unlock* Online Workbook for more practice with this unit's learning objectives.

UNLOCK ONLINE

WORDLIST		
adaptive (adj) ⊙	longevity (n) ⊙	renovation (n)
affluent (adj)	long-term (adj) ⊙	retrieve (v)
anonymous (adj) ⊙	memorabilia (n)	scenario (n) ⊙
compatible (adj) ⊙	one-way (adj)	state-of-the-art (adj)
demolition (n)	opt for (v)	vibrant (adj)
energy-efficient (adj)	out-of-date (adj)	vulnerable (adj) ⊙
fast-growing (adj)	practice (n) ⊙	well-known (adj) ⊙
irreversible (adj)	prompt (v)	

⊙ = high-frequency words in the Cambridge Academic Corpus

LEARNING OBJECTIVES	IN THIS UNIT YOU WILL ...
Watch and listen	watch and understand a video about the importance of fonts.
Reading skill	take notes in outline form; challenge ideas in a text.
Critical thinking	determine and apply criteria.
Grammar	use non-defining relative clauses; use appositives.
Academic writing skills	structure a summary—response essay; write a conclusion.
Writing task	write a summary—response essay.

UNLOCK YOUR KNOWLEDGE

Work with a partner. Discuss the questions.

1 How many different brands of shoes are in this photo? Can you tell? Why / Why not?

2 What does a logo tell you about the product it appears on? When you are shopping, do you look for any particular logos? If so, which ones? If not, why not?

3 Which logos would you recognize from these industries?
- sportswear
- fast food
- car manufacturing

PLUS

WATCH AND LISTEN

PREPARING TO WATCH

ACTIVATING YOUR
KNOWLEDGE

1 Work with a partner. Discuss the questions.

1 When you are typing a document, do you choose your font carefully? Why / Why not?

2 Do you use exclamation marks when you write in English? If so, where do you use them? If not, why not?

3 Do you read advertisements? If so, which ones do you like best? If not, do you think you are immune to advertising?

PREDICTING
CONTENT
USING VISUALS

2 You are going to watch a video about design in advertising. Look at the photos and discuss the questions with a partner.

1 Which advertisements do you think are more effective? Why?

2 How does the look of the letters – the font – differ in each photo?

3 How do you think the font affects the look of a logo, advertisement or sign?

4 Do you think the font affects the way people perceive the information? If so, how big a difference does it make?

5 What are the benefits of simple lettering?

GLOSSARY

endemic (adj) regularly found and very common

exclamation point (US n phr) exclamation mark

cursive (n, adj) joined-up writing

typography (n) the design of writing in a piece of printing or on a computer screen

period (US n) full stop

be in full swing (idiom) be fully underway; be at the highest level of activity, popularity, etc.

come off (as) (phr v, informal) seem a particular way to other people; create a particular impression

authoritarian (adj) demanding total obedience

WHILE WATCHING

UNDERSTANDING MAIN IDEAS

3 ▶ Watch the video and check your predictions from Exercise 2. Which sentence best expresses the main idea of the video?

1 The advertisement for Coca-Cola is the most effective advertisement ever.

2 Many corporations today use Helvetica because it communicates a clear message.

3 Slogans use Helvetica font today so they appear authoritarian.

UNDERSTANDING DETAIL

4 ▶ Watch the video again. Write examples for each main idea.

1 In the 1950s, bad typography was prevalent.

_____

_____

2 Helvetica has several characteristics which make it successful.

_____

_____

MAKING INFERENCES

5 Work with a partner. Discuss the questions.

1 Why do you think there was a wide variety of lettering designs in the 1950s?

2 How do you think the man feels about the use of exclamation marks? How do you know?

3 What public image do governments and corporations who use Helvetica hope to create?

DISCUSSION

6 Work with a partner. Discuss the questions.

1 Which type of lettering do you prefer, the typography in the advertisements from the 1950s, or the ones of today? Why?

2 Do you think the lettering in an advertisement, logo or sign is crucial to the success of a business?

3 Think of an advertisement, logo or sign that you find attractive. What is it? Why do you think it appeals to you?

4 Think of an advertisement, logo or sign that you find difficult to read or unpleasant to look at. What is it? What is the problem with it?

READING 1

PREVIEWING

UNDERSTANDING
KEY VOCABULARY

PREPARING TO READ

1 You are going to read a chapter from a marketing textbook about logos. Work with a partner. Preview the text on pages 44–45 and discuss the questions.

1 How would you answer the title question?
2 Would you say the logos pictured are successful? Why / Why not?

2 Read the sentences. Write the correct form of the words in bold (1–8) next to their definitions below (a–h).

1 The researchers used specific **criteria** to rate the quality of the products.
2 The initial report said that the business had made a 10% profit last year, but a **subsequent** report corrected the amount to 7%.
3 The new smartphone has **aroused** tremendous interest in consumers in Kuwait.
4 The president's speech was an effort to **reinforce** a positive image of the company.
5 The advertisement **conveys** the message that these products use the most advanced technology.
6 Advertisements that are **evocative** of childhood adventure have been successful for us in the past.
7 We should stop using plastic and find a way to package our products that is more **sustainable**.
8 The best way to **retain** customers is to give them a good price and good service.

a _____ (v) to provide more proof or support for an idea or opinion and make it seem true
b _____ (adj) making a person remember or feel a particular thing
c _____ (adj) next; happening after something else
d _____ (adj) causing little or no damage to the environment and therefore able to continue for a long time
e _____ (n) standards used for judging something
f _____ (v) to keep; to continue having
g _____ (v) to express an idea so that it is understood by other people
h _____ (v) to make someone have a particular feeling or reaction

WHILE READING

3 Read the textbook chapter. Then circle the statement that gives the most complete and accurate description of a good logo.

READING FOR MAIN IDEAS

  a A good logo is easy for anybody to recognize and understand.

  b A good logo expresses a company's identity in a way that is easy to recognize.

  c A good logo will last forever in the public's mind.

  d A good logo helps the company to make a profit.

SKILLS

Taking notes in outline form

Using an outline to take notes on a text can help deepen your understanding of the text and help you remember more of the details. Main ideas provide the basic organization for an outline, with supporting details and examples listed below them.

4 Complete the outline with information from the textbook chapter. Complete the main ideas, details and examples. Use examples from the text.

READING FOR DETAIL

Criteria for a successful logo

I. Efficient form of visual communication
   A. Simple and easy to remember
   B. _____ so it is unlikely to be confused
     with other logos.
     Example: _____
   C. Arouses _____
     Example: _____

II. _____ and adaptable
   A. Across _____
     Example: _____
   B. Across _____
     1. Can shrink
       Examples: _____
     2. _____ from a distance

III. Tells a _____
   A. Conveys company's _____
     1. Example: _____
     2. Example: _____
   B. Evokes_____
     Example: _____

Chapter 5 — What makes a successful logo?

1 A logo is an efficient visual form that **conveys** an organization's message. Logos may seem quite simple. After all, they are often just a name or very basic image, but in fact, designing a good logo takes a lot of time and thought. So, what are the **criteria** that define a good logo? If you ask ten different graphic designers, you may get ten different answers. However, there are some common themes.

2 A good logo is clear and simple. Simple logos are easy to remember. In studies where participants were shown hundreds of unfamiliar logos, the ones they remembered later all had simple designs. Some designers advise the use of no more than two colours.

A good logo must also be unique so it will not be confused with the logo from another organization. For example, the logo for IKEA is so familiar that any new logo in those shades of blue and yellow would probably remind people of IKEA. A unique logo also **arouses** curiosity when people see it for the first time. They want to know more about it. When tennis star Novak Djokovic began wearing shirts by the Japanese clothing manufacturer UNIQLO, people unfamiliar with the company became curious about the odd combination of letters that make up its logo.

3 Logos should be flexible enough to adapt across time and placement. Apple's iconic logo was originally rainbow coloured, which worked in the 1970s, but today it would look dated. The **subsequent** grey and black Apple logo looks more contemporary, yet it **retains** the original design. Designers also need to consider where the logo will appear. Will it be on shopping bags? Coffee cups? Does it need to shrink down to a tiny icon on a digital device, like the Twitter bluebird or the Facebook f? Will people be able to recognize it from far away on the side of a lorry?

4 More than anything else, a logo needs to tell a story – to convey the company's identity and evoke an emotional response in the people who see it. But to be successful, the message and the response must be appropriate for the organization that the logo represents. The Toys R Us

logo, with its childish handwriting and backwards R, conveys a message of fun. It is childlike and playful. It works for a toy company, but it probably would not be effective for a bank or an insurance company.

5 In contrast, the FedEx logo, with its block letters forming a forward pointing arrow between the 'E' and the 'x', looks like it belongs to a serious business. Its aim is to inspire confidence: we are a company you can trust to deliver your package.

6 An emotional response is particularly important for charitable organizations. The World Wide Fund for Nature (WWF) hopes that its iconic black and white panda resonates with the public, and encourages people to make a donation to support its global conservation work saving endangered species and their habitats, and reducing people's footprint for a **sustainable** future.

7 Once a logo becomes widely recognized, businesses and organizations often rely more on the logo than their name. The public immediately recognizes the Nike swoosh, the McDonald's golden arches or Apple's apple. Research has shown that the more **evocative** the logo, the more positive the impact on customer loyalty – suggesting that the most powerful logos are those which forgo[1] lettering to rely on symbols.

8 Making a brand stand out from the crowd is key to the survival of a business – and

a logo is one powerful tool in achieving this. For other types of organizations, it is the public's connection to the role the organization plays in society that is important, and logos can help to **reinforce** this. Whatever the type of organization, those who get their logos right will reap the benefits[2] for many years to come.

[1] **forgo** (v) not use/have/do something that is usual
[2] **reap the benefits** (v phr, idiom) to get something good as the result of your own actions

SKILLS

Challenging ideas in a text

Not every idea you read in a text is equally valid. When writers present their arguments, they present facts, opinions and analysis. You may not agree with everything in a text. It is important to read all texts critically. As you read, ask yourself, 'Does this make sense based on my own experience and knowledge?' 'Does my experience and knowledge contradict what I have read?' Be ready to challenge ideas in a text before you accept them, but be ready to support your challenge with evidence.

5 Work with a partner. Read the quotes from the textbook chapter and answer the questions for each one.

> - A good logo is clear and simple.
> - Simple logos are easy to remember.
> - A good logo must also be unique so it will not be confused with the logo from another organization.
> - A unique logo also arouses curiosity.
> - A logo needs to tell a story – to convey the company's identity and evoke an emotional response.

1 Do you agree with the statements?
2 What evidence is there to support these statements?
3 Can you think of examples of successful logos that contradict the statements? Why are they successful?
4 Do you think the text is trustworthy based on the statements above?

6 Work with a partner. Complete the tasks.

1 Review your outline in Exercise 4. Write three criteria for a successful logo below.

_____

_____

_____

2 Look online and find a logo that is not in the textbook chapter, and that meets each of these three criteria.
3 Present your logo to the class. Explain how it meets your criteria.

DISCUSSION

7 Work in small groups. Discuss the questions.

1 Choose one of the logos discussed in the textbook chapter. What story do you think it is meant to tell?
2 Think of another logo. Choose one that you think is not as successful as those in the textbook chapter. Explain why you think so.

READING 2

PREPARING TO READ

PREVIEWING

1 You are going to read another chapter in the textbook. Preview the chapter on pages 48–49 and discuss the questions with a partner.

  1 The chapter title uses the word *brand* to describe an action and adds the prefix *re-*. What do you think the process of *rebranding* involves?

  2 Why would companies need to rebrand themselves?

  3 How would you approach rebranding a business?

UNDERSTANDING KEY VOCABULARY

2 Read the sentences and choose the best definition for the words in bold.

  1 There has been **opposition to** our latest design – people really don't like it.
    a doubt about
    b disagreement with
    c misunderstanding about

  2 The design closely **resembles** a successful product, so we must rethink it.
    a looks like
    b sounds like
    c competes with

  3 The display was placed in a **strategic** location so that shoppers would see it.
    a likely to result in problems
    b helping to achieve a plan
    c unusual; unpredictable

  4 She is the country's **foremost** expert and will provide reliable advice.
    a most controversial
    b most wealthy
    c best known

  5 The company has **refined** the design several times, making it more attractive and energy efficient.
    a improved by making small changes
    b invested a lot of money in
    c carefully chosen from a range of options

  6 Many people **associate** specific products with experiences in their childhood.
    a prefer
    b consider
    c connect

  7 A logo must have a **distinctive** design that people remember.
    a influential
    b easy to recognize
    c fashionable

Chapter 6 — Rebranding and logos

1 Businesses need to be able to change as markets change. To keep up with changes, they frequently update their brands and advertising in a process called rebranding. Rebranding often prompts these companies to redesign their logos at the same time. Take, for example, NBC (the National Broadcasting Company of the United States) – this company started in the days of radio, hence the microphone in its original logo from 1944. Moving into television and then colour television, the company adopted its **distinctive** peacock design in 1956. Since then, it has updated 'the Bird' several times to reflect the tastes and styles of the times.

  NBC

2 Rebranding and new logo designs are always **strategic** decisions. They may be needed because a company has changed its focus. For example, Xerox, a company whose primary product was once photocopiers, wanted to call attention to the fact that it handles a much wider range of document technology now. Some companies may want to change their image because there have been some negative associations with their old one. For example, Kentucky Fried Chicken hoped to distance itself from unhealthy fried foods. When it redesigned the product's logo, the word 'fried' disappeared and only the initials, KFC, remained. The logo for oil company British Petroleum (BP) looked like any sign you might see at a petrol station. Customers often **associate** fossil fuels with climate change and a negative impact on the environment, so BP opted for a 'greener' logo, one that **resembles** a sunflower.

3 Some brands simply mature and need a new logo to show this. Many high-tech companies, often founded by young entrepreneurs, begin with logos that reflect the age of their founders. If the companies are successful and begin to appeal to a wider audience, they may want to **refine** their logo. Both Spotify, the music and video streaming service, and Snapchat, the image messaging app, have gone through this process. Spotify's earlier, youthful logo has recently evolved into a simple graphic that evokes sound waves. Snapchat's cute ghost has lost its silly face, retaining only the figure's outline.

4 The public generally resists changes to familiar logos at first. However, **opposition to** the new design usually dies down after a while, especially if the new logo retains some familiar elements. For example, the new BP logo kept the colour scheme of the old logo, and the new KFC logo retains the familiar bearded face of its founder, Colonel Sanders. If there is too much change, however, customers may become confused or reject the change. Executives at PepsiCo found this out when they changed the logo for one of their brands: Tropicana orange juice.

Customers were looking for the familiar orange with a straw; they did not recognize the product with the new logo as Tropicana. Sales dropped dramatically, and PepsiCo brought back the old logo.

5 A final reason for a new logo design comes from technology. New platforms[1] may necessitate modifications. As devices become smaller, logos need to be simpler and easier to recognize on a small scale. Companies like Airbnb and PayPal dropped their names and chose simpler graphics for their latest logos so that users can identify them more easily on their mobile devices.

6 Changes in technology can place limits on logo designs, but can also offer new options. In particular, as more business and personal interactions take place in digital environments, more companies are creating logos that are animated and interactive. The **foremost** example of this is Google's latest logo, which appeared in 2015. The new logo has the same four basic colours as the old logo, but it transforms into a number of different images, depending on the product. For example, at the start of a Google voice search, the logo transforms into four dots in the Google colours, then into four wiggling lines that look like sound waves.

7 New logos can be expensive. The sunflower logo cost BP £4.6 million to design and a further £132 million to rebrand all its assets. New logos can also be risky. PepsiCo lost $33 million in revenue on top of the cost of rebranding twice with its short-lived Tropicana logo. Yet, for most companies, the process can inject new energy into a brand, and is therefore considered worth the investment.

[1] **platform** (n) the type of system a computer or smartphone uses

WHILE READING

READING FOR MAIN IDEAS

3 Read the textbook chapter. Then circle all the circumstances that might prompt a company to redesign its logo.

a The company wants to appeal to younger consumers.
b Changes in technology require it.
c The public does not like the old logo.
d The company wants the public to forget about something negative.

READING FOR DETAIL

4 Match the reasons for a logo redesign (1–6) to the companies (a–f).

1 need to fit logo on mobile devices
2 company and founders have matured
3 wider range of products
4 opportunities provided by new technology
5 negative associations
6 need to refresh their look over time

a British Petroleum
b Google
c Snapchat
d Xerox
e NBC
f PayPal

5 Read the textbook chapter again. Take detailed notes on each point I–IV. Compare your notes with a partner.

I. Change in focus

II. Brand has matured

III. Problems with rebranding

IV. Impact of changing technology

READING BETWEEN THE LINES

MAKING INFERENCES

6 Work with a partner. Choose the statement(s) that can you infer from the textbook chapter. Discuss your reasoning.

a A peacock can be associated with the idea of colour.
b The founders of Spotify were young when they started the company.
c The new BP logo was a success.
d The face on KFC's logo is an important element of the brand.
e Other companies now have animated logos like Google's.

DISCUSSION

SYNTHESIZING

7 Work with a partner. Use ideas from Reading 1 and Reading 2 to answer the following questions.

1 How important do you think a logo is for a brand? Explain your answer.
2 Choose one of the pairs of logos discussed in Reading 2. Analyze and describe the difference between the old and new logo.
3 Think of a famous logo, for example a car, clothing or fast food company. What changes would you suggest to improve the logo?
4 Think of a company or product that you believe should begin the rebranding process. Explain why you chose that product or company. How would you rebrand it?

⊙ LANGUAGE DEVELOPMENT

DESCRIBING EMOTIONAL RESPONSES

1 Look at the table of common verb + noun collocations used to describe emotional responses. Decide if each group of expressions describes positive, negative or mixed responses.

verbs	nouns	descriptions
1 evoke	feeling(s), memories, emotions	mixed
2 inspire	confidence, awe, fear	
3 arouse	interest, curiosity, suspicion, anger	
4 stir up	trouble, opposition, feelings, anger	
5 generate	interest, excitement, enthusiasm	
6 provoke	controversy, outrage, anger, anxiety	

2 Complete the sentences with an appropriate collocation from the table in Exercise 1. In some items, more than one answer is possible.

1 The man in the campaign wore a hat pulled down over his eyes and a large coat that seemed to be covering something. His appearance immediately _____ _____ .
2 The new advertising campaign for the law that requires safety seats for all children under the age of two has _____ _____ .
3 The new line of computer products and accessories has _____ a lot of _____ among tech-savvy buyers.
4 After being associated with the party for over a hundred years, the old-fashioned logo _____ _____ among voters.
5 The change from a recognizable logo to a new design _____ an angry _____ from many consumers.
6 Songs from the past often _____ happy _____ .

3 Write three sentences of your own using some of the collocations in the table in Exercise 1 to describe emotional responses to unusual or difficult situations. You can describe a friend's responses or your own.

1 _____

_____

2 _____

_____

3 _____

_____

PLUS

PARAPHRASING

GRAMMAR

Paraphrasing is an important and useful writing skill, especially when you write a summary. When you paraphrase, you put another person's ideas into your own words. To write a paraphrase, use synonyms and different grammatical structures to express the ideas in a new form without changing their meaning. You may also need to arrange the ideas in a different order.

Changes in technology can place limits on logo designs but they can also offer new options.

At the same time that emerging technology restricts logo designs, it can also open up new possibilities.

The public generally resists changes to familiar logos at first.

In the beginning, people usually don't like it when logos they know well change.

If you use identifiable phrasing from the original text, you must use quotation marks.

PLUS

4 Paraphrase the sentences below.

1 Logos are symbols commonly used by organizations to promote their identity and to increase public recognition.

2 Many companies choose logos that reflect their names, origins or products so that consumers can easily associate the logo with the company.

3 Colour is a crucial element of any logo because colours help anchor the logo in consumers' memories, allowing them to distinguish the logo from other similar logos.

4 Some of the most famous logos in the world are those of sporting brands, which inspire brand loyalty in consumers by the prominence of their logos on each item they sell.

5 Paraphrase the three sentences from Reading 1 below.

1 A good logo must also be unique so it will not be confused with the logo from another organization.

2 Logos should be flexible enough to adapt across time and placement.

3 More than anything else, a logo needs to tell a story – to convey the company's identity and evoke an emotional response in the people who see it.

WRITING

CRITICAL THINKING

At the end of this unit, you will write a summary–response essay. Look at this unit's writing task in the box below.

> Summarize the information in Reading 1, 'What makes a successful logo?' Then choose a logo that is not mentioned in either reading text and analyze it in terms of the criteria given in Reading 1.

Determining and applying criteria

Understanding criteria can help you organize an essay and ensure that you address the most relevant issues. To choose and use criteria effectively, you must first understand what you are evaluating – its components, purpose and goals. Then you can identify the criteria that show if its purpose has been fulfilled and its goals have been met.

1 Review the entire outline (Parts I, II and III) of the criteria for a successful logo on page 43. Write the criteria below.

REMEMBER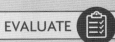

_____

_____

_____

_____

_____

2 Complete the tasks.

EVALUATE

1 Which criteria do you think are crucial for a successful logo? Which are important but not essential? Based on your discussion in Exercise 5 on page 46, are some criteria not valid at all? Choose the top five criteria and rank them in order of importance.

1 _____

2 _____

3 _____

4 _____

5 _____

2 Compare your ordered list with a partner's. Discuss any differences between the two lists. Explain your order to your partner. Make any changes that you agree on.

3 Work with a partner. Are there additional criteria that you think are important or helpful in creating a logo? Add them to your list. Reorder your list if necessary.

3 Work with a partner. Complete the tasks. Make notes.

1 Choose a logo for your analysis. _____

2 Apply the criteria from the list you made in Exercise 1. Does your logo meet each of the criteria completely, partly or not at all?

_____

_____

_____

_____

_____

4 Work with a partner. Answer the questions.

1 How successful do you think the logo is? Explain your answer.

_____

_____

2 Is your judgment based on the criteria in the chapter or were other criteria important? If so, what were they? Why were they important?

_____

_____

GRAMMAR FOR WRITING

NON-DEFINING RELATIVE CLAUSES

GRAMMAR

Writers use non-defining relative clauses to provide additional information about a noun. These details are not essential because the clause can be removed without affecting the sense of the sentence. Commas are used to separate a non-defining clause from the rest of the sentence.

The non-defining relative clause in the example below gives additional information about IKEA, but it does not identify the company, nor is the information necessary for understanding the meaning of the rest of the sentence.

IKEA, **which is a multinational company**, has a logo that is recognized around the world.

PLUS

1 Rewrite the sentences to include the additional information.

1 Apple's logo has been redesigned several times in the past 40 years. Additional information: The logo was once rainbow coloured.

_____

_____

_____

2 The letters in the logo for FedEx form an arrow moving forward.
   Additional information: FedEx provides delivery services.

   _____

   _____

   _____

3 A Serbian designer, Predrag Stakić, won an international competition.
   Additional information: His design encapsulated the features of a dove
   and a hand.

   _____

   _____

   _____

4 Rebranding is only one of many options available to the marketing
   department. Additional information: Rebranding can revive interest in
   a company's products.

   _____

   _____

   _____

5 High-tech companies have realized that they need to reconsider and
   revise their logos. Additional information: High-tech companies often
   have very young founders.

   _____

   _____

   _____

APPOSITIVES

GRAMMAR

An appositive is a noun phrase that provides more information about another noun.

Appositives are commonly used with proper nouns.
IKEA, **a multinational company**, has a logo which is recognized around the world.
Tennis star **Roger Federer** wears UNIQLO shirts.
The CEO of Facebook, **Mark Zuckerberg**, is one of the world's youngest billionaires.

Like relative clauses, if an appositive provides information which is not essential to the sentence, it requires commas around it.
The CEO of Facebook, **Mark Zuckerberg**, is one of the world's youngest billionaires.
(There is only one CEO of Facebook, so the information is not essential to the sentence.)

When the appositive is essential to the meaning of the sentence there are no commas.
Tennis star **Roger Federer** wears UNIQLO shirts.
(Readers need to know which tennis star is being described.)

2 Rewrite the sentences using the additional information as an appositive. Then write two sentences of your own with appositives, using the proper nouns given (5–6).

1 The golden arches have achieved international recognition as a symbol of fast food. Additional information: The golden arches are the McDonald's logo.

_____

_____

2 The design of logos requires careful thought before release. Additional information: Logos are a company's public face.

_____

_____

3 A media mogul has announced he will turn over his empire to his son next year. Additional information: Rupert Murdoch is the media mogul.

_____

_____

4 Microsoft has lost some of its market share to Google in the past five years. Additional information: Microsoft is a software giant.

_____

_____

5 Lionel Messi

_____

_____

6 Nike

_____

_____

ACADEMIC WRITING SKILLS

STRUCTURING A SUMMARY–RESPONSE ESSAY

There are two basic formats for a summary–response essay.

- **Format 1:** Summarize then respond. Summarize the entire source text first. Then respond with your own ideas or an application of the ideas from the source.
- **Format 2:** Integrate the summary and the response. Summarize the source text point by point, responding to each point with your own ideas or an application of the ideas from the source.

Remember that the *summary* should include only the most important points, not details.

The *response* usually consists of impersonal statements of the writer's point of view, followed by justified support for that point of view.

1 Work with a partner. Summarize the second paragraph of Reading 2. Then, on your own, write a response to that summary, in one or two sentences.

2 Work on your own. Summarize the fourth paragraph of Reading 2. Add a response, again in one or two sentences.

3 Compare your summaries and responses with a partner.

WRITING A CONCLUSION

The conclusion is your opportunity to make a final impression on your readers – to remind them of the point you are trying to make and to leave them with something to think about.

Do ...

✔ refer to your main idea and emphasize its importance, without repeating your thesis statement.

✔ refer to something in your introduction; for example, if you began with a story, you could come back to it in your conclusion.

✔ give your readers something to think about:
  - point out wider implications of the ideas you have presented.
  - point out the personal relevance to your readers of the ideas you have presented.
  - refer to future possibilities.

Do not ...

✘ repeat your thesis statement or summarize your supporting points. In a very long essay, this might be appropriate, but it is not necessary in a short essay like the one you will write in this unit.

✘ undermine your argument with expressions such as 'This is only one interpretation.'

4 Work with a partner. Complete the tasks.

1 Review the main idea activities after the two readings in this unit. Use them to help you write one sentence that expresses the main idea of each text.

'What makes a successful logo?' (pages 44–45)

Main idea: _____
_____

'Rebranding and logos' (pages 48–49)

Main idea: _____
_____

2 Read the last paragraph of Reading 1 again. Underline the phrase that refers to the main idea of the full text. Circle any parts of the paragraph that leave the reader with something new to think about.

3 Read the last paragraph of Reading 2 again. Underline the phrase that refers to the main idea of the full text. Circle any parts of the paragraph that leave the reader with something new to think about.

WRITING TASK

▶ Summarize the information in Reading 1, 'What makes a successful logo?' Then choose a logo that is not mentioned in either reading text and analyze it in terms of the criteria given in Reading 1.

PLAN

1 Which format will you use for your summary–response essay, format 1 or format 2? See Academic writing skills, page 57.

_____

2 What logo will you discuss in your essay? See Critical thinking, Exercise 3, page 54. If possible, include a picture of it in your essay as a visual reference for your reader.

_____

3 Review your list of criteria from Critical thinking, Exercise 2, page 53. Paraphrase each point here and use your paraphrases in your essay.

_____
_____
_____
_____
_____

4 Review the information that applies to the format you will follow.

Format 1: summary and then response

Opening paragraph: Review the main idea that you wrote down (Academic writing skills, Exercise 4 on page 58) and use it as the basis of your one-paragraph summary of Reading 1. Make sure you have explained the criteria.

Body paragraphs: Write one paragraph or more applying the criteria for a successful logo to your choice of product or service.

- Add details from Reading 2 if they are relevant to your essay.
- Review your notes on applying the criteria to the logo you have chosen (see Critical thinking, Exercises 2 and 3 on pages 53–54). You probably will not need a separate paragraph for each criterion.
- Refer to the criteria in your introduction, but do not explain them again here.

Logo X is indeed simple but not unique, so it may easily be confused with other, more famous logos.

Conclusion: Make sure your conclusion answers this question: *After considering all of the criteria, do you believe the logo you selected is successful? Why / Why not?*

Format 2: integrated summary and response

Opening paragraph: Review the main idea that you wrote down (Academic writing skills, Exercise 4 on page 58) and use it as the basis of your opening paragraph.

Body paragraphs: Write one or more paragraphs explaining and applying each of the criteria for a successful logo to your choice of product or service. If there are any additional criteria that you think are important, discuss them as well.

Conclusion: Make sure your conclusion answers this question: *After considering all of the criteria, do you believe the logo you selected is successful? Why / Why not?*

---

5 Refer to the Task checklist on page 60 as you prepare your essay.

WRITE A FIRST DRAFT

6 Write your essay. Use your notes and the essay plan in Exercise 4 to help you. Write 400–450 words.

REVISE

7 Use the Task checklist to review your essay for content and structure.

TASK CHECKLIST	✔
Does your essay contain a summary of the criteria – either in a separate paragraph (format 1) or point by point (format 2)?	
Does your summary include the most important information from the original textbook chapter?	
Did you use your own words to paraphrase the points in the original texts?	
Did you apply the criteria from Reading 1 to a new logo?	
Does your conclusion contain an evaluation of the logo's success?	
Have you left your reader with something to think about?	
Does each paragraph include a topic sentence?	

EDIT

8 Use the Language checklist to edit your essay for language errors.

LANGUAGE CHECKLIST	✔
Have you used words and phrases for describing emotional responses correctly?	
Have you paraphrased any information you used from Reading 1 and Reading 2?	
Have you used quotation marks and cited your source if you used the exact words from a source text?	
Did you add extra information in non-defining relative clauses with commas?	
Did you punctuate appositives correctly according to how each one is used?	

9 Make any necessary changes to your essay.

OBJECTIVES REVIEW

1 Check your learning objectives for this unit. Write *3, 2* or *1* for each objective.

3 = very well   2 = well   1 = not so well

I can ...

watch and understand a video about the importance of fonts.   _____

make notes in outline form.   _____

challenge ideas in a text.   _____

determine and apply criteria.   _____

use non-defining relative clauses.   _____

use appositives.   _____

structure a summary–response essay.   _____

write conclusions.   _____

write a summary–response essay.   _____

2 Go to the *Unlock* Online Workbook for more practice with this unit's learning objectives.

UNL⌀CK
ONLINE

WORDLIST		
anxiety (n) ⊙	evoke (v)	resemble (v) ⊙
arouse (v)	foremost (adj)	retain (v) ⊙
associate (v) ⊙	generate (v) ⊙	stir up (phr v)
controversy (n) ⊙	inspire (v)	strategic (adj) ⊙
convey (v) ⊙	opposition to (n)	subsequent (adj) ⊙
criteria (n) ⊙	outrage (n)	suspicion (n)
curiosity (n)	provoke (v)	sustainable (adj) ⊙
distinctive (adj) ⊙	refine (v) ⊙	
evocative (adj)	reinforce (v) ⊙	

⊙ = high-frequency words in the Cambridge Academic Corpus

LEARNING OBJECTIVES	IN THIS UNIT YOU WILL ...
Watch and listen	watch and understand a video about online harassment.
Reading skills	preview a text; identify purpose and tone.
Critical thinking	analyze problems and solutions.
Grammar	use impersonal passive constructions; use passives for continuity.
Academic writing skills	write about problems; write about solutions.
Writing task	write a problem–solution essay.

UNL**O**CK YOUR KNOWLEDGE

Work with a partner. Discuss the questions.

1 How much time do you spend on the internet every day?
What kinds of site do you spend the most time on?

2 In what ways do you interact publicly on the internet other than
social media? For example, do you comment on articles or blog posts?

3 Do you know everyone you interact with online? How easy
is it to communicate with total strangers? Is this positive
or negative? Why?

PLUS

WATCH AND LISTEN

PREPARING TO WATCH

ACTIVATING YOUR KNOWLEDGE

1 Complete the sentences with your own ideas. Compare your ideas with a partner.

1 Social media is a useful tool for _____ .
2 A common misuse of social media is _____ .
3 Children should be taught how to avoid _____ online.
4 One way to deal with trolls or bullies online is to _____ .

USING YOUR KNOWLEDGE TO PREDICT CONTENT

2 You are going to watch a video about an anti-bullying campaign. Before you watch, discuss the questions with your partner.

1 What age groups do you think the campaign is aimed at?
2 What specific types of behaviour might the campaign be trying to stop?
3 What suggestions might the experts involved with the campaign make?

GLOSSARY

to someone's face (adv, idiom) directly, without trying to hide anything or be kind

fake (adj) not real, but made to look or seem real

counter (v) to defend yourself against something

unflattering (adj) making someone look less attractive or seem worse than usual

awareness (n) understanding of a situation or subject at the present time

surge (n) a sudden and great increase

WHILE WATCHING

UNDERSTANDING MAIN IDEAS

3 ▶ Watch the video. Write *T* (true) or *F* (false) next to the statements below. Correct the false statements.

_____ 1 Charlotte Thomas used to be a victim of online bullying.
_____ 2 The Safer Internet campaign wants to help children fight back against bullies.
_____ 3 The Safer Internet campaign needs to find more supporters.
_____ 4 Nicola Sturgeon believes that children's access to the internet should be limited.

4 ▶ Watch again. Match the speakers (1–5) to the main points they make (a–g). Some speakers make more than one point.

1 Reporter
2 Charlotte Thomas
3 Kevin Gourlay
4 Teenager in workshop
5 Nicola Sturgeon

a The internet makes bullying easier. _____
b People have been putting more photos and videos online. _____
c People don't always consider what they post online carefully. _____
d The place to teach children about the internet is in schools. _____
e Children need to learn about how social media profiles work. _____
f The campaign has changed its approach this year. _____
g Asking for help from adults does not always prevent online bullying. _____

5 ▶ Watch again. Answer the questions.

UNDERSTANDING
DETAIL

1 What example does Charlotte Thomas give of how the internet makes bullying easier? _____
2 What does Kevin Gourlay suggest children do if somebody bullies them online? _____
3 What has Charlotte Thomas been unable to get removed from social media? _____
4 What does the teen in the workshop say can happen if you are not cautious? _____
5 Why does Nicola Sturgeon say politicians are talking to young people?
_____
6 What warning does the reporter end his piece with?
_____

DISCUSSION

6 Work in a small group. Discuss the questions.

1 What online dangers are there for children in your country? What can parents, governments and schools do to protect children?
2 Is it a good idea to ban children from using the internet? Why / Why not?
3 What skills do you think it is most useful to teach children who are using the internet regularly?

READING

PREPARING TO READ

UNDERSTANDING KEY VOCABULARY

1 Read the sentences. Write the words in bold (1–6) next to their definitions (a–f) below.

1 His **hostile** response to the questions made people in the audience feel unwelcome.

2 She felt deep anger and **humiliation** when she learned that her private emails and photos had been published on the internet.

3 Children may be excluded from school for physically or verbally **abusive** behaviour towards teachers.

4 She decided to **withdraw** from the competition because of continuous complaints about her participation.

5 This new policy sets an important **precedent** that other companies may follow.

6 In order to protect members' **anonymity**, the website uses a number system for identification.

a _____ (adj) rude and offensive; causing another person mental or physical harm

b _____ (n) an action or decision that becomes an example for future actions or decisions

c _____ (adj) unfriendly; showing strong dislike

d _____ (n) the situation in which somebody's name is not given or known

e _____ (n) shame and loss of self-respect

f _____ (v) to stop participating

USING YOUR KNOWLEDGE

2 You are going to read an article about cyber harassment. Work with a partner. Complete the task below. Then explain to a partner what you think cyber harassment means.

Use a dictionary to find the meaning of each of the words in *cyber harassment*.

cyber: _____

harassment: _____

_____

Previewing a text

It is useful to know something about the topic before you begin reading. Quickly reading the first sentence of each paragraph will help you remember and consider what you know about the topic. This knowledge will make the article easier to read critically.

3 Preview the article on page 68 by reading the first sentence in each paragraph. Circle the topics you think will be discussed in the article. Compare your answers with a partner.

PREVIEWING

a a comparison between online and face-to-face harassment
b reasons why cyber harassment continues to occur
c a description of cyber harassment
d how victims can fight against people who harass them
e a description of people who engage in cyber harassment
f an explanation of the legal issues in cyber harassment

WHILE READING

4 Read the article and check your predictions in Exercise 3.

READING FOR MAIN IDEAS

5 Read the article again. Decide if the statements in the table are main ideas (M) or supporting details (D). Match the statements (a–j) with the paragraphs (1–5).

READING FOR MAIN IDEAS AND DETAIL

	M or D	paragraph
a Complaints about cyber harassment by victims are sometimes considered too dramatic.		
b Trolls engage in disruptive behaviour for a variety of reasons.		
c Forty percent of internet users have experienced some form of cyber harassment.		
d It is difficult to stop cyber harassment.		
e Victims of cyber harassment often do not get a lot of support.		
f Cyber harassment takes many forms.		
g Limiting offensive speech may be considered a violation of the right to free speech.		
h Many internet users experience cyber harassment.		
i Cyber harassment includes physical threats.		
j Trolls harass other internet users because they enjoy causing pain.		

6 Use your work in Exercise 5 to create an outline of the article. (See page 43 for help and an example outline.)

CYBER HARASSMENT

1 Bloggers like Amanda Hess know about it. Journalist Caroline Criado-Perez is also familiar with it. Online gamer Jenny Haniver knows it all too well. They all know about cyber harassment because they have all been victims. Cyber harassment ranges from

Journalist Caroline Criado-Perez

behaviour such as name-calling online to more disturbing behaviour, including threats of violence, posting embarrassing photos and spreading personal or false information online. In the most serious cases, as in those of Hess, Criado-Perez and Haniver, the harassment continues over a long period of time, with numerous offensive and threatening posts every day.

2 A 2014 survey revealed that this kind of harassment is quite common. Almost three-quarters of all internet users have seen it happen, and 40% have experienced it personally. It has been suggested that even these figures may not reflect the full extent of the problem. Falling victim to cyber harassment is particularly common among younger internet users, and women are more likely to experience its more serious forms. Criado-Perez made the suggestion online that the Bank of England should put more women on their banknotes. For this idea, she received hundreds of **hostile** comments against her personally and against women more generally. Haniver was the victim of ongoing **abusive** comments and threats for no other reason than she was an assertive female gamer. Blogger Hess received similar treatment. You can easily find examples of cyber harassment on social media, in the comments section of blogs and websites and, especially, in the online gaming world.

3 Who is saying and doing all of these nasty things and why? The worst behaviour is believed to come from so-called trolls, internet users who disrupt internet communication with negative and offensive actions and comments. These individuals take pleasure in insulting other users, causing them **humiliation** and pain. Studies suggest that some of these people have mental or emotional problems; however, experts believe that many people who engage in online abuse are otherwise unremarkable people. Harassing others simply brings them the attention and

excitement that their lives in the offline world may lack. The **anonymity** of the internet allows them, and perhaps even encourages them, to behave in ways that they never would in face-to-face situations. Technology makes all of this very easy. New mobile apps, designed to allow users to provide anonymous feedback in the business world, are often used to send abusive messages to users in other settings. Sarahah, which means 'frankly' in Arabic, is an example of these apps. Created by a Saudi programmer, it has become popular, particularly in the Middle East.

4 Legal recourse against trolls varies from country to country. In Europe, exceptions to free speech include threatening, abusive or insulting words or behaviour. In the UK, an average of five trolls a day were prosecuted in 2015 for improper use of public electronic communications networks. In the USA, however, the constitutional right to free speech which guarantees all people the right to say what they want, even if it is unpopular or offensive, may protect trolls. People argue that limiting what people can say online or anywhere else could set a dangerous **precedent**. Furthermore, it can be seen that eliminating anonymity and limiting what people can say on the internet present problems of their own. Many people prefer not to reveal their identity online, not because they are trolls, but because they want to protect their own privacy. For example, you may want to ask questions online about a health problem that you do not want others to know about.

5 Because the harassment takes place online, it is not always taken seriously. A threat online may not seem as real as a threat that occurs face-to-face. Victims are often told not to be 'drama queens[1]'. Yet, the impact of this harassment on its victims is very real and very damaging. They often suffer serious psychological shock and pain. They may lose their confidence and **withdraw** from all interaction on the internet because they fear that they or their families will also suffer abusive treatment. Recovery can be difficult, and for some, it never comes. For others, the experience prompts them to speak out. Jenny Haniver blogs, tweets and speaks about her experiences of harassment in the gaming world in the hope of bringing more public attention to this issue.

[1]**drama queen** (n) someone who gets too upset or angry over small problems

READING BETWEEN THE LINES

Identifying perspective and purpose

Understanding the writer's perspective on the topic can help you determine the purpose of a text. Positive or negative words, such as those underlined in the examples below, can help you establish the writer's perspective, specifically if he or she is offering praise or criticism.

... the harassment continues over a long period of time, with numerous <u>offensive</u> and <u>threatening</u> posts every day.

Yet, the impact of this harassment on its <u>victims</u> is very real and very <u>damaging</u>.

IDENTIFYING PURPOSE

7 Work with a partner to complete the tasks.

1 Choose the phrase that best describes the writer's perspective regarding cyber harassment.
   a positive, offering praise
   b negative, offering criticism
   c neutral and informative

2 Choose the idea that best describes the writer's main purpose in writing this article.
   a to find and punish trolls
   b to change the laws that govern cyber harassment and behaviour on the internet
   c to explain cyber harassment to readers and persuade them that it is a problem
   d to convince the government to punish people who engage in cyber harassment
   e to help the victims of cyber harassment

3 Skim read the article. Find words and phrases that support your ideas about the writer's perspective and highlight or circle them. Explain your choices to another pair of students.

DISCUSSION

8 Work in small groups. Discuss the questions.

1 How does the legal system deal with cyber harassment and trolls in your country?

2 Have any cases of cyber harassment been covered by the media in your country? If so, what happened?

3 What are the benefits of having chat functions on online games? What are the drawbacks?

READING 2

PREPARING TO READ

1 You are going to read an essay about possible solutions to cyber harassment. Work with a partner. Discuss the questions.

1 The title of the essay is 'Combatting cyber harassment'. What solutions to cyber harassment do you think it will offer?

2 What kinds of advice do you think the essay will give to victims of cyber harassment?

3 Who do you think is responsible for stopping offensive behaviour on the internet?

2 Read the sentences and choose the best definition for the words in bold.

1 Our leaders must be held **accountable** for the promises they have made.

   a punished   **b** aware   **c** responsible

2 The police announced they would **prosecute** anybody who made threats online.

   a search for in order to arrest

   b take to court to argue the guilt of

   c commit a crime against

3 For weeks, he has been receiving **malicious** letters and phone calls, filled with lies that could destroy his career.

   a legal but inappropriate

   b untruthful

   c intentionally hurtful

4 We will probably never be able to **eliminate** cybercrime, but we can take steps to reduce it.
  a remove; get rid of completely
  b find an appropriate punishment for
  c weaken significantly

5 The research institute has **assembled** a team of top experts in an effort to find the cause of the problem.
  a gathered   **b** attracted   **c** interviewed

6 The government has announced a new programme to **combat** the increase in cybercrime.
  a evaluate   **b** try to stop   **c** destroy

7 The government has just passed a set of laws to help **regulate** the growing online market.
  a control   **b** encourage   **c** tax

8 After long weeks of hard work, the team began to **exhibit** signs of stress.
  a create   **b** accept   **c** show

WHILE READING

3 Read the essay on page 72. Match each main idea (a–e) to the correct paragraph (1–5).

Read the essay on page 72.

  a The online gaming community is taking steps to reduce abuse. _____
  b Legal measures against cyber harassment have not been very effective. _____
  c We need to do more to fight abusive online behaviour. _____
  d People are starting to take cyber harassment more seriously. _____
  e Online communities are beginning to make rules against cyber harassment. _____

4 Read the essay again. Complete the table with the actions that each group has taken to combat cyber harassment.

group	actions
online gaming communities	
Twitter	
Google	
the US government	

READING FOR MAIN IDEAS

READING FOR DETAIL

PLUS

COMBATTING CYBER HARASSMENT

1   Cyber harassment can have a serious and destructive impact on its victims and their families. Yet, until recently, it was not taken seriously in the US. Instead, it was widely believed that this behaviour was similar to childish fights, but this attitude is changing. Media attention on several recent cyber harassment cases has prompted the public to demand that trolls be held **accountable** for their behaviour. Additionally, as offensive and **malicious** behaviour has become more prevalent, and the threats by internet trolls have become more frightening, social media apps and sites, as well as online gaming communities, are taking notice. They worry that their users will begin to abandon their sites if trolls are allowed to operate freely. In short, taking responsibility for cyber harassment has become an economic issue.

2   The effort to **combat** cyber harassment requires a two-pronged approach: prevention and penalties; however, to date, most of the focus has been on the first. Prevention can be controversial. The anonymity of the internet makes harassment easy, yet placing any limits on online interaction could threaten the benefits of both the anonymity and free speech that we value. Online gaming communities want to provide maximum freedom to their participants, but these are the places where a great deal of harassment occurs, especially of female players. To try to address this problem, one hugely popular gaming site, *League of Legends*, **assembled** a team of behaviour experts to study its 67 million monthly users. What they discovered surprised them. They expected to find a small group of badly behaved players – users who were responsible for most of the abuse and hostile behaviour. Their plan was to suspend these players in hopes of **eliminating**, or at least reducing online harassment. They did find a few 'bad apples', but they discovered that most of the offensive behaviour came from players who were usually good internet citizens. They only acted badly occasionally. The research team had greater success when the chat function on the game was turned off as default, although players could choose to turn it on. This resulted in abusive comments dropping by 30%. This study suggests that creating even a small barrier to bad behaviour can often stop abuse before it starts.

3   Other online communities and sites have already taken steps in this direction. Twitter has had a 'report abuse' button since 2013. Some gaming sites have systems that allow players to establish their reputations in the same way that sellers on online market sites, such as eBay, must do. They rate one another as 'good player' or 'avoid me'. In other words, the communities are beginning to **regulate** themselves. They are also using the latest technology to identify the worst offenders. Google has sponsored a research study to find an algorithm for identifying them. Their posts are more frequent and generally contain negative words, poor grammar and misspelled words, allowing researchers to identify and ban users who **exhibit** troll behaviour.

4   The United States government have updated their laws to cover threats and stalking over the internet. Nevertheless, these laws still lag disturbingly behind emerging technology. What is more, so far, very few people have been **prosecuted** under the laws that do exist. Experts offer advice that is familiar to anybody who has been the victim of bullying: ignore it. Do not respond to the harassment.
    By responding to it, you give the trolls what they want – attention. Although this is generally considered to be good advice, unfortunately it often does not stop ongoing abuse.

5   As we spend more and more time on the internet, addressing offensive and threatening behaviour online is becoming increasingly important. As Laura Hudson wrote in *Wired* magazine in 2014, '… the internet is now where we socialize, where we work. It's where we meet our spouses, where we build our reputations. Online harassment isn't just inconvenient, nor is it something we can walk away from with ease. It's abhorrent behaviour that has real social, professional and economic costs.'

READING BETWEEN THE LINES

5 Work with a partner to complete the tasks.

1 Which phrase best describes the writer's perspective on cyber harassment? Circle the correct answer.
   a neutral and objective
   b informative and argumentative
   c negative and emotional

2 What is the writer's purpose? Circle all of the correct answers.
   a to eliminate cyber harassment
   b to inform readers about current steps to stop cyber harassment
   c to tell readers about specific cases of cyber harassment
   d to help victims fight against and recover from cyber harassment
   e to convince readers that more must be done to stop cyber harassment in the US

3 Skim read the essay. Find words and phrases that support your ideas about the writer's perspective and underline them. Explain your choices to another pair of students.

DISCUSSION

6 Work in small groups. Use ideas from Reading 1 and Reading 2 to answer the following questions.

1 What advice would you give to a victim of cyber harassment?
2 Do you think technology will find a solution to the problem? How?
3 What kind of penalty do you think that people who in engage in cyber harassment should face?
4 What do you think are the consequences of cyber harassment, beyond its effect on victims?

COLLOCATIONS FOR BEHAVIOUR

1 Complete each sentence with one verb (in the correct form) and one noun to describe behaviour or responses to behaviour. In some items, more than one answer is possible.

verbs	nouns
build exhibit experience lose suffer take	abuse behaviour confidence pain a reputation responsibility

1 When you have done something wrong, it is important to _____ _____ for your actions.

2 My online service provider has _____ _____ for protecting its users from abusive behaviour.

3 People who have _____ _____ online often decide to withdraw from any interaction (n) at all on the internet.

4 It is not only trolls who _____ hostile and offensive _____ online. Some ordinary users have also been known to act badly.

5 The stress of online abuse can cause people to _____ _____ that is both physical and psychological.

6 Even a single hostile or abusive online post can cause a user to _____ _____ and feel bad.

PLUS

2 Work with a partner. Discuss the questions. Use the words in the box to describe online activity, behaviour, comments or posts.

abhorrent   disturbing   insulting   negative threatening   abusive   hostile   malicious   offensive

1 Have you heard about cases of cyber harassment among your friends or acquaintances, or in the news? What happened?

_____

_____

2 What kind of online behaviour do you believe is the most damaging? Why?

_____

_____

3 Do you think damaging online behaviours can be eliminated? Why / Why not?

_____

_____

PROBLEM–SOLUTION COLLOCATIONS

VOCABULARY

There are many nouns and verbs that describe problems and solutions. Some form typical or frequent collocations.

		verbs	nouns
stating the existence of a problem		become, face	an issue, a problem
		face, pose, present, represent	a challenge, a danger, a problem, a risk, a threat
		cause, run into	trouble, problems
describing solutions		address, confront, eliminate, face, respond to	a challenge, a danger, an issue, a problem, a risk, a threat
		fix, resolve, solve	a problem
		resolve	an issue

3 Complete each sentence with one verb (in the correct form) and one noun from the Explanation box. In some items, more than one answer is possible.

1 Phishing is an internet crime that _____ _____ to the almost four billion people who interact on the web.

2 If we do nothing, this could easily get worse and so we should _____ the _____ as soon as possible.

3 We have been ignoring cyber harassment for far too long and it is time that we finally _____ this _____ .

4 Everything on the project was going so well until last week, when we started to _____ _____ with our computer systems.

5 It is impossible to _____ _____ of cyber attacks but it is possible to increase your protection against them.

4 Work with a partner. Read the scenarios. Retell each scenario using the language in the table to describe the problems and solutions.

---

1 Arriving passengers at an airport complained constantly about the length of time they had to wait for their baggage. Airport officials tried several approaches to reduce the waiting time, including hiring extra staff. With these adjustments, the wait was reduced to about the average at most airports, but passengers still complained. Eventually, the officials moved the baggage claim area farther away, so passengers had to walk farther to reach it.

---

2 A city neighbourhood was having a problem with rats. The rats lived on the rubbish people had thrown out. The neighbours considered using poison, but they worried about pets or even children coming into contact with it. They tried traps, but the rats were too intelligent. The neighbours contacted an organization that brings feral cats (cats that live on the streets) into areas with rat problems. They delivered five feral cats. A week later, the rats were gone.

WRITING

CRITICAL THINKING

At the end of this unit, you will write a problem–solution essay. Look at this unit's writing task in the box below.

> Describe an online behaviour that you think is a problem and explain what you think should be done to prevent or eliminate it.

Analyzing problems and solutions

Framing a text in terms of problems and their possible solutions can be an effective form of analysis. First identify the problem. Analyze the problem and look at it from different angles. How did the problem arise? What conditions allow it to continue? Consider a range of possible ways to reduce or eliminate the problem and, finally, decide which solution is best.

 **EVALUATE**

1 Work with a small group. Think of examples of problematic online behaviour. Give a clear explanation of each of the behaviours. Look back at the two reading texts for ideas or think of examples from your own experience. Two examples are provided for you below (doxxing and phishing).

Then, discuss how difficult it would be to control each behaviour. Rank each behaviour: (1) Impossible to control, (2) Possible to control but not stop, (3) Possible to stop.

doxxing: publishing private information about people online in order to expose them to abuse and possible threats
phishing: pretending to be a trustworthy contact, such as a bank, and attempting to trick the victim into revealing information, such as bank details, over the internet

 **ANALYZE**

2 Work in pairs. Choose two of the behaviours you thought of in Exercise 1. Discuss the questions and make notes. Use the tables on page 77 to organize your notes.

  1 What is the origin of the behaviour? Why do people behave this way? What technology allows people to behave this way?
  2 What are the consequences for victims of allowing this behaviour to continue? What are the consequences for internet users in general?

Problem 1 _____

origins of and reasons for behaviour	consequences	
	victims	internet users

Problem 2 _____

origins of and reasons for behaviour	consequences	
	victims	internet users

3 Discuss the questions about each behaviour in Exercise 2 and make note of any good ideas you have. Use the tables to organize your notes.

1 What can individual internet users do to help control and/or prevent this behaviour?
2 Do you know of any organizations that are responsible for preventing or responding to this behaviour? What do they currently do? What more could they do?

Problem 1 _____

	responses/solutions	
	individuals	organizations
current		
proposed		

Problem 2 _____

	responses/solutions	
	individuals	organizations
current		
proposed		

EVALUATE

4 Exchange your tables with another pair of students. Give each other feedback about the solutions that you have proposed. Which one(s) do you think are most likely to be effective? Which one(s) will be the most likely to happen? Why?

5 Revise your solutions based on the feedback from other students.

GRAMMAR FOR WRITING

IMPERSONAL PASSIVE CONSTRUCTIONS

Writers often choose the passive voice when the agent is 'people'. As a subject, 'people' may be too general or repetitive.

People say that cyber harassment is most common in the male–dominated online gaming world.

When reporting what people think or say, writers create a passive which has no apparent agent. Two constructions are commonly used:

*Cyber harassment **is said to be** most common in the male–dominated online gaming world.*

***It is said that** cyber harassment is most common in the male–dominated online gaming world.*

These passive constructions often appear with the verbs *agree, argue, believe, claim, consider, decide, expect, say, think* and *understand*. Note, however, that not all of these verbs allow both constructions.

*Removal of online anonymity **is believed to be** one of the best ways to prevent online abuse.*

***It is argued that** laws relating to online abuse are old–fashioned and don't reflect how the internet is used.*

1 Rewrite sentences 1–4 in the impersonal passive in two ways. For sentences 5 and 6, only one of the constructions is possible.

1 People believe that these figures underestimate the size of the problem.
2 People claim that trolls are responsible for the most abusive forms of cyber harassment.
3 People expect that victims of online harassment will speak out against their abusers.
4 People understand that self-regulation is the best way to control bad behaviour.
5 People consider 'just ignore it' to be sensible advice to victims of online harassment.
6 People have argued that these problems will require a legal solution.

2 Now write three sentences of your own using an impersonal passive construction with *say*, *believe* or *think*.

PASSIVE FOR CONTINUITY

GRAMMAR

One reason a writer might choose to use the passive is to maintain continuity within and across sentences. In other words, the passive allows writers to continue using the same noun phrase as the subject across clauses and sentences. It is easier for readers to follow ideas when the subject remains the same.

Because the **harassment** takes place online, <u>the public</u> do not always take it seriously.
    SUBJECT OF THE FIRST CLAUSE   SUBJECT OF THE SECOND CLAUSE

Because the **harassment** takes place online, **it** is not always taken seriously.
    SUBJECT OF THE FIRST CLAUSE   SUBJECT OF THE SECOND CLAUSE

In the second sentence, the passive allows *harassment* to be the subject of both clauses, providing greater continuity. Notice that the *by* phrase is omitted.

3 Read the sentences below. Rewrite the second clause or sentence using the passive. Omit the *by* phrase if it is not necessary.

1 Although the stalker had been harassing students for weeks, the police did not catch him until yesterday.
2 A full year after the troll's attacks began, a journalist discovered their identity.
3 These cyber stalkers were not very careful. Security experts found evidence of their activity quite quickly.
4 The news generally includes positive stories about technology, but in recent months stories of cybercrime have dominated the media.

4 Read the paragraph. Underline all the instances in which the subject of one sentence appears in another role in subsequent sentences. Then rewrite the paragraph using the passive where appropriate. Omit the *by* phrase if it is not necessary.

> Identity theft is a growing problem. It occurs when somebody uses your personal information to open bank accounts, borrow money or make purchases. Almost 17 million people reported identity theft last year. The elderly are especially likely to become victims. Criminals targeted over 2.6 million older people in 2014. Stolen credit cards were the most common source of identity theft. Unfortunately, police do not usually recover the stolen cards.

ACADEMIC WRITING SKILLS

WRITING ABOUT PROBLEMS

SKILLS

When presenting problems, writers use a range of strategies to demonstrate to their readers that these problems are important. Facts, statistics and examples (especially ones that will resonate with readers) can highlight the seriousness of each problem.

Here are some examples of these strategies.
Facts (F): Many countries do not have laws against cyber harassment.
Statistics (S): Almost 75% of all internet users have witnessed cyber harassment.
Examples (E): Jenny Haniver was subjected to months of violent threats.

1 Read the statements and label the strategy the writer uses: *F, S* or *E.*

1 Three-quarters of all cyber stalking victims are female. _____
2 After several abusive reviews, business at the hair salon decreased dramatically. _____
3 In a recent survey, 34% of students reported that they had experienced cyber bullying. _____
4 Most teens and children do not tell their parents when they experience cyber bullying. _____
5 Laura Hosmer lost her entire life savings when somebody found her social security number and other personal information online. _____
6 A cyber stalker has been harassing an Emirati teacher for more than ten years. _____

7 In some cases, doxxing has led to physical harm against victims. _____
8 The most widely used platform for cyber harassment is social media. _____

2 Read the extract from Reading 1 below. Find one example, one statistic and one fact. Compare your extract to a partner's.

> A 2014 survey revealed that this kind of harassment is quite common. Almost three-quarters of all internet users have seen it happen, and 40% have experienced it personally. It has been suggested that even these figures may not reflect the full extent of the problem. Falling victim to cyber harassment is particularly common among younger internet users, and women are more likely to experience its more serious forms. Criado-Perez made the suggestion online that the Bank of England should put more women on their banknotes. For this idea, she received hundreds of hostile comments against her personally and against women more generally.

3 Work in small groups. Write four sentences, including at least one fact, one statistic, one example and one opinion about cyber harassment. Share your sentences with the class.

1 _____
_____
_____

2 _____
_____
_____

3 _____
_____
_____

4 _____
_____
_____

WRITING ABOUT SOLUTIONS

When a writer offers recommendations or solutions, they may do it in several ways:

- cite experts or research (R)
- cite generally held views (G)
- make direct suggestions of their own (S)

4 Read the statements and label the strategy the writer uses: *R, G* or *S*.

1 A recent study suggests that a minor change in a game's design can significantly reduce abusive behaviour. _____

2 One solution is to require social media sites to do a better job of regulating their members' behaviour. _____

3 These new, stricter laws are considered effective tools for combatting cyber scams. _____

4 Most internet users prefer self-regulation to government intervention. _____

5 Technology created the problem, so technology should provide a solution. _____

6 Media professionals believe we need to provide more public support for victims and harsher penalties for trolls. _____

5 Work in small groups. Offer somebody advice on what they should do when facing cyber harassment. Write three pieces of advice. Use each strategy from the Explanation box once. Share your sentences with the class.

R _____

_____

G _____

_____

S _____

_____

WRITING TASK

Describe an online behaviour that you think is a problem and explain what you think should be done to prevent or eliminate it.

PLAN

1 Review your tables from Critical thinking, Exercise 2 on pages 76–77. Choose one of the problematic online behaviours to write about.

2 Use your notes from Critical thinking to write your introductory paragraph.

- Describe the problem.
- Explain its consequences.
- End with a thesis statement that suggests there are possible solutions, but do not list what those solutions are. You will present those in the body of your essay.

_____

_____

_____

_____

_____

3 Now review the tables of responses/solutions you proposed in Critical thinking, Exercise 3 on pages 77–78. Which two or three of the solutions from Critical thinking do you think are most likely to be successful? Present one possible solution per paragraph.

- State a possible solution and explain how it works.
- Explain what steps need to be taken to carry out this solution.

Solution 1: _____

_____

_____

Solution 2: _____

_____

_____

Solution 3: _____

_____

_____

4 Think about your concluding paragraph. Write two or three sentences.

- Refer back to your main idea.
- Emphasize the importance of acting against this behaviour.
- Leave your readers with something to think about.

_____

_____

_____

_____

_____

5 Refer to the Task checklist on page 84 as you prepare your essay.

WRITE A FIRST DRAFT

6 Write your essay. Use your essay plan to help you structure your ideas. Write 400–450 words.

REVISE

7 Use the Task checklist to review your essay for content and structure.

TASK CHECKLIST	✔
Have you explained the negative online behaviour and its consequences in your introductory paragraph?	
Does your thesis statement suggest that solutions are possible but not list them?	
Have you provided at least two possible solutions in separate body paragraphs?	
Do you refer to research or generally held views?	
Does each paragraph have a topic sentence and are all points in the paragraph related to that topic?	
Does your conclusion refer back to the main idea of your essay?	
Does each paragraph include a topic sentence?	

EDIT

8 Use the Language checklist to edit your essay for language errors.

LANGUAGE CHECKLIST	✔
Have you used appropriate vocabulary to describe behaviour and responses to behaviour?	
Have you used problem–solution collocations?	
Have you used impersonal passive statements in your essay?	
Have you used the passive, where appropriate, to create continuity of subject?	
Have you used a combination of facts, statistics, examples and opinions?	

9 Make any necessary changes to your essay.

OBJECTIVES REVIEW

1 Check your learning objectives for this unit. Write *3*, *2* or *1* for each objective.

3 = very well   2 = well   1 = not so well

I can ...

watch and understand a video about online harassment. _____

preview a text. _____

identify purpose and tone. _____

analyze problems and solutions. _____

use impersonal passive constructions. _____

use passives for continuity. _____

write about problems. _____

write about solutions. _____

write a problem–solution essay. _____

2 Go to the *Unlock* Online Workbook for more practice with this unit's learning objectives.

WORDLIST		
abhorrent (adj)	disturbing (adj)	offensive (adj)
abuse (n) ⦿	eliminate (v) ⦿	precedent (n) ⦿
abusive (adj)	exhibit (v)	prosecute (v)
accountable (adj)	hostile (adj) ⦿	regulate (v) ⦿
anonymity (n)	humiliation (n)	resolve (v) ⦿
assemble (v)	insulting (adj)	run into (phr v)
combat (v) ⦿	malicious (adj)	threatening (adj)
confront (v) ⦿	negative (adj) ⦿	withdraw (v)

⦿ = high-frequency words in the Cambridge Academic Corpus

LEARNING OBJECTIVES	IN THIS UNIT YOU WILL ...
Watch and listen	watch and understand a video about problems faced by small, independent businesses.
Reading skill	work out meaning from context.
Critical thinking	analyze advantages and disadvantages.
Grammar	express contrast; use reductions of subordinate clauses.
Academic writing skill	write about similarities and differences.
Writing task	write a comparison and contrast essay.

UNL⌀CK YOUR KNOWLEDGE

Work with a partner. Discuss the questions.

1 Are there a lot of street food vans and other mobile retail businesses where you live? Do you ever buy from these businesses?

2 What makes you choose to shop at one business instead of another?

3 If you were going to start your own small business, what would it be? Give reasons for your answer.

PLUS

WATCH AND LISTEN

PREPARING TO WATCH

ACTIVATING YOUR KNOWLEDGE

1 Work with a partner. Discuss the questions.

  1 What kinds of small businesses can you find in most town centres?
  2 What kind of challenges do you think the people who own small businesses face?
  3 How do small businesses promote themselves in your country?

USING YOUR KNOWLEDGE TO PREDICT CONTENT

2 Complete the questionnaire. Work in a small group and compare your answers.

	agree	not sure	disagree
1 Small shops and market stalls are popular places to shop.			
2 It is a good time to start a new business.			
3 It is hard to make a profit in a new retail business.			
4 Small shops and market stalls are cheap to run.			

GLOSSARY

private sector (n) businesses that are not owned or controlled by the government

afloat (adj) having enough money to pay what you owe

deposit (n) an amount of money that you pay when you rent something, and is returned to you when you return the thing you have rented

premises (n) the building(s) that a company uses for their business activities

relief (n) money or other services that provide help for people who need it

regulatory burden (n phr) laws that business owners have to obey, including laws regarding the amount of tax they pay

WHILE WATCHING

UNDERSTANDING MAIN IDEAS

3 ▶ Watch the video and take notes. Write one or two sentences to summarize why the UK's small businesses are in the news.

_____

_____

4 ▶ Watch again. Complete the table.

1 Type of shops on UK high streets	_____
2 Number of small businesses in the UK	_____
3 Proportion of sales in private sector by small businesses	_____
4 Date of Small Business Saturday	_____
5 Amount spent in small businesses on Small Business Saturday	_____
6 Proportion of businesses that have fewer than ten workers	_____
7 Amount it cost Eve to start her shop	_____
8 Why it was cheap for Eve to start her business	_____
9 How Jamie's father financed his business	_____
10 What Jamie feels business rates pay for	_____
11 How tax on Kate's shop is calculated	_____
12 How much tax Kate pays	_____
13 Two things small businesses need in order to grow	_____ _____

5 Choose the best meaning for each of the phrases in bold.

1 Visit any UK high street or market place and you will find **an array of** specialist shops.
   a a large number of   b several   c a variety of

2 ... the retailers **are bustling with** customers ...
   a are attracting   b are full of   c are competing for

3 If you **look ahead**, it's going to be a small firm's world.
   a are optimistic   b work hard   c think about the future

4 It's a huge **chunk**; it's over half of what our rent is.
   a amount   b proportion   c number

DISCUSSION

6 Work in a small group. Discuss the questions.

1 How similar is the situation for small businesses in your country to that in the UK regarding finances and taxes?

2 Would you be prepared to take a risk like selling your home to start a business? If so, in what circumstances? If not, why not?

3 David Young says that 'it's going to be a small firm's world'. Do you agree with him? Why / Why not?

READING

READING 1

PREPARING TO READ

1 You are going to read an article about mobile businesses. Discuss the statements with a partner. Rate each statement on a scale of 1 (completely disagree) to 5 (completely agree).

1 It is easy to turn a hobby into a business. _____
2 It usually only costs about £3,000 to start a mobile business. _____
3 Street food van owners usually make a profit more quickly than new restaurant owners. _____
4 The number of mobile businesses is increasing. _____
5 Street food vans are the most common type of mobile business in the world. _____

2 Read the words and their definitions below. Use the correct forms of the words in bold to complete the sentences below.

> **aspiring** (adj) wishing to become successful
> **break even** (idiom) to have no profit or loss at the end of a business activity
> **component** (n) one of the parts of something
> **fluctuating** (adj) changing frequently from one level to another
> **outweigh** (v) to be greater or more important than something else
> **proposition** (n) a proposal or suggestion, especially in business
> **revenue** (n) the money that a business receives regularly
> **transition** (n) a change from one form or type to another

1 The price of oil has _____ dramatically since 2000, going from £30 a barrel to almost £120, then down to £25!
2 The most interesting business _____ are a little risky.
3 My daughter is an _____ chef. She has just started her career working in a food van.
4 The potential profits _____ the potential risks.
5 One _____ of the machine has broken so we have had to stop production.
6 It can be difficult for small family businesses to make the _____ to large public companies.
7 The first year, our business lost money; the second year, it _____ .
8 Amazon's UK _____ in 2015 was over £6 billion (£6,000,000,000).

3 Read the article on page 92 quickly to find the answers to the questions below.

Read the article on page 92

1 What are the average start-up costs for a street food van? _____

2 What kind of mobile business can you find in Jeddah? _____

3 What are some other examples of mobile retail?

_____

4 How much did mobile retail in the US grow between 2009 and 2014?

_____

5 What are some of the problems that mobile retail owners face?

_____

6 How much money do street food vans bring in annually in the US?

_____

4 Read the article again. Decide whether this article would be worth reading for each of these people. Write *Y* (yes), *N* (no) or *M* (maybe).

1 A small business owner who wants to find a bigger location _____

2 A small business owner who wants to expand into other parts of the city, but is not sure where _____

3 A person who wants to open a restaurant, but does not have much money _____

4 A person looking for a job with a tech company _____

5 A researcher looking for current economic trends _____

6 A researcher looking for information on traffic flow in a city _____

WHILE READING

5 Read the article and summarize the writer's main argument in one sentence. Compare your ideas with a partner.

_____

_____

STARTING OUT MOBILE

1 Maybe you make the world's best pies, or you have always helped your friends and neighbours by mending their computers, or perhaps you have green fingers and your garden is the envy of the street. A lot of businesses are started by people who have hobbies or special talents and want to turn these interests into a business. But scaling up from a hobby to a real business, such as a bakery, restaurant or shop, requires business know-how and a substantial investment. Many people do not have enough of either of these, so they never take the first step.

2 An increasing number of **aspiring** business owners have found a way to take a first step that makes this **transition** from hobby to business more gradual, less expensive and less risky. They are taking their dreams and talents on the road – in vans and lorries, and even horse trailers. The first entrepreneurs to do this have been in the food business. In recent years a wave of street food vans has arrived on the scene, serving everything from gourmet cupcakes and burgers to Vietnamese street food. Street food vans have become a way for aspiring chefs to try out recipes and test the water before making a big investment in a traditional, brick-and-mortar business[1].

3 Beginning on a small scale has its advantages, the most important of which is the relatively modest size of start-up costs. These costs, which consist primarily of the vehicle and any required equipment, usually come to about £5,000–£10,000, a fraction of what it would cost to start a shop or restaurant. Similarly, overhead costs[2] are generally low. Mobile business owners must pay for fuel, of course, but other utility payments are modest. With such tightly controlled costs, mobile businesses often **break even** in a year or two; in contrast, success comes to brick-and-mortar businesses much more slowly, and they often fail within the first two years. In short, mobile businesses are relatively low-risk **propositions**.

4 The mobile food vendor trend in the US and Europe has spread to other parts of the globe. Today, you can get waffles and pancakes from a lorry in Jeddah, Saudi Arabia and tacos from an old school bus in Dubai. The success of these street food vans has inspired other entrepreneurs to consider starting out on wheels. Rich Harper once ran a chain of gyms, but his real interest was boxing. In 2005, he bought an old lorry, equipped it with some gym equipment and

took to the streets – all for a total start-up cost of just under £5,000. His business quickly made a profit and is still going strong, as he brings the boxing ring to customers all over his state.

5 UK entrepreneurs could take inspiration from the US where, today, there are vehicles that sell flowers, shoes, clothes and all kinds of specialty food items. There are also mobile businesses that provide services, such as hair styling, pet grooming and repair of high-tech devices. Mobile retail has grown steadily, declaring a 12% increase between 2009 and 2014. Mobile retail is not without problems, however. Weather, the **fluctuating** price of fuel, and just finding a place to set up are all challenges that mobile entrepreneurs have to deal with. These business owners, however, feel the advantages **outweigh** the disadvantages. In the US, the mobile food business alone – the largest in the mobile retail sector – generates an average annual **revenue** of $857 million.

6 Once convinced that their business has achieved sufficient success, some successful mobile entrepreneurs move on to a brick-and-mortar business. Others, like Rich Harper and his boxing gym, are satisfied to stay mobile. In an interesting twist, some brick-and-mortar business owners, observing the success of mobile retailers, have added a mobile **component** to their business. The vehicle acts as a marketing tool to bring business into the shop. As stand-alone businesses or as extensions of shops, mobile retail has huge future potential in these economic times.

[1]**brick-and-mortar business** (n phr) a business with a physical location in a building
[2]**overhead costs** (n) the regular costs, such as rent and heating, that are involved in operating a business

READING BETWEEN THE LINES

Working out meaning from context

Most texts will contain words and phrases that you don't know, but stopping to look up each unfamiliar word will make it more difficult to understand the whole text. Instead you should keep reading. You can try to work out the general meaning of unfamiliar words and phrases by looking for examples, contrasts, comparisons or in-text definitions. There may also be some other words in the context that indicate their general meaning. Understanding the general meaning of unfamiliar words and phrases can enable you to carry on reading.

In recent years a wave of street food vans has arrived on the scene, serving everything from **gourmet cupcakes** *and burgers to Vietnamese street food.*

The context allows you to guess that *gourmet cupcakes* are a type of food. It is not important to know exactly what kind of food.

WORKING OUT MEANING FROM CONTEXT

6 Find the phrases (1–8) in the article. Work out the meaning from the context. Match the phrases with their definitions (a–h).

1 have green fingers (para 1)
2 the envy of the street (para 1)
3 scale up (para 1)
4 arrive on the scene (para 2)
5 test the water (para 2)
6 going strong (para 4)
7 move on to (para 6)
8 stand-alone (para 6)

a try out in a safe way or on a small scale
b be good at growing plants
c appear
d doing very well
e something your neighbours wish they had
f independent
g increase in size, amount or importance
h progress to

7 Work with a partner. Write a sentence for each phrase in Exercise 6, using the phrase in context correctly. Share your sentences with the class.

_____

_____

_____

_____

_____

_____

_____

_____

DISCUSSION

8 Work with a partner. Discuss the questions.

1 What role do you think social media plays in the rise of mobile retail?
2 In what way, if any, do you think the rise of mobile retail is related to the state of the economy?

READING 2

PREPARING TO READ

USING YOUR
KNOWLEDGE

1 You are going to read an essay about customer loyalty. Circle the strategies that would be successful in keeping you as a loyal customer. Then compare your choices with a partner. Discuss your reasons.

a special prices that are only available to loyal customers
b free delivery
c a scheme that rewards you for buying more merchandise
d special products that are only available to loyal customers
e the opportunity to buy products in high demand before the general public
f prizes or free gifts

UNDERSTANDING
KEY VOCABULARY

2 Read the sentences and choose the best definition for the words in bold.

1 When petrol prices are low, drivers have no **incentive** to leave their cars at home and take public transport.
   a alternative
   b encouragement
   c argument
2 Some investors **shrewdly** bought shares in the company when prices were very low.
   a in a way that is based on good judgment
   b in a way that is based on illegal actions
   c in a way that is based on luck or coincidence
3 It is important to set goals that are **attainable**; otherwise, you will just get discouraged.
   a possible to achieve
   b practical; sensible
   c simple; able to be explained clearly
4 There is an **ongoing** debate in this business community about the future of mobile retail.
   a formal
   b highly emotional
   c continuing

5 We have been in this office for more than 30 years, so we have **accumulated** a lot of equipment.
  a gradually collected
  b rid ourselves of
  c increased the value of

6 If their pay is low, employees look for work in other companies. Higher salaries are the best way to improve employee **retention**.
  a performance
  b the ability to keep something
  c quality or standards

7 Jeff Bezos was a **pioneer** in online retail, establishing Amazon.com in 1994.
  a one of the first people to do something
  b one of the most famous people in a field
  c an international expert

8 After one company started to offer free shipping to its customers, other companies soon **followed suit**.
  a made a more attractive offer
  b competed against one another
  c did the same thing

PLUS

WHILE READING

3 Read the essay on page 96. Which of the statements are consistent with the claims made in the essay? Write *C* (consistent) or *NC* (not consistent). Compare your answers with a partner.

READING FOR MAIN IDEAS

Example: Subscription services give customers fewer choices. C
Claim in essay: *the service makes decisions for consumers who may have difficulty making decisions for themselves.*

  a Businesses are less concerned with keeping customers than with finding new ones. _____
  b Reward schemes are a good way to keep customers loyal. _____
  c Customers will not participate in loyalty schemes if the rewards are too difficult to get. _____
  d The main reason customers become members of subscription services is the low price of joining them. _____
  e Subscription services are more successful than loyalty schemes in attracting and keeping customers. _____
  f Subscription services can increase sales. _____

KEEPING YOUR CUSTOMERS

It costs five to ten times more to sell a product to a new customer than to an existing one. So what are businesses doing to hold on to their customers? The answer is – everything they possibly can. Two popular business strategies with successful track records for customer **retention** are reward schemes, often also referred to as loyalty schemes, and subscription services.

Loyalty schemes encourage customers to continue buying products or services from one particular company by offering customers rewards. Airlines, **pioneers** of loyalty schemes, provide a good example. When customers fly with one airline on multiple trips, that airline rewards them with free travel. Generally, customers have to **accumulate** a specific number of 'air miles' in order to receive their reward, providing an **incentive** to continue flying with one airline. Other companies, from Starbucks to Tesco, have **followed suit**, offering rewards to loyal customers.

Consumers often belong to multiple loyalty schemes, yet most people participate actively in only a few. Companies are interested in understanding the reasons behind this behaviour. The most successful loyalty schemes have several features in common. They are simple and easy to understand, but most important, their rewards are **attainable**. Customers receive rewards often enough that they see the benefit of remaining loyal to the company. The schemes not only keep customers buying the company's products or services, they also provide the company with valuable information about their customers' behaviour and preferences.

A second successful strategy for maintaining customer relationships is the subscription service. In these schemes, customers sign up to purchase items, such as shaving products, snacks or make-up, on a regular basis. These items are delivered to the customer's home. The convenience of home delivery is an idea with a long history, but subscription services offer more than a convenient way to replace household necessities. They offer customers products that are tailored to their own personal needs and desires. This kind of treatment makes customers feel special and deepens their connection to the brand. In a retail environment where consumers are faced with a dizzying array of[1] products, this kind of service can combat what has been referred to as 'the paralysis of choice'. In other words, the service makes decisions for consumers who may have difficulty making decisions for themselves. For the company, subscription services offer guaranteed regular sales, an **ongoing** relationship with their customers and, like loyalty schemes, a rich source of data about buying behaviour.

Some companies, such as Amazon, even charge their customers for their subscription services. In return, customers get what they value most, for example, free delivery or access to digital content. It may seem as if Amazon would lose money by not charging their customers for delivery, but the company has **shrewdly** calculated that customers, having paid for the subscription service, will even shop on Amazon for items they might otherwise buy at the local supermarket. One study showed that Amazon subscription customers spent 100% more after becoming a member of their subscription service.

Reward schemes and subscription services are just two of the marketing tools that businesses use to hold on to customers. They have learned that it makes better business sense to devote attention and even money to their current customers than to try to attract new ones.

[1] **a dizzying array of** (quantifier) a confusingly large number of different things on display

4 Read the essay to find the information to complete the summary.

> The most effective loyalty schemes are (1)_____ and have (2)_____ rewards. Keeping customers loyal is not the only reason for such schemes. They also provide (3)_____ information about what (4)_____ like. (5)_____ were the first to offer reward schemes, and they are probably still the most familiar to the public. Subscription services offer more than (6)_____ ; they also offer products that are specific to customers' needs and (7)_____ . They offer a limited selection, which helps customers make (8)_____ . Research suggests that customers buy more products when they have a subscription. Amazon subscription members spend (9)_____ more than non-subscription customers.

READING BETWEEN THE LINES

5 Work with a partner. Discuss the questions.

1 How do you think loyalty schemes provide companies with data on customer behaviour?
2 Why might customers join a loyalty scheme but then not participate actively in it?
3 What do you think the term *the paralysis of choice* means?
4 Why might products such as snacks, razors for shaving and make-up be popular items for subscription services?

DISCUSSION

6 Work with a partner. Use ideas from Reading 1 and Reading 2 to answer the following questions.

1 Do you participate in a loyalty scheme? If so, what do you like or not like about it? If not, why not?
2 Do you participate in a subscription service? If so, do you think having the subscription has encouraged you to buy more? If not, why not?
3 What important information do you think a shop owner could get from a loyalty scheme or subscription service before opening a mobile operation?
4 Which do think would be more successful among your peers – a loyalty scheme or a subscription service? How about among your parents and their peers? Why?

EXPRESSING CONTRAST

There are many different ways to connect contrasting ideas. Contrast connectors may differ in both structure and meaning.

Structure

Unlike other companies, Amazon charges for its subscription service.

Many subscription services are free. **However**, Amazon charges a substantial fee for its scheme.

Despite the director's best efforts, the company was unable to make a profit. The director made a huge effort. **Nevertheless**, the company was unable to make a profit.

Instead of reducing the number of staff to save money, the café's owner hired more to try to make more money.

The café's owner didn't reduce the number of staff. **Rather**, he hired more to try to make more money.

Meaning

Contrast connectors typically express one of three somewhat different meanings.

	to connect a contrasting idea in a noun phrase with another in the same sentence	to connect contrasting ideas in two sentences
direct contrast	*unlike* *in contrast to*	*by contrast* *however* *on the other hand*
concession: to show that the contrast might be unexpected	*despite* *in spite of*	*nevertheless* *however*
correction or replacement: to show that the first clause or phrase is wrong or insufficient and that the clause that follows is correct	*instead of* *rather than*	*instead* *on the contrary* *in fact* *rather* *however*

1 Read the sentences. Choose the best contrast connector to complete each sentence. Pay attention to structure and meaning.

1. _____ the convenience of subscription services, these schemes are not as popular as loyalty schemes.
   a Instead of
   b In spite of
   c Nevertheless

2. One company has decided to avoid the points system in their loyalty scheme. _____ , they give their loyal customers their rewards immediately.
   a Instead
   b However
   c On the other hand

3. About a quarter of all new restaurants fail in their first year. _____ , hundreds of entrepreneurs open restaurants every year, hoping to beat the odds.
   a Rather
   b Despite
   c Nevertheless

4. _____ loyalty schemes, subscription services restrict membership to special customers, giving those customers the sense that they belong to an exclusive club.
   a Unlike
   b Instead of
   c However

5. Mobile businesses are not as risky as they seem; _____ , they are less likely to lose money than brick-and-mortar businesses.
   a by contrast
   b in fact
   c on the other hand

PLUS

BUSINESS AND MARKETING VOCABULARY

2 Complete the text below with the correct form of the words and phrases from the box. In some items, more than one answer is possible.

> break even   brick-and-mortar   generate revenue
> make a profit   marketing tool   on a large/small scale
> start-up costs   track record   utility bills

For many people, the dream of a lifetime is owning their own business. If you are one of them, it is a good idea to start (1)_____. You may want to begin with a mobile business, where (2)_____ and (3)_____ are low. Whatever you decide, you should set goals for your new business. For example, how long do you expect it to take before your business (4)_____? How much longer after that will it take for the business to (5)_____? Even for an established (6)_____ business with a good (7)_____, there comes a time when sales start to slow down and you need to find a new way to (8)_____. The question is, 'What do your customers want?' There are lots of online (9)_____ that can help you learn more about your customers. So do not wait – start thinking about your marketing strategy today!

PLUS

WRITING

CRITICAL THINKING

At the end of this unit, you will write a compare and contrast essay. Look at this unit's writing task in the box below.

> Not all products and services fit the same business model. Some might have a more successful introduction in a mobile setting. For others, a mobile setting would not be appropriate. Compare and contrast two products or services regarding their potential as a mobile business.

Analyzing advantages and disadvantages

Many comparison essays involve a discussion of the ways in which one thing is better or worse than another. When you discuss advantages and disadvantages, consider all the aspects of the situation, including all the people involved. This will mean that you consider all the possible advantages and disadvantages and have the widest possible view of the situation you are analyzing.

1 Work in small groups. Complete the tasks.

ANALYZE

1 List the advantages and disadvantages of starting a business in a mobile setting that are discussed in Reading 1. Add your own ideas.

advantages of a mobile setting	disadvantages of a mobile setting

2 Write what factors might contribute to the operation's success or failure in the table below. Consider the customers' perspective as well as the business owner's interests.

factors that contribute to success of mobile operation	factors that contribute to failure of mobile operation
lower financial risk	location unpredictable for customers

3 What type of customer would be best served by a mobile operation and why? How would going mobile affect the customer experience?

2 Work in small groups. Complete the tasks.

1 Read the list of products and services below. Brainstorm ideas for five others and add them to your list.

- a yoga studio
- minor surgery
- architecture studio
- art classes for children
- mobile phone and tablet repair

2 Decide whether each one would work better as a mobile or a traditional business or either. Place them in the diagram below. Give reasons for your choice.

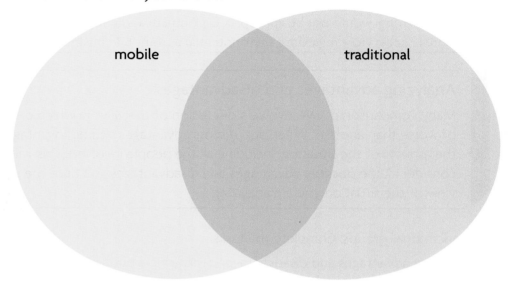

mobile   traditional

3 Choose two products or services that you would like to write about.

3 Complete the table with all the advantages and disadvantages of going mobile for your two chosen products. Think about all the advantages and disadvantages to different people involved in a business and its customers.

	advantages of mobile operation	disadvantages of mobile operation
product 1: _____		
product 2: _____		

4 Work with a partner. Compare your tables in Exercise 3. Add any of your partner's ideas that are also true for the products you are going to write about.

GRAMMAR FOR WRITING

REDUCTIONS OF SUBORDINATE CLAUSES

> Many subordinate clauses that contain the auxiliary verb *be* can be reduced to participle phrases if the subject of the subordinate and main clauses are the same. To form the participle phrase, the subject in the subordinate clause and auxiliary verb *be* are deleted.
>
> 1 subordinate clause with a continuous verb
> <u>While she was surfing the web</u>, she discovered a new loyalty scheme.
> <u>While surfing the web</u>, she discovered a new loyalty scheme.
>
> 2 subordinate clause with a passive verb
> <u>Once they are convinced</u> that their business has achieved sufficient success, some successful mobile entrepreneurs move on to a brick-and-mortar business.
> <u>Once convinced</u> that their business has achieved sufficient success, some successful mobile entrepreneurs move on to a brick-and-mortar business.

1 Underline the participle clauses in the sentences. Rewrite the participle clauses as full clauses.

1 Although impressed by the presentation of the sales manager, Nour decided not to make the initial investment. _____
_____

2 While working in a street food van, Kwan developed enough experience to start his own business. _____
_____

3 While interviewing dozens of mobile phone users, Isabelle got an idea for a new mobile business – a phone-charging service at the park!
_____
_____

4 Once discovered by the writer of a local food blog, the Vietnamese street food van had more business than its owners could handle.
_____
_____

5 When supported by good reviews and positive feedback, a subscription service can become part of a successful plan.
_____
_____

2 Rewrite the sentences. Reduce the first clause to a participle clause. In some items, more than one answer is possible.

1 When you are considering the mobile option for your business, you need to be flexible in the planning phase.

_____

_____

2 While he was researching marketing tools, Ali was surprised to learn about the inconsistent track record of loyalty schemes.

_____

_____

3 Unless they are embraced by a large number of customers, loyalty schemes are not a very effective marketing tool.

_____

_____

4 Although they were worried about the risks, the Smith brothers decided to begin their business online.

_____

_____

5 If it is taken seriously, this advice can improve a company's chances of success.

_____

_____

ACADEMIC WRITING SKILLS

WRITING ABOUT SIMILARITIES AND DIFFERENCES

In essays and reports, writers often compare or contrast people, things or ideas in order to make an argument. There are two common ways to structure a text that includes comparison and/or contrast:
- **Block organization:** the writer discusses all the features (cost, appearance, size) of one thing and then those same features of a second thing.
- **Point-by-point organization:** the writer compares one feature at a time, usually one feature per paragraph. Point-by-point organization works best when there are clear parallel points for comparison.

1 Work with a partner. Complete the tasks.

   1 Look at the two outlines below. Which structure does each one represent?

Structure: _____

Job A

Feature 1: _____

Feature 2: _____

Job B

Feature 1: _____

Feature 2: _____

Structure: _____

Feature 1: _____

Job A

Job B

Feature 2: _____

Job A

Job B

---

   2 Think about the features of a job opportunity that can influence an applicant's choice. List as many as you can. Choose the two that you think are most important. Complete both outlines above with the features you have chosen.

2 Read the preparatory notes for a report about the food industry. Then answer the questions below with a partner.

---

1 Starting out in the baking industry — Mobile or
  Brick-and-mortar — Background info
2 Mobile business
  Different to other street food vans — impossible to bake
  on site, can't bake and sell at same time, need staff to
  bake/sell or work 24/7, no enticing smell for customers,
  small space to work in, need access to kitchen space
  with oven, ingredients storage space
  Much cheaper start-up costs than brick-and-mortar,
  able to go on site at events/functions, fewer competitors,
  more varied customer base, larger area covered, lower
  overheads
3 Brick-and-mortar
  Huge initial overheads, significant investment, very
  competitive industry, need to find right location
  All business on one site, large kitchen, time for product
  development
4 Conclusion

---

1 Which structure do these notes follow?
  a point-by-point organization
  b block organization
2 How could you reorganize the information to follow the other structure?
3 A report usually contains recommendations or considerations for the future. Which of the conclusions below would be best for this report? Give reasons for your choice.
  a In conclusion, brick-and-mortar is the most familiar model for this business. However, mobile is cheaper.
  b Today, the street food van business is an enormously successful industry, which could lead aspiring bakers to try their luck with a mobile business. However, a mobile bakery would require more investment than another type of street food van.
  c A mobile bakery has potential as a business model. Although the initial investment may be higher than with other street food vans, it is significantly lower than that of a brick-and-mortar bakery and there is an opportunity to be a pioneer of street food baking.
  d Brick-and-mortar bakeries are a thing of the past and the market is already saturated. The future is mobile, although this business model has yet to fully prove itself.

WRITING TASK

> Not all products and services fit the same business model. Some might have a more successful introduction in a mobile setting. For others, a mobile setting would not be appropriate. Compare and contrast two products or services regarding their potential as a mobile business.

PLAN

1 Review your table of the advantages and disadvantages of a mobile operation for two products/services in Exercise 3 on page 102. Which structure is more appropriate for your essay? (See Academic writing skills, page 105.)

- block
- point-by-point

2 Prepare an outline for your essay using the block or point-by-point organization given in Academic writing skills. Provide evidence for each point you want to make in your essay.

_____

_____

_____

_____

_____

_____

3 Prepare the background information for your introduction and recommendations you are going to make in your conclusion.

_____

_____

_____

_____

_____

_____

4 Refer to the Task checklist on page 108 as you prepare your essay.

WRITE A FIRST DRAFT

5 Write your essay. Use your plan to help you structure your ideas. Write 400–450 words.

REVISE

6 Use the Task checklist to review your essay for content and structure.

TASK CHECKLIST	✔
Did you give some background information on mobile retail operations?	
Have you used an appropriate organizational structure for comparison and contrast?	
Have you provided evidence to support your argument in your body paragraphs?	
Does your concluding paragraph make recommendations or refer to considerations for the future?	
Does each paragraph include a topic sentence?	

EDIT

7 Use the Language checklist to edit your essay for language errors.

LANGUAGE CHECKLIST	✔
Have you chosen appropriate contrast markers for your intended meaning?	
Are your contrast markers grammatically correct?	
Have you used business and marketing vocabulary correctly? Did you hyphenate the terms correctly?	
Have you reduced some subordinate clauses with *be* to participle clauses, for sentence variety?	

8 Make any necessary changes to your essay.

OBJECTIVES REVIEW

1 Check your learning objectives for this unit. Write *3*, *2* or *1* for each objective.

3 = very well   2 = well   1 = not so well

I can ...

watch and understand a video about the problems
faced by small, independent businesses.   _____

work out meaning from context.   _____

analyze advantages and disadvantages.   _____

express contrast.   _____

use reductions of subordinate clauses.   _____

write about similarities and differences.   _____

write a comparison and contrast essay.   _____

2 Go to the *Unlock* Online Workbook for more practice with this unit's learning objectives.

WORDLIST		
accumulate (v)	generate revenue (v phr)	proposition (n) ⊙
aspiring (adj)	incentive (n) ⊙	retention (n) ⊙
attainable (adj)	make a profit (v phr)	revenue (n) ⊙
break even (idiom)	marketing tool (n)	shrewdly (adv)
brick-and-mortar (adj)	on a large/small scale (adv)	start-up costs (n)
component (n) ⊙	ongoing (adj) ⊙	track record (n)
fluctuating (adj)	outweigh (v)	transition (n) ⊙
follow suit (idiom)	pioneer (n)	utility bills (n)

⊙ = high-frequency words in the Cambridge Academic Corpus

LEARNING OBJECTIVES	IN THIS UNIT YOU WILL ...
Watch and listen	watch and understand a video about an artist who creates sculptures from plastic bricks.
Reading skills	annotate a text; interpret quotes.
Critical thinking	synthesize information from more than one text.
Grammar	use complex noun phrases with *what*.
Academic writing skills	cite quoted material; write an expository essay.
Writing task	write an expository essay.

UNL⊙CK YOUR KNOWLEDGE

Work with a partner. Discuss the questions.

1 Who do you think the person in the photo is? What do you think she does? Why?

2 Do you consider yourself a creative person? Why / Why not? What does it mean to be creative?

3 Name three famous people, living or dead, whom you consider to be highly creative. In what ways are such people different from the rest of the population? What do they have that most people do not? Explain your answer.

PLUS

  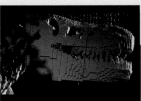 

PREPARING TO WATCH

ACTIVATING YOUR
KNOWLEDGE

1 Complete the questionnaire about creativity. Work with a partner and compare your answers.

> **1** Number the creative activities in your order of preference.
>
> ☐ making a model or sculpture
> ☐ painting or drawing
> ☐ cooking without a recipe
> ☐ making a useful object, e.g. clothing or furniture
> ☐ decorating something, e.g. a room or a cake
>
> **2** What creative activities did you do as a child?
> _____
>
> **3** How often do you do creative activities now?
> _____
>
> **4** What was the last thing you (or someone you know) created?
> _____

PREDICTING
CONTENT USING
VISUALS

2 Look at the pictures. Discuss the questions with your partner.

1 What kind of toy will be discussed in the video? Is this toy popular in your country? Why / Why not?

2 What do you think the man in the picture's job is? Where do you think he works?

3 Do you think the man is successful at his job? Why / Why not?

GLOSSARY

irresistible (adj) impossible to ignore or refuse because it is too pleasant or attractive

creative medium (n phr) a method or way of expressing an artistic idea such as writing or painting

vision (v) the ability to imagine how something could be developed and to plan for this

boardroom (n) a room where the people who control a company or organization meet

creative release (n phr) an artistic activity somebody does to feel free of negative emotions such as stress

commission (n) a request to do a special piece of work

WHILE WATCHING

3 ▶ Watch the video. Circle the ideas you hear.

UNDERSTANDING
MAIN IDEAS

1 According to psychologists, Lego is popular because it is easy to make things from.
2 Nathan's work is difficult to transport to other countries.
3 Nathan gave up his career as a lawyer to become a Lego sculptor.
4 Nathan gets asked to build Lego sculptures by a variety of people.
5 Nathan doesn't make much profit from his work.

4 ▶ Watch again. Write two details for each main idea.

UNDERSTANDING
DETAIL

1 There are several reasons Lego is popular with children.

_____

2 Nathan Sawaya's work shows that Lego is not just for children.

_____

3 Nathan has built some very large Lego models.

_____

4 Nathan used to be a lawyer.

_____

5 Nathan builds each model from the bottom up.

_____

6 Recently Nathan has been very busy.

_____

7 Nathan sells his work.

_____

DISCUSSION

5 Work in a small group. Discuss the questions.

1 What do you think of Nathan Sawaya's models? Which models in the video did you like the most? Why?
2 Why do you think Nathan's models are so popular? Why do you think Nathan's models are so expensive to buy?
3 What do you think of Nathan's decision to change careers? Would you have agreed with that choice at the time he made the decision? Why / Why not?
4 If you needed a creative release at the end of a day, what would you do?
5 Is the amount of creativity required an important factor in your choice of career? Why / Why not?
6 Would you say that being creative is generally an advantage in life? Why / Why not?

READING

PREPARING TO READ

UNDERSTANDING KEY VOCABULARY

1 You are going to read an article about what makes people creative. Read the definitions. Use the correct forms of the words in bold to complete the sentences below.

> **attribute to** (phr v) to say that something is caused by something else
> **cognition** (n) the use of conscious mental processes
> **genius** (n) someone with great and rare natural ability
> **label** (v) to assign a (usually negative) characteristic to somebody or something
> **norm** (n) accepted standard or way of doing something
> **stimulation** (n) an action that causes someone to become active, interested or enthusiastic
> **suppress** (v) to prevent something from being expressed or known
> **trauma** (n) severe emotional shock or physical injury that affects you for a long time

1 His violent behaviour has been _____ a brain injury.
2 This kind of behaviour is definitely not the _____ for traditional society, but it is more acceptable among young people.
3 Scientists hope that this new medication will improve _____ in older people who have experienced problems with memory.
4 She tried to _____ all her other thoughts in order to concentrate completely on the exam questions.
5 If you always complain and do not work well with others, you will be _____ an unsatisfactory employee.
6 Many children who live in extreme poverty suffer significant _____ that can last a lifetime.
7 After she started working, she found that she missed the intellectual _____ of student life at the university.
8 Many people consider Einstein the greatest mathematical _____ of all time.

2 Read the first sentence only of each paragraph of the article on pages 116–117. Then circle the topics you think will be discussed in the article. Compare your answers with a partner.

a the connection between pain and creativity
b how ordinary people can become more creative
c how and why creative people behave differently
d how psychologists test people to determine whether they are creative
e how creative people think differently from other people
f how experts define creativity
g the disadvantages of being a creative person

WHILE READING

3 Read the article and check your predictions from Exercise 2.

Annotating a text

Annotating a text includes marking it up with highlighting or underlining, and writing notes and comments in the margins. Annotating can help you understand the text's main argument, as well as its organization. It is especially helpful in longer texts. You will find that it is much easier to review a text that you have annotated than one you have not.

When you annotate, it is important that you highlight, underline or bracket only the most important parts of the text. If you highlight almost everything, the process will not be useful. Make short notes in the margins to indicate main ideas, supporting examples, definitions and quotes. You can also make a note of words you need to look up.

If you need to synthesize ideas across two or more texts, it is helpful to annotate them all in the same way and to note the parts of each text that are different and that are the same.

SKILLS

4 Read the first and second paragraphs of the article again. Notice the annotations. How has the student used highlighting, underlining, etc. in their annotations?

5 Annotate the rest of the article. Compare your annotations with a partner's.

THE CREATIVE MIND

1 What is the secret to the world's most creative minds – the minds of resourceful inventors, innovative scientists and inspired artists? Are they simply lucky to be born with the right genes? That may be part of the explanation, but most studies suggest that only about ten percent of creativity can be **attributed to** a person's genes. So, are they simply smarter than the rest of us? Such individuals are certainly intelligent, but intelligence cannot be the key, as numerous studies have shown that a high IQ[1] alone does not lead to creativity. Creative thinkers seem to have a special way of thinking. Creativity researcher and neuroscientist Nancy Andreasen, in a 2014 *Atlantic Magazine* article, describes creative people as ['better at recognizing relationships, making associations and connections, and seeing things in an original way – seeing things that others cannot see.'] For example, in the early 2000s, Jack Dorsey, one of the founders of Twitter, tried to use text messages to improve the system for reserving and sending out taxis. He made a connection between two seemingly unrelated systems, but he was too far ahead of his time – the necessary technology was not yet available. Today, most taxi services use a version of Dorsey's original idea.

look up

supporting detail

main idea

quote, definition

example

2 So what are the requirements for creativity? First of all, creativity takes time. We tend to think of breakthroughs as coming in a sudden flash of brilliance, but this is rarely the case. Ideas often evolve and form over a long period. Andreasen, who conducted a study of creative thinking, described her findings this way, ['... almost all of my (research) subjects confirmed that when Eureka moments occur, they tend to be precipitated by long periods of preparation and

supporting detail

quote

Martin Luther King, Jr

incubation[2]], and to strike when the mind is relaxed.' In fact, many of history's most creative people

look up have a reputation as daydreamers or procrastinators. Martin Luther King, Jr,

example reportedly wrote his 'I Have a Dream' speech at ten o'clock the night before he delivered it, although it is likely to have gone through a long period of 'preparation and incubation' in his mind before that.

3 In a surprising twist, creativity may also be sparked by suffering, such as a serious illness or the loss of a loved one. We can see examples of this in the lives of many great creative **geniuses**. Artist Paul Klee suffered great pain for much of his life, as did many other artists, and composer Johann Sebastian Bach lost both his parents when he was only nine years old. Research by Hungarian scientist Szabolcs Keri confirms this. He says, 'We found that many individuals with artistic creativity suffered from severe **traumas** in life.' He and other researchers believe that this trauma affects brain structure and expands the brain's ability to make the diverse and multiple connections that underlie much of creative thinking.

4 Those investigating the sources of creativity have noted that some creative geniuses do not always fit in well with societal **norms**. They don't seem able to **suppress** the fountain of ideas that bubble up in their minds, some of which may seem irrelevant or inappropriate to others. Creative

people are also curious; they seem wired[3] to seek novelty, take risks and push limits in their explorations. The reward centres in their brains seem to need more than the average amount of **stimulation** in order to release dopamine, the chemical that triggers feelings of pleasure. In 2013, psychologist Barry Kaufman, writing in a blog in the journal *Scientific American*, summarized the implications of a study in this way, 'It seems that the key to creative **cognition** is opening up the flood gates and letting in as much information as possible. Because you never know: sometimes the most bizarre associations can turn into the most productively creative ideas.'

5 As children, creative people are often unable to sit still, unable to focus on their lessons, instead, always looking for something new and interesting to capture their attention. Today, many children who display this kind of behaviour are often **labelled** as trouble makers. However, their characteristics were probably extremely useful in the past – when humans depended on hunting, a risky and unpredictable but exciting activity – and researchers suspect they may also contribute to creativity.

6 The search for the source of creativity continues. Most researchers agree that the answer will be complex and that there is probably no single characteristic which can explain the world's most creative minds.

[1]**IQ** (n) quotient: a measure of someone's intelligence found from special tests
[2]**incubation** (n) protected development
[3]**wired** (adj) biologically programmed

SKILLS

Interpreting quotes

Writers often include quotations from other people, especially experts. This allows writers to add another voice in support of their perspective. It is important for readers to interpret these quotations – understand what they mean and think about why they are relevant to the text – because they often contain key ideas.

MAKING INFERENCES

6 Work with a partner. Read each quotation in the table below and write your interpretation. Read the article again for context, if needed. Look up any words you do not know, especially the words in bold.

source	quote	your interpretation
Keri	'... almost all of my (research) subjects confirmed that when **Eureka moments** occur, they tend to be precipitated by long periods of preparation and incubation ...' (paragraph 2)	
Kaufman	'... the key to creative cognition is **opening up the flood gates** and letting in as much information as possible ...' (paragraph 4)	

7 Discuss your interpretation of the quotations in Exercise 6 with the rest of the class. Answer the questions.

   1 Did you all have a similar interpretation of the quotes?
   2 Why do you think the writer included each of the quotes in the text?

DISCUSSION

8 Work in small groups. Discuss the questions.

   1 Why do you think people who don't fit in with society's norms are more likely to be tolerated in a community of artists?
   2 How would you define creativity?

PLUS

PREPARING TO READ

PREDICTING
CONTENT
USING VISUALS

1 You are going to read an article about learning to be creative. Work in small groups. Complete the task. How do you think this task relates to creativity?

Imagine that you have only these items: a candle, a box of matches and some drawing pins.

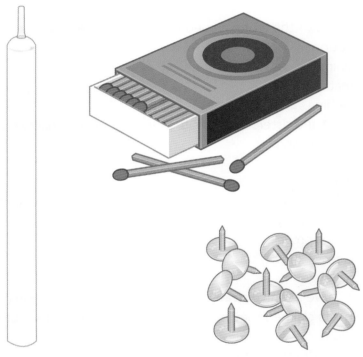

Using only these items, how would you attach the candle to the wall so that wax will not drip onto anything below it? (see page 133 for a solution)

2 Work with a partner. Discuss whether each task is creative or not. Why? / Why not?

USING YOUR
KNOWLEDGE

1 Playing a piece of music
2 Writing a play
3 Baking a cake using a recipe
4 Designing a building
5 Building a model using a kit
6 Making an animation
7 Making a video game
8 Gardening

3 Read the sentences and choose the best definition for the words in bold.

1 I really admire my professor, so I have tried to **emulate** her energy and creativity.
   a carry on a tradition of
   b justify; make an argument for
   c copy and try to do as well as

2 Too many rules are likely to **constrain** a child's creativity and emotional development.
   a limit
   b reverse
   c assist

3 Members of the group argued for hours before finally **arriving at** a resolution.
   a signing
   b creating
   c reaching

4 Brothers and sisters often share physical and personality **traits**.
   a characteristics
   b ideas
   c genes

5 In his book, the psychologist **contends** that there is no limit to the human memory.
   a cannot prove
   b claims
   c challenges

6 There have been **contradictory** reports about the research study. First, scientists claimed they had found a gene for creativity, but later they denied it.
   a having different or opposite ideas
   b not helpful
   c likely to create interest

7 Scientists are trying to **reproduce** these exciting results to make sure they are valid.
   a do or make again
   b expand
   c publish widely

8 When you are a young teenager, **conformity** is the norm; teens want to be just like all their friends.
   a hard work
   b obedience
   c behaviour that follows the usual standards

PLUS

Can we learn to be more creative?

1 Most of us would like to be more creative, but we assume there is little we can do about it. Is creativity indeed something that only some of us are born with? Perhaps, but current thinking suggests we should not be satisfied with our inborn talents. Psychology professor K. Anders Ericsson claims that with enough practice, any of us can become experts, in ice skating, piano or anything else. However, he is quick to add that this requires a specific kind of practice and lots of it – about 10,000 hours. To develop expertise, simple repetition is not enough; what Ericsson calls 'deliberate practice', is required: that is, pushing beyond one's comfort zone[1] and setting goals that are above one's current level of performance. The more deliberate practice, the better the performance. In his 2016 book, *Peak: Secrets from the New Science of Expertise*, Ericsson says he has spent 30 years looking 'for kinds of limits that would actually **constrain** some individuals from being successful…' He says he has yet to find those limits and he doesn't believe they exist. Not everyone agrees, however. A 2014 study concluded that practice explains only about 25% of the difference between top performers and performers who were just 'very good'. The rest was due to natural ability. Still, 25% is not insignificant.

2 Ericsson has looked primarily at artistic and athletic expertise, but can these findings apply to creativity? Is it a skill, like ice skating or playing the piano? Can we learn to be more creative? Most experts agree that even if most people cannot hope to become creative geniuses, they can learn to become more creative through practice. Psychologists **contend** that there are actually two levels of creativity, which they refer to as 'Big C' and 'small c'. Big C creativity applies to breakthrough ideas, ones that may change the course of a field or even history. It's unlikely that any amount of practice can lead ordinary thinkers to Big C creativity. Small c, however, is a different story. Small c creativity refers to everyday creative problem solving, like creating a new recipe or improving a process, which psychologists subdivide further into convergent and divergent thinking. Convergent thinking involves examining all the facts and **arriving at** a single solution. In contrast, divergent thinking involves coming up with many possible solutions – for example, thinking of many different uses for a brick or a paper clip. What most people think of as creativity generally involves divergent thinking. And divergent thinking can be taught, practised and learnt.

3 Even with practice, divergent thinking alone cannot make one creative, however. Scott Barry Kaufman, a cognitive psychologist, says that most creative people share one personality **trait**: openness to new experience. Since this trait and these processes have been identified, less creative people can try to **emulate** them. Creativity experts advise that we be open to many different and possibly **contradictory** ideas, that we take time to let our own ideas form and develop, allowing new connections to become apparent. Normally, we tend to **reproduce** what we already know because **conformity** is comfortable, and new ideas – in other words, creative ones – move us into unfamiliar territory.

4 This unfamiliar territory involves risks – risk of failure and risk of criticism – as well as a willingness to carry on in the face of failure. Creative thinkers accept that not all their ideas will work. In general, creative artists, inventors and scientists come up with a huge number of ideas, knowing that many of them will not succeed. Ernest Hemingway wrote 47 different endings for his novel *A Farewell to Arms* before he found one that worked. Thomas Edison came up with dozens of inventions that failed and over a thousand versions of his lightbulb before he found success.

5 Moving outside of our comfort zone, engaging in deliberate practice and tolerating contradictory ideas, risk and failure are all things we can learn to do better. It is unlikely that doing so will transform any of us into creative geniuses, but it does have the potential to increase our level of creativity.

[1]**comfort zone** (n phr) a familiar place or situation in which you feel at ease

WHILE READING

ANNOTATING

4 Read the article on page 121. Annotate the reading, making a note of main ideas, supporting details, definitions, examples and words you need to look up.

5 Using your annotations, decide if the statements below are *M* (main ideas), *D* (supporting details) or *X* (not included in this article).

1 Divergent thinking means finding many different ways to solve a problem. _____

2 Creative people often engage in divergent thinking. _____

3 Creative thinking is often a rapid process. _____

4 Many creative people take risks. _____

5 Creative thinkers seek new experiences. _____

6 Kaufman's research explores the connection between practice and creativity. _____

7 The inventor Thomas Edison failed many times. _____

8 We can learn to be more creative. _____

SUMMARIZING

6 Using your annotations, write a summary of the research of the two researchers mentioned in the article.

Anders Ericsson	
Scott Barry Kaufman	

READING BETWEEN THE LINES

MAKING INFERENCES

7 Work in small groups. Discuss the questions.

1 Ericsson says he has 'yet to find those limits'. Limits on what? Why does he believe he will never find these limits?

2 What contradictory evidence does the author offer to Ericsson's claim? Does the author believe this evidence is truly contradictory?

3 Why is conformity comfortable?

DISCUSSION

8 Work in small groups. Make a list of three examples. Then compare your list with another group.

1 Big C ideas

_____
_____
_____

2 Small c ideas

_____
_____
_____

9 Work in the same group. Use ideas from Reading 1 and Reading 2 to answer the following questions.

SYNTHESIZING

1 Some people say they get their best ideas in the shower. When are you at your most creative? Can your creativity be explained in terms of any of the ideas presented in this unit?
2 Are you more of a convergent or divergent thinker? Give an example to explain your answer.
3 What different kinds of tasks or professions are more appropriate for convergent thinkers? For divergent thinkers? Why?

EXPERIMENTAL SCIENCE TERMINOLOGY

1 Read the summary of a child development study. Write the correct form of the words and phrases in bold next to their definitions below.

A study that began in 1986 **established a causal link** between the behaviour of parents and the success of their children. The **research subjects** in this study were the families of 129 children living in poverty in Jamaica. There were two **experimental groups** and each group received a different treatment. In one, the children received extra food and milk. In the other, the families received visits from an expert in early childhood development, who encouraged the parents to spend more time engaging with their children: reading books, singing songs or simply playing. A third set of families, the **control group**, received no treatment.

The experiment itself only lasted for two years, but the researchers who **conducted the study** continued to follow the children. They found that the **intervention** that made the most difference in the children's lives was the early parental interaction. In an interview with the World Bank in 2015, one of the authors of the 1986 Jamaica study, Elaine Burke, explained, 'Even before we could stimulate the children, we had to stimulate the parents and get them to understand the importance of toys and appropriate language.' As they were growing up, the children in this group exhibited more positive behaviour and had higher IQ scores than the children in the other groups. As adults, they earn 25% more than the other participants in the study. The researchers **contend** that their findings have clear **implications**. To ensure the future success of children living in poverty, educate their parents about the importance of parent–child interaction.

1 _____ (v phr) to do academic research, such as an experiment

2 _____ (n) action taken to deal with a problem

3 _____ (n) conclusions suggested by the results of an academic study

4 _____ (n phr) participants in an experiment who do not receive experimental treatment

5 _____ (n phr) participants in an experiment who receive experimental treatment

6 _____ (n) all the participants in an experiment

7 _____ (v phr) to show a cause-and-effect connection

8 _____ (v) to claim

PLUS

WRITING

CRITICAL THINKING

At the end of this unit, you will write an expository essay. Look at this unit's writing task in the box below.

> What is creative thinking? Explain the current understanding of this concept by synthesizing information from different sources.

Synthesizing information from more than one text

When you synthesize ideas from more than one text, you draw ideas from both (or all of them), evaluating each text. If the texts make similar claims about a point, you can report where they converge. If the texts contain contradictory claims, you may need to acknowledge that as well. When you do this, make sure the texts are addressing the same information. Annotating the original texts can help you prepare a synthesis. Synthesizing information from more than one text is an important skill because it shows your understanding of texts beyond a simple summary.

1 Review Reading 1 and Reading 2. As you read, review your annotations. Then summarize the topics that are discussed and the main points the writer is making about them. Compare your summaries with a partner.

ANALYZE

_____

_____

_____

_____

_____

_____

_____

_____

_____

_____

_____

_____

_____

_____

_____

_____

_____

_____

_____

_____

APPLY

2 Use your annotations on Reading 1 and Reading 2 to complete the table below for each topic. If one of the articles does not address a particular topic, write an X. Add any other topics that you think are important. Compare your table with those of other students.

topic	Reading 1	Reading 2
a sources of creativity		
b research findings		
c descriptions of creative behaviour		
d specific examples of creative individuals		
e different kinds of creativity		
f traits that creative thinkers share		
g disadvantages of creativity		
h suggestions for increasing an individual's creativity		

3 Conduct outside research on creative thinking. Make notes on the ideas in your research that make similar claims or converge from the ideas in Readings 1 and 2.

EVALUATE

4 Think about the table above and your outside research and complete the tasks.

1 Select three topics from the table and/or your outside research. The topics should be the ones that are the most important for describing our current understanding of creativity. Make sure you include some topics that are discussed in more than one source.

2 Consider the entries in your chart for those topics. Are they facts, opinions or examples? Which will provide the strongest support?

3 Scan Reading 1 and Reading 2 and highlight any quotes that can help you make your points.

GRAMMAR FOR WRITING

COMPLEX NOUN PHRASES WITH *WHAT*

A complex noun phrase with *what* can perform the same function as a noun + relative clause.

In a complex noun phrase beginning with *what*, the pronoun *what* replaces both the relative pronoun and the noun (phrase) it refers to. However, *what* can only be used to replace general terms like 'the things/stuff/activities that ...'

These complex noun phrases can appear as subjects or objects. Notice that, although 'the things/stuff/activities' are plural, *what* always takes a singular verb.

Subject: **What most people think of as creativity** generally involves divergent thinking.
Object: We tend to reproduce **what we already know**.

Complex noun phrases with *what* add variety to a writer's sentences. This structure is also an efficient and elegant way to draw attention to a point.

1 Rewrite the sentences so that they contain a complex noun phrase with *what*. Make sure you use the correct verb form after *what*.

1 The articles describe the activities that the research subjects in the study did in order to demonstrate their creativity.

_____

_____

2 We are largely unaware of the processes that go on in our own brains to create our perception of reality.

_____

_____

3 We still do not know for certain the things that lead to creativity.

_____

_____

4 The researchers were looking for the things that single out the most creative people in the population.

_____

_____

5 One of the goals of the study was to find out the activities that creative people are doing when they come up with their best ideas.

_____

_____

2 Write three sentences of your own about creativity using complex noun phrases with *what*.

1 _____

_____

2 _____

_____

3 _____

_____

ACADEMIC WRITING SKILLS

CITING QUOTED MATERIAL

Using a variety of sentence types can be particularly useful in summaries and syntheses when you want to distance your own writing from the original text.

You can increase variety by changing the length, type, order and pattern of sentences you use. You can also add variety by using direct quotations, which can provide interesting details and important support in an essay.

When you use somebody's exact words, make sure you use quotation marks and cite the source of the quotation. The source may include the person's name as well as when and where the words appeared.

In an interview with the World Bank in **2015**, one of the authors of the 1986 Jamaica study, **Elaine Burke**, explained, 'Even before we could stimulate the children, we had to stimulate the parents and get them to understand the importance of toys and appropriate language.'

1 Scan Reading 1 and Reading 2 to find the quotations attributed to each of these experts and the source information. Then write a sentence of your own citing the quotation.

1 Nancy Andreasen (Reading 1)

Year: _____ Source: _____

_____

_____

_____

2 Anders Ericsson (Reading 2)

Year: _____ Source: _____

_____

_____

_____

2 Do some research to find two or three more quotes about creativity or creative thinking that you could cite in your essay.

1 Name: _____

   Quote: _____

   _____

   _____

   Year: _____ Source: _____

2 Name: _____

   Quote: _____

   _____

   _____

   Year: _____ Source: _____

3 Name: _____

   Quote: _____

   _____

   _____

   Year: _____ Source: _____

WRITING AN EXPOSITORY ESSAY

SKILLS

An expository essay is an essay that synthesizes information from two or more sources. In this type of essay you should summarize the key points about the topic from all texts, analyze how the texts are different and similar and make an evaluation of them – this can be your own opinion of the texts, but this isn't an argumentative essay so you don't need to convince the reader of your point of view. You must weave information from the source texts together to make a coherent new text.

Because you are reporting the work of other writers, you will not make a claim based on your own views. However, you will still need a thesis statement to give your readers an idea about the content of your essay.

As you prepare to write your essay, a simple table can help you gather and organize your ideas.

3 Look at the three topics you chose in Critical thinking, Exercise 4 on page 126. For each topic, use your notes to write one or two sentences that bring together (synthesize) the ideas from all sources, using the table below as an example. These will be your topic sentences.

topic	topic sentences	notes
creative behaviour	Creative thinkers see unexpected connections between ideas and find a range of ways to approach a problem or task.	R1: seeing connections between ideas open to as much info as poss. seeking novelty Dorsey ex. R2: openness to experience accepting contradictory info

4 Gather all the details: write the facts, expert opinions and quotes that belong with each topic sentence in the *notes* column.

WRITING TASK

What is creative thinking? Explain the current understanding of this concept by synthesizing information from different sources.

PLAN

1 Look at the three topics you chose in Critical thinking, Exercise 4 on page 126. Using those three topics, write a thesis statement for your essay. Remember that in an expository essay you don't need to give a strong opinion, but your thesis statement should give the reader a general idea of the topic of the essay.

2 Think about your introductory paragraph. Review your table in Critical thinking, Exercise 2 on page 126. What will you mention in your introductory paragraph?

_____

_____

_____

_____

3 Decide on the order of your body paragraphs. Which point is most important?

First body paragraph: _____
Second body paragraph: _____
Third body paragraph: _____

4 Think about your conclusion. What thoughts do you want to leave your readers with?

_____
_____
_____

5 Refer to the Task checklist below as you prepare your essay.

WRITE A FIRST DRAFT

6 Write your essay. Use your essay plan to help you structure your ideas. Write 400–450 words.

REVISE

7 Use the Task checklist to review your essay for content and structure.

TASK CHECKLIST	✔
Have you introduced and explained your topic?	
Have you included information from all your sources?	
Have you paraphrased the information in the articles in your own words?	
Have you used quotations from experts?	
Have you used a variety of sentence structures?	
Does your concluding paragraph leave your readers with something to think about?	

EDIT

8 Use the Language checklist to edit your essay for use of appropriate language and style.

LANGUAGE CHECKLIST	✔
Did you use terminology from experimental science correctly?	
Did you draw attention to a point by using a complex noun phrase with *what*?	
Did you cite the source and year of any quotations properly?	
Did you punctuate quotations accurately?	

9 Make any necessary changes to your essay.

OBJECTIVES REVIEW

1 Check your learning objectives for this unit. Write 3, 2 or 1 for each objective.

3 = very well   2 = well   1 = not so well

I can ...

watch and understand a video about an artist who creates sculptures from plastic bricks.   _____

annotate a text.   _____

interpret quotes.   _____

synthesize information from more than one text.   _____

use complex noun phrases with *what*.   _____

cite quoted material.   _____

write an expository essay.   _____

2 Go to the *Unlock* Online Workbook for more practice with this unit's learning objectives.

WORDLIST

arrive at (phr v)
attribute to (phr v)
cognition (n)
conduct a study (v phr)
conformity (n)
constrain (v)
contend (v)
contradictory (adj)

control group (n)
emulate (v)
establish a causal link (v phr)
experimental group (n)
genius (n)
implications (n)
intervention (n)
label (v)

norm (n)
reproduce (v)
research subjects (n)
stimulation (n)
suppress (v)
trait (n)
trauma (n)

 = high-frequency words in the Cambridge Academic Corpus

Answer to the puzzle on page 119:

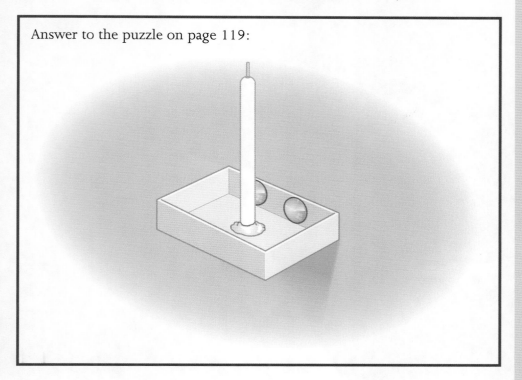

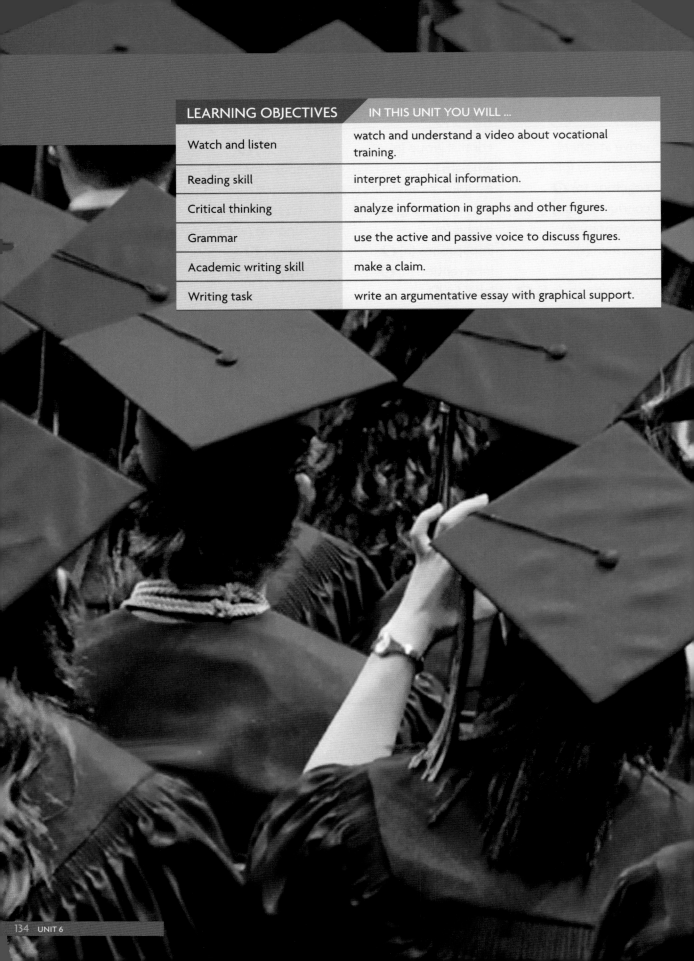

LEARNING OBJECTIVES	IN THIS UNIT YOU WILL ...
Watch and listen	watch and understand a video about vocational training.
Reading skill	interpret graphical information.
Critical thinking	analyze information in graphs and other figures.
Grammar	use the active and passive voice to discuss figures.
Academic writing skill	make a claim.
Writing task	write an argumentative essay with graphical support.

UNL⌀CK YOUR KNOWLEDGE

Work with a partner. Discuss the questions.

1 What is happening in this picture? Have you experienced something similar? What was it like?

2 What kind of job do you have or hope to have?

3 How closely is, or was, your education connected to your professional goals?

4 What do you think is the main purpose of a university education?

PLUS

PREPARING TO WATCH

ACTIVATING YOUR
KNOWLEDGE

1 Work with a partner. Discuss the questions.

1 Are there vocational colleges / secondary schools for teenagers in your country? How might vocational training benefit school-leavers?

2 What do most young people do after completing secondary school?

3 What job opportunities exist for young people after secondary school?

4 What industries do you think are in need of more workers?

PREDICTING
CONTENT
USING VISUALS

2 You are going to watch a video about vocational training. Look at the photos and complete the table. Discuss your table with a partner.

	photo 1	photo 2	photo 3	photo 4
1 What job does this person have?				
2 What kind of training is needed for this job?				

GLOSSARY

not dig something (v phr, informal US) not enjoy something

second shift (n) working hours from approximately 4pm to midnight

welder (n) a person whose job is joining metal parts together

hydrogen (n) a chemical element that is the lightest gas, has no colour, taste, or smell, and combines with oxygen to form water

instrument technician (n) someone who works repairing, maintaining and adjusting industrial controlling and measuring systems

vo-tech education (US n phr) education in which students get vocational training (training for a specific career) and/or technical training (training using the tools, machinery, manual techniques, etc. involved in a particular field)

federal (adj) of, or connected with, the central government of some states, including in the USA

career path (n) the way that you progress in your work, either in one job or in a series of jobs

WHILE WATCHING

3 ▶ Watch the video. Circle the ideas you hear.

UNDERSTANDING MAIN IDEAS

1 Nick had more than one job offer when he graduated from a career and technical high school.
2 The need for technical workers is increasing.
3 Air Products manufactures high tech equipment.
4 John McGlade has to train the skilled workers he needs himself.
5 Government support for vocational education is decreasing.
6 Not many young people are interested in vocational education.

4 ▶ Watch the video again. Write details for each main idea.

UNDERSTANDING DETAIL

1 Air Products has 7,500 workers, and not all are skilled.

_____

2 John McGlade's company often has positions available.

_____

3 Career and technical education has been cut, and more cuts may be on the way.

_____

4 Vocational schools train students to work in technical careers.

_____

5 Work with a partner. Discuss the questions.

MAKING INFERENCES

1 Do you think Nick likes his job? Why / Why not?
2 Why do you think John McGlade is worried?
3 Why do you think more skilled workers will be needed in the future?
4 What do you think are some other jobs that students can train for at a career and technical high school?

DISCUSSION

6 Work with a partner. Discuss the questions.

1 Do you think entering into a career and technical high school is a good idea? Why / Why not?
2 Would you have been interested in attending a career and technical high school? Why / Why not?
3 What are the advantages of young people entering the workforce shortly after secondary school? Are there any disadvantages?

READING 1

PREPARING TO READ

Interpreting graphical information

Academic texts often include tables, graphs or other diagrams to support and extend the content of the text. In a good academic text the graphical information is always discussed and interpreted in the body of the text – graphs and diagrams are not just put in a text and not discussed.

As a first step to understanding information presented in graphical form, read the title, headings and the labels on the axes on any graphs. This will provide some context for the information presented there. If the axes of a graph are not labelled, try to work out what the labels would be.

PREDICTING CONTENT USING VISUALS

1 You are going to read an article about the demand for workers with appropriate skills. Work with a partner. Look at the graph and discuss the questions below.

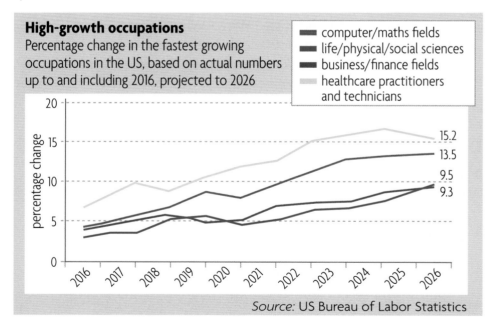

High-growth occupations
Percentage change in the fastest growing occupations in the US, based on actual numbers up to and including 2016, projected to 2026

- computer/maths fields
- life/physical/social sciences
- business/finance fields
- healthcare practitioners and technicians

Source: US Bureau of Labor Statistics

1 What kinds of jobs does each category include? Name some.
2 What sorts of skills and education are required for the jobs in these fields?
3 Why do you think these occupational areas are predicted to be the fastest growing in the near future?
4 What implications might this prediction have for school curriculum development?

2 Now look at Figures 1 and 2 in the article on pages 140–141 and answer the questions about each graph.

Now look at Figures 1 and 2 in the article on pages 140–141

1 What does the horizontal axis (the x-axis) measure?
2 What does the vertical axis (the y-axis) measure?
3 What information does the whole graph express?

3 Based on the information in the graphs in the article, answer the questions.

1 Look at Figure 1. Why do you think companies are struggling to recruit employees?
2 What problem does Figure 2 illustrate?
3 How does the information in Figure 2 explain the problems that the employers in Figure 1 are experiencing?

4 Read the definitions. Use the correct forms of the words in bold to complete the sentences below.

> **assertive** (adj) forceful; bold and confident
> **comprise** (v) to have things or people as parts or members; to consist of
> **expertise** (n) a high level of knowledge or skill
> **labour** (n) workers, especially people who do practical work with their hands
> **mismatch** (n) things that do not work well together
> **persistent** (adj) (of a problem) lasting for a long time, difficult to resolve
> **pose** (v) to cause
> **prospective** (adj) wanted or expected to do a particular thing in the future

1 Professors at this technical institute are known for their _____ in robotics and high-tech electronics.
2 This situation _____ a real problem for our company because we can't find skilled applicants to fill our positions.
3 There is an unfortunate _____ between the organization's goals and its actions.
4 Experts are studying the youngest sector in the labour force, which _____ workers between the ages of 18 and 24.
5 You have to be more _____ if you want people to listen to your ideas.
6 Our _____ costs were way too high, so we moved our operation to Vietnam, where workers' salaries are lower.
7 The staff in the admissions office regularly meet with _____ students to answer their questions and give campus tours.
8 For the last five years, there has been a _____ shortage of job applicants with skills in a wide range of technical areas.

THE SKILLS GAP

1 All over the world, business leaders and government officials complain about the 'skills gap'. Businesses have plenty of job openings, but they cannot find enough qualified applicants to fill the positions because workers' skills do not match those needed by employers. Figure 1 shows the results of an annual survey of about 42,000 companies worldwide.

2 For the most part, the employees that employers in western countries are seeking fall into two categories. The first category includes professionals in STEM fields (Science/Technology/Engineering/Mathematics) that require advanced training and **expertise**, especially in Information Technology (IT). The second category is much larger, **comprising** workers in the 'skilled trades'. Workers in the skilled trades have expertise in, for example, manufacturing, computers, electronics and construction. There are simply not enough workers with training in these areas to meet the growing demand. These jobs require more than a secondary education (for example, a training course to develop the required skill), but often they do not require a university education. In the United States, almost half of the **labour** force works in these kinds of jobs.

Causes of the skills gap

3 Why have we been unable to bridge this gap and prepare workers for the jobs of the future, or even the jobs of today? The answer lies in both the job market and the education system in many western countries. The job market is changing more quickly than ever before. Many of the jobs that companies need to fill today did not exist when current job applicants were in school, making it difficult for curriculums to keep up with the demands of the market. Nevertheless, numerous business leaders argue that schools are not doing enough to provide the technical training that many jobs demand. For example, only a quarter of all schools in the United States teach computer science. Most schools and universities continue to offer the same type of education that they have provided in the past. As a result, lots of students graduate with degrees that do not prepare them for the jobs that are available. Given this **mismatch** between the education system and the job market, several labour experts say we cannot and perhaps should not depend on traditional schooling to close the skills gap and should instead find alternative solutions.

Closing the skills gap

4 Both industry and academic experts argue that businesses themselves need to take a more **assertive** role in the preparation of the labour force they require. Businesses have the best information about what skills their employees will need, so it makes sense for them to participate in training **prospective** employees. First, they need to communicate better with schools and universities about the skills they require. Second, they should establish relationships with future employees earlier, perhaps through partnership schemes that begin training future employees while they are still students. Finally, businesses may need to develop and provide their own in-house training.

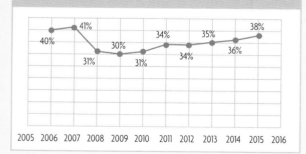

Figure 1. Percentage of companies with difficulty filling positions

40% 41% 31% 30% 31% 34% 34% 35% 36% 38%

2005 2006 2007 2008 2009 2010 2011 2012 2013 2014 2015 2016

Source: Manpower (2014)

5 Technical skills, particularly computer science skills, are in high demand, but developing these skills is not necessarily best accomplished by means of a traditional university education. There are a wide range of schools, courses and training schemes that have opened in response to the demand for computer science professionals, some in brick-and-mortar classrooms and others online – technical colleges for the digital age. The top computer science schools are expensive, but some boast a 99% placement rate for their graduates, many of whom find positions that pay $100,000 a year or more. Figure 2 displays the predicted job growth in computing jobs.

6 The skills gap is both **persistent** and expensive. One business expert estimates that a company loses $14,000 when a position remains open for three months. The skills gap is the result of many factors, and there is no single solution to the problems it **poses**. It is likely that a combination of approaches will be needed before the supply of qualified workers will be able to meet demand for them.

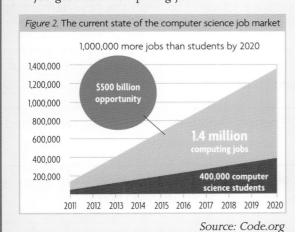

Figure 2. The current state of the computer science job market

1,000,000 more jobs than students by 2020

$500 billion opportunity

1.4 million computing jobs

400,000 computer science students

Source: Code.org

WHILE READING

5 Read the article. Then match the main ideas (a–f) with each paragraph (1–6).

READING FOR MAIN IDEAS

a Schools that provide training in IT can help fill the skills gap. _____
b Employees in the skilled trades and with STEM training are in the greatest demand. _____
c There is no single solution to the skills gap. _____
d Current job applicants do not have the skills that employers are looking for. _____
e Businesses need to participate more in preparing future employees. _____
f Universities do not always offer an education with a clear career path. _____

6 Which of the statements in Exercise 5 expresses the main idea of the whole article? _____

7 Read the article again. Write *T* (true), *F* (false) or *DNS* (does not say) next to the statements below. Then correct the false statements.

_____ 1 Globalization has led to labour shortages in some developing countries.

_____

_____ 2 The most critical labour shortages are in IT fields.

_____

_____ 3 The positions that companies are trying to fill all require a university education.

_____

_____ 4 About 50% of workers in the United States are in the skilled trades.

_____

_____ 5 School curriculums have adapted to meet the new demand for technical skills.

_____

_____ 6 Businesses have the most accurate knowledge of the kinds of employees that are in demand.

_____

_____ 7 More than 1,000 IT schools and training schemes have opened to meet demand.

_____

_____ 8 An unfilled position that remains open for more than three months can cost a company more than $10,000.

_____

READING BETWEEN THE LINES

8 Work with a partner. Answer the questions.

1 What is the purpose of this article?
   a to persuade universities to change their courses
   b to offer general information
   c to warn employers
2 Where might you find an article like this?
   a in a print or online magazine
   b in a textbook
   c in an academic journal

DISCUSSION

9 Work with a partner. Discuss the questions.

1 What do you think the $500 billion opportunity is in Figure 2?
2 Who do you think should take action to improve this situation?

READING 2

PREPARING TO READ

PREDICTING
CONTENT
USING VISUALS

1 Work with a partner. You are going to read an article about the value of a university education. Look at the graphs on page 145. Then discuss the questions.

1 Based on Figure 1, what generalization can you make about university education?

2 Look at Figure 2. What does *median income* mean? Are university-educated workers more likely to earn above or below the median income?

3 What do you think the topic of this article will be? What argument do you think it will make?

UNDERSTANDING
KEY VOCABULARY

2 Read the sentences. Write the correct form of the words in bold next to their definitions below.

1 There is a **chronic** shortage of skilled workers in the technology sector. It's been impossible to hire enough workers.

2 Steve Jobs was a **founder** of Apple, Inc.

3 Business leaders **dispute** the government's claim that the number of jobs has grown.

4 The new training programme provides a good **illustration** of how the government and private sector can work together.

5 There is some **ambiguity** in the law, so it is difficult to know whether the company actually did anything wrong.

6 The Chief Technology Officer's responsibilities extend beyond IT; he plays **multiple** roles in the company.

7 The company's Chief Executive Officer **asserts** that profits will exceed expectations in the coming year.

a _____ (v) to disagree with an idea, a fact, etc.

b _____ (n) the state of being unclear or having more than one possible meaning

c _____ (n) someone who establishes an organization

d _____ (adj) very many

e _____ (adj) lasting for a long time, especially something bad

f _____ (v) to say that something is certainly true

g _____ (n) an example that explains something

PLUS

WHILE READING

READING FOR MAIN IDEAS

3 Read the article and check your ideas from Exercise 1.

4 Read the article. Write *T* (true), *F* (false) or *DNS* (does not say) next to the statements below. Then correct the false statements.

_____ 1 A university education is worth the investment.

____

_____ 2 Graduates in the US make twice as much as those with just secondary school qualifications.

____

_____ 3 Graduates generally have healthier lifestyles than those without a degree.

____

_____ 4 Graduates are more likely to vote than those without a degree.

____

_____ 5 Arts graduates have higher incomes than graduates with an engineering degree.

____

_____ 6 Arts graduates have some advantages over graduates with technical degrees.

____

5 Read the article again. Which of the statements in Exercise 4 expresses the main idea of the whole text? _____

READING FOR DETAIL

6 Look at the graphs in the article and answer the questions.

Figure 1

1 Which country had the highest percentage of graduates in 2012?
____

2 Which country had the largest increase in the percentage of graduates between 2000 and 2012? ___________

3 What percentage of the Mexican population (25–64) had a degree in 2012? ___________

Figure 2

1 Which country had the highest percentage of graduates with incomes more than twice the median? ___________

2 Which country had the highest number of graduates with incomes at the country median or below? ___________

3 What percentage of graduates in Brazil earned more than twice the median income? ___________

WHAT IS THE VALUE OF A UNIVERSITY EDUCATION?

1 A university education is a significant investment, so it makes sense to consider carefully whether it is worth the time and money. In good economic times and bad, and in spite of its rising cost, the answer is 'yes'. According to the Organization for Economic Cooperation and Development (OECD), around the world the number of people getting a university education is rising steadily (see Figure 1).

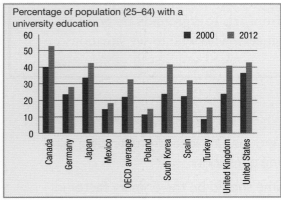

Figure 1   *Source: OECD Indicators*

The impact of a university education

2 A university education has a broad and positive impact. People with a degree are by far the most likely to enter and remain in the labour force. In OECD countries, average participation in the labour force for those without secondary school qualifications is about 55%. For those with secondary school qualifications, the figure is about 70%, and for graduates, it is about 83%. Graduates also earn more than those with only secondary school qualifications. In the United States, individuals leaving education with only secondary school qualifications earned on average $28,000 per year in 2013, whereas those with a degree made about $45,000. Over a lifetime, that difference adds up to about a million dollars. Figure 2 provides a dramatic **illustration** of the impact of a degree on income in selected OECD countries.

3 The consequences of getting – or not getting – a university education extend beyond income. There is a strong association between education and health. **Chronic** diseases, such as heart disease and diabetes, pose the greatest threats to public health in developed countries today. These diseases are caused, at least partly, by lifestyle choices, such as poor diet or smoking. In general, people with higher levels of education make healthier lifestyle choices and have greater access to high-quality healthcare.

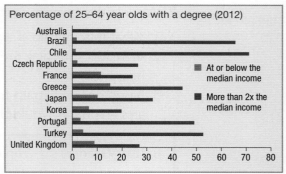

Figure 2   *Source: OECD Indicators*

Income variance between degrees

4 It is evident that a university degree provides an economic advantage, but not all degrees have the same earning power. Most analyses suggest that degrees in STEM fields (Science, Technology, Engineering and Maths) have the greatest potential impact on future income. In the United States, a graduate with, for example, a Chemical Engineering degree can expect to earn about $70,000 annually, whereas a graduate with a Literature or Art degree may be lucky to get $36,000 for an entry-level position. Marc Andreessen, the **founder** of the internet company Netscape, once declared that somebody who studies a non-technical field like literature will probably end up 'working in a shoe store'.

5 Yet, technical knowledge alone may not be sufficient for success. Steve Jobs, one of the founders of Apple, famously **asserted** that it was technology married with the arts '... that yields the results that make our hearts sing'. Other major employers in the technology field agree. Industry leaders say employees from arts backgrounds are good at managing **ambiguity**, unlike engineers, who tend to see situations in black and white. Arts graduates can see a problem from **multiple** perspectives.

It is interesting to note that the income disparity between arts and STEM graduates gradually diminishes as they continue in their careers. In fact, arts degrees are quite common among the world's most highly paid workers. About one-third of the directors of Fortune 500 companies[1] have an arts background.

Students, parents, politicians and industry leaders may argue over which are the most valuable degrees, but the value of a university degree in general cannot be **disputed**.

[1] **Fortune 500 companies** (n) the businesses ranked by *Fortune* magazine as the 500 most profitable companies in the US for a particular year

READING BETWEEN THE LINES

7 Work with a partner. Discuss the questions.

1 What relationship, if any, exists among education, income and health?

2 What do you think Steve Jobs meant by 'the results that make our hearts sing'?

3 Based on the extract from the article below, what are some jobs that arts graduates would be good at? Why?

> Industry leaders say employees from arts backgrounds are good at managing ambiguity, unlike engineers, who tend to see situations in black and white.

DISCUSSION

8 Work with a partner or in small groups. Use ideas from Reading 1 and Reading 2 to answer the following questions.

1 Do you think that future income should be the primary factor in deciding on a course of study? Why / Why not?

2 Why do you think the impact of a university education on income is greater in some countries than in others?

⊙ LANGUAGE DEVELOPMENT

COMPOUND NOUNS

English, especially academic English, uses a large number of compound nouns as they are the most efficient way of expressing complex concepts concisely.

Compound nouns are formed of two or more words and can be formed with several different parts of speech. They also take different forms:

Single words: *healthcare, lifestyle, throwback, earthquake, homeowner*

Hyphenated words: *right-of-way, dry-cleaning, build-up, passer-by, well-being*

Separate words: *learning curve, world leader, drinking water, student identification number*

Noun + noun compounds are very common.

In the United States, almost half of the **labour force** works in these kinds of jobs.

There are a wide range of schools, courses and **training schemes**.

The top computer science schools are expensive, but some boast a 99% **placement rate** for their graduates.

1 Form noun + noun compound nouns with the words from the box to complete the sentences below. Use a dictionary to help you.

first noun	second noun
earning	balance
placement	market
entry	force
training	power
job	level
work–life	scheme
labour	rate

1 The training centre offers a _____ _____ for people who hope to become airplane mechanics.

2 Statistics clearly demonstrate that a college degree increases lifetime _____ _____ .

3 Our course has an excellent _____ _____ . More than 90% of our graduates find a job within a month.

4 The _____ _____ has been very weak this year, as can be seen from the steady increase in unemployment.

5 The _____ _____ is defined as all the people in the population who are able to work.

6 Recent college graduates usually join a business at _____ _____ , but some graduates with a STEM background are able to find more senior positions.

7 Salary is an important consideration in choosing a career, but a career that offers a good _____ _____ is just as important.

2 Rearrange the words to create complex noun phrases (a–e). Then use them correctly to complete the sentences (1–5).

a information / professional / technology _____

b training / graduate / scheme _____

c participation / rate / force / labour _____

d university / trends / enrolment _____

e household / income / median _____

1 The 2013 _____ in Kuwait was $40,854 per year.

2 A local car parts factory announced that it will be recruiting for its new _____ this summer.

3 If you want a secure future, you may want to consider a career as a(n) _____ .

4 The _____ in Saudi Arabia reached 55% in 2016.

5 The Department of Education publishes a report on _____ every January.

WRITING

At the end of this unit, you will write an argumentative essay. Your essay should include some form of graphical support. Look at this unit's writing task in the box below.

> Considering the job market in your country, what is a good choice for a career path with a secure future?

Analyzing information in graphs and other figures

SKILLS

Information in academic texts is often presented visually – in graphs or other types of figure. This information usually extends what is in the text or illustrates points that may be more difficult to understand in words. It is important to be able to connect this information with the information in the text, but, as with everything you read, you should process the information in graphs and figures critically. When describing a graph you don't need to discuss all the information – you just need to mention the most important data that supports your main point.

 UNDERSTAND

1 Work with a partner. Read the information about the annual 100 Best Jobs report and look at the pie chart below. Complete the tasks.

1 Explain why the author chose a pie chart to display this information.
2 Explain the meaning of each section of the pie chart in your own words.

> Every year, the news magazine *US News and World Report* publishes a report on the year's 100 best jobs. Figure 5 shows how the authors of the report measured job quality.

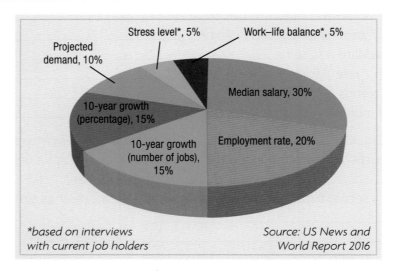

Figure 5. Components of *Best Job* measure

2 Work with a partner. Complete the tasks.

1 Look at Figure 1 below. Based on what you have learned in this unit, explain the wide range of median salaries for the jobs in the table. Which information surprises you most?

2 The highest ranked job is also the highest paid, but this relationship is not consistent throughout the list. Choose two examples and explain what other components in the measure could be responsible for the ranking.

Figure 1. The 100 best jobs in the US, with median salary

rank	job title	median salary in USD
2	dentist	150,000
13	software developer	96,000
22	nurse	67,000
24	accountant	66,000
36	pharmacist	121,000
38	mechanical engineer	83,000
49	medical secretary	32,000
66	laboratory technician	38,000
71	lawyer	71,000
73	social worker	52,000
81	high school teacher	56,000
84	insurance salesperson	48,000
91	manicurist	20,000
93	anthropologist	59,000

Source: US News and World Report 2016

3 You have read about the skills gap situation and the value of higher education, primarily as they apply to western countries. Investigate these issues in your own country or region focusing on the questions below. Keep a record of your sources.

1 Which kinds of jobs are most in demand?

2 Which kinds of jobs are easiest for employers to fill? Which are the most difficult?

3 Is there a skills gap? If so, explain the gap.

4 If there is a skills gap, what kind of training would address this gap?

5 What are the job prospects for university graduates? Do most of them get jobs in their fields?

4 Gather some statistics on employment in your country or region. Keep a record of your sources.

1 What is the average participation rate in the labour market? Has this changed in recent years?
2 What percentage of young people go to university?
3 What is the unemployment rate? If possible, find out if there are different rates for people with different levels of education. Has this rate changed?
4 What are average salaries for university graduates? For those without a university education? Have these figures changed?

 **EVALUATE**

5 Imagine you are a careers adviser and some students have asked you to advise them about which job they should do in the future. Choose one of the top five jobs, and identify the key reasons why they should choose this job. Compare your advice with a partner's and discuss how the two sets of advice differ and why.

GRAMMAR FOR WRITING

ACTIVE VS. PASSIVE VOICE TO DISCUSS FIGURES

Within an academic text, supporting images and graphical elements (graphs, tables, diagrams) are usually all referred to as *figures*.

When writers discuss figures, they use specific words and phrases, sometimes in the passive voice.

To introduce an idea by discussing a figure, the active voice is usually preferred.
Every year, the news magazine US News and World Report publishes a report about the year's 100 best jobs. Figure 5 **shows** how the report's authors measured job quality.

If you have already introduced an idea and wish to explore it in more detail using a figure, the passive is a useful way to avoid repetition.
Judgment of job quality has several components. These **are illustrated** in Figure 5.

These verbs are frequently used when discussing figures:

demonstrate	display	illustrate	reveal
depict	list	indicate	show

Last year's employment rate, **as depicted** in the figures on the slide, was lower than average.

Students who graduated with scientific degrees had a higher starting salary, **as demonstrated** in Figure 2.

1 Work with a partner. Match the figures (A–D) to their descriptions below (1–4). Write A, B, C or D.

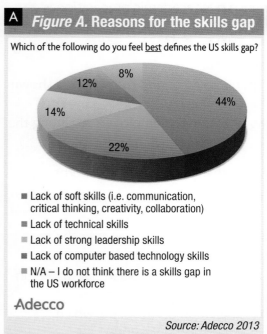

A *Figure A.* **Reasons for the skills gap**

Which of the following do you feel <u>best</u> defines the US skills gap?

44%
8%
12%
14%
22%

- Lack of soft skills (i.e. communication, critical thinking, creativity, collaboration)
- Lack of technical skills
- Lack of strong leadership skills
- Lack of computer based technology skills
- N/A – I do not think there is a skills gap in the US workforce

Adecco

Source: Adecco 2013

B *Figure B.* **US labour force participation**

63.20%

1950 1960 1970 1980 1990 2000 2010

Source: Washington Post / Bureau of Labor Statistics 2013

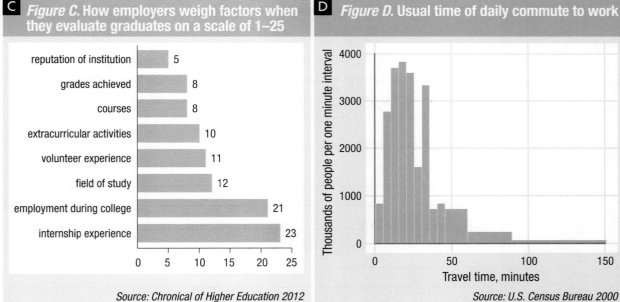

C *Figure C.* **How employers weigh factors when they evaluate graduates on a scale of 1–25**

reputation of institution	5
grades achieved	8
courses	8
extracurricular activities	10
volunteer experience	11
field of study	12
employment during college	21
internship experience	23

0 5 10 15 20 25

Source: Chronical of Higher Education 2012

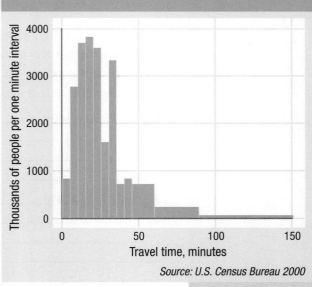

D *Figure D.* **Usual time of daily commute to work**

Thousands of people per one minute interval

4000
3000
2000
1000
0

0 50 100 150
Travel time, minutes

Source: U.S. Census Bureau 2000

1 A *line graph* usually shows change over time. _____

2 A *pie chart* shows the proportion that each category in the chart represents, usually as percentages of a whole. _____

3 A *histogram* displays frequency data, usually in columns, with the y-axis as the counter. _____

4 A *bar graph* compares the amounts or frequency of categories that are not part of a whole. _____

2 Match the figures in Exercise 1 (A–D) to the sentence which best expresses the content (1–4). Write A, B, C or D. Notice the words in bold.

1 Employer preference for experience over academic preparation is **clearly indicated** by Figure _____.

2 Figure _____ **depicts** the steep rise in labour force participation during the final quarter of the twentieth century.

3 The length of time employees spend going to and from work **is shown** in Figure _____.

4 Figure _____ **illustrates** the views of 500 major employers regarding the reasons for the skills gap.

3 Complete the sentences below with either passive or active verbs.

1 The table on p. 111 _____ the results of our employer survey on the skills gap.

2 The dramatic increase in specialized IT training courses over the past ten years _____ in Fig. 1.

3 The figure on the left _____ the various sectors in our market in 1980 and the one on the right _____ our market today.

4 You can see this steady growth in the graph on this slide, which _____ the nation's labour participation since 2000.

5 The jobs with the highest salaries last year _____ in the accompanying table.

PLUS

4 For each of the figures in Reading 1 and Reading 2, write one sentence that summarizes the information and one sentence that introduces the material in the graph. You may write them in either order. Pay attention to passive and active voice. Compare your sentences with a partner.

Figure 1 (page 140): _____

_____

_____

_____

Figure 2 (page 141): _____

_____

_____

_____

Figure 1 (page 145): _____

_____

_____

_____

Figure 2 (page 145): _____

_____

_____

_____

ACADEMIC WRITING SKILLS

MAKING A CLAIM

In an argumentative essay, a writer makes a claim and then provides support for that claim. The claim is delivered in the thesis statement. So the claim is the writer's argument and the thesis statement is the way that argument is expressed in words.

An effective thesis statement does several things:
- It gives readers an idea of what the paper will be about, but it does *not* list every supporting idea that will be offered.
- It narrows down a broader topic so that the writer can fully explore it in an essay.
- It helps readers understand and interpret information about the topic.
- It presents a claim that the readers could argue with. For this reason, facts do not make effective claims.

The thesis statement will generally appear in the first paragraph of an essay. Usually it is expressed in a single sentence, but a complex claim may require two sentences.

To check if you have written an effective thesis statement, ask yourself these questions:
- Does my thesis statement make a claim that my readers can have an opinion about?
- Does it give readers an idea of what my paper will be about without listing every point?
- Is the claim specific enough to be effectively supported in a short essay?

1 Choose the best thesis statement for an essay about the skills gap in the labour market.

   a The skills gap is an economic problem that has developed over several decades.
   b Addressing the skills gap will require significant changes in the education system and the participation of the business community.
   c The skills gap is a consequence of the changing economy.
   d We understand the causes of the skills gap; now it is time to find a way to end it.
   e The skills gap has developed because the job market changed, schools are not providing training in technical areas and businesses have not communicated their needs to educational leaders.

2 Work with a partner. Review the thesis statements in Exercise 1. For each one, answer the following questions.

   1 Does the statement make a claim? If so, what is it?
   2 Is the claim something readers could have an opinion about?
   3 Is the claim specific enough to be developed in a short essay?
   4 Are there other reasons the sentence is not an effective thesis statement?

WRITING TASK

Considering the job market in your country, what is a good choice for a career path with a secure future?

PLAN

1 Review your research results and the career path you chose in Critical thinking, Exercises 3–5 on pages 149–150. Make notes in the table below. Now reread the two articles in this unit and note any information which is relevant to your essay in the table.

introduction and claim	
body points	

2 Work with a partner. Discuss the considerations you are basing your claim on. Think about each factor below. Add notes to your table in Exercise 1.

- form of education needed (university, vocational training, secondary education)
- if university is needed, field of study
- salary potential
- market demand – which positions are in demand now and will continue to be in demand in the future
- job satisfaction factors

3 Write a thesis statement for your essay.

_____

_____

_____

4 Organize the body paragraphs of your essay.

1 Highlight the notes in your table that support your claim.

2 Organize the notes into groups around themes or topics by numbering, circling or highlighting them in different colours. Topics might include:
- current and future trends in the labour market
- salary potential
- educational requirements
- work–life balance

3 Choose two or three topics to write about in your essay. Decide on the order of your topics. Write a topic sentence for each of your body paragraphs.

First body paragraph: _____

_____

_____

Second body paragraph: _____

_____

_____

Third body paragraph: _____

_____

_____

4 Create a figure, based on the statistics you have gathered, to help explain a supporting point in one of your body paragraphs or find one that already exists. Include the source of your information. Write a sentence that explains what your chosen figure shows.

_____

_____

_____

5 Think about your conclusion. What thoughts do you want to leave your readers with?

_____

_____

6 Refer to the Task checklist on page 156 as you prepare your essay.

WRITE A FIRST DRAFT

7 Write your essay. Use your essay plan to help you structure your ideas. Write 450–500 words.

REVISE

8 Use the Task checklist to review your essay for content and structure.

TASK CHECKLIST	✔
Have you introduced and explained your topic?	
Does your thesis statement make a claim that people could argue about?	
Have you paraphrased the information in the articles?	
Do your body paragraphs have topic sentences?	
Do your body paragraphs support your claim?	
Have you included a figure to support at least one of the points in your essay?	
Have you explained the figure and said why it is important?	
Does your concluding paragraph leave your readers with something to think about?	

EDIT

9 Use the Language checklist to edit your essay for language errors.

LANGUAGE CHECKLIST	✔
Have you used compound nouns correctly in your essay?	
Did you use appropriate verbs to introduce information from graphics?	
Did you use active and passive voice correctly to introduce or refer to information shown in graphics?	
Did you give your graphics a figure number and title? Did you cite the source below them?	

10 Make any necessary changes to your essay.

OBJECTIVES REVIEW

1 Check your learning objectives for this unit. Write *3, 2* or *1* for each objective.

3 = very well   2 = well   1 = not so well

I can ...

watch and understand a video about vocational training.   _____

interpret graphical information.   _____

analyze information in graphs and other figures.   _____

use the active and passive voice to discuss figures.   _____

make a claim.   _____

write an argumentative essay with graphical support.   _____

2 Go to the *Unlock* Online Workbook for more practice with this unit's learning objectives.

 UNLOCK ONLINE

WORDLIST		
ambiguity (n) ⊙	expertise (n) ⊙	multiple (adj) ⊙
assert (v) ⊙	founder (n) ⊙	persistent (adj) ⊙
assertive (adj)	illustration (n) ⊙	placement rate (n)
chronic (adj) ⊙	job market (n)	pose (v) ⊙
comprise (v) ⊙	labour (n) ⊙	prospective (adj) ⊙
dispute (v) ⊙	labour force (n)	training scheme (n)
earning power (n)	mismatch (n)	work life balance (n phr)
entry level (n, adj)		

⊙ = high-frequency words in the Cambridge Academic Corpus

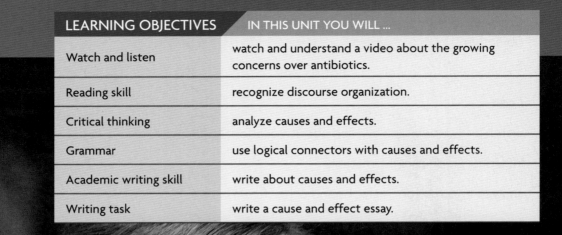

LEARNING OBJECTIVES	IN THIS UNIT YOU WILL ...
Watch and listen	watch and understand a video about the growing concerns over antibiotics.
Reading skill	recognize discourse organization.
Critical thinking	analyze causes and effects.
Grammar	use logical connectors with causes and effects.
Academic writing skill	write about causes and effects.
Writing task	write a cause and effect essay.

UNLOCK YOUR KNOWLEDGE

Work with a partner. Discuss the questions.

1 What do you think is happening in this photo?

2 Which diseases do you think are the greatest threats to global health today?

3 Do you think the world's population is healthier now than a hundred years ago? Why / Why not?

4 The world's population is more interconnected than ever before. What effect do you think this has on global health?

PLUS

   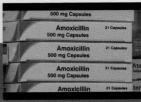

PREPARING TO WATCH

ACTIVATING YOUR KNOWLEDGE

1 Complete the sentences with your own ideas. Work in a small group and compare your ideas.

1 In order to avoid catching an illness, I _____ and
_____ .

2 When people have _____ , the doctor usually prescribes _____ .

3 To prevent the spread of infection in hospitals, visitors must
_____ , otherwise _____ .

4 Scientists are trying to develop drugs to treat _____
and _____ .

PREDICTING CONTENT USING VISUALS

2 You are going to watch a video about clinical drug development. Before you watch, look at the pictures, read the glossary and discuss the questions with your partner.

1 What problem do you think the scientists are trying to address?
2 What do you think has caused this problem?
3 What approach are the scientists taking in their research?

GLOSSARY

antibiotic resistance (n) the ability of harmful bacteria to fight against drugs designed to destroy them

basis (n) the most important facts, ideas, etc. from which something is developed

hamper (v) to prevent someone from doing something easily

overuse (v) to use something too often or too much

predator (n) an animal that hunts, kills and eats other living things

hypothesis (n) an idea or explanation for something that is based on known facts but has not yet been proved

---

WHILE WATCHING

3 ▶ Watch the video and check your predictions from Exercise 2. Write a sentence to summarize the answer to each question.

UNDERSTANDING MAIN IDEAS

1 _____

2 _____

3 _____

4 ▶ Watch again. Note the answers to each item.

UNDERSTANDING DETAIL

1 Two health problems Matthew Hawksley had.

_____   _____

2 Two areas where antibiotic use has increased.

_____   _____

3 Two reasons why new antibiotics haven't been developed.

_____   _____

4 Three ways the government hope to tackle the problem.

_____   _____   _____

5 Four types of predators that prey on plants.

_____   _____

_____   _____

5 ▶ Watch again. Work with a partner and explain the words in bold in each sentence.

WORKING OUT MEANING FROM CONTEXT

1 I was **pumped full of** antibiotics to help me **counter** the MRSA.
2 There's been very much a sense of **crying wolf** over this – **academics**, **microbiologists**, doctors have been saying this is going to happen for over ten years …
3 … change public attitudes from being seen as a 'cure-all' to a 'last resort' medicine …
4 Plants have a **distinct** disadvantage as they can't move out of the way of predators – and they have **no end of** predators.

DISCUSSION

6 Work with a partner. Discuss the questions.

1 Do you think it is important to invest more money into the research and development of new antibiotics? Why / Why not? Who should pay for more research and development?
2 How do you think people in the UK came to see antibiotics as a 'cure-all'? Do you think the situation is the same in your country?
3 What medical campaigns have you seen to change public attitudes or behaviours? How were the messages communicated? Do you think they were effective? Why / Why not?
4 What do you think the most effective way(s) to change public attitudes to antibiotics would be?

READING

PREPARING TO READ

USING YOUR KNOWLEDGE

1 You are going to read an article about superbugs. Work with a partner. Discuss the questions.

1 When you are feeling sick and go to a doctor's office or clinic, do you usually get antibiotics? Why / Why not?

2 Do you always finish all the medication the doctor prescribes even if you are feeling better? Why / Why not?

3 Why do you think antibiotics are commonly given to livestock (animals that produce food for humans)?

UNDERSTANDING KEY VOCABULARY

2 Read the sentences and choose the best definition for the words in bold.

1 The discovery of penicillin and other antibiotics **revolutionized** the treatment of infectious diseases.
   a made easier
   b completely changed
   c made more accessible

2 The news report presented a **grim** picture of the public health crisis people are living through.
   a worrying; without hope
   b dangerous
   c conflicting, unclear

3 Mosquitoes **thrive** in warm, wet conditions, so they are more common in summer.
   a live and develop successfully
   b compete with each other more easily
   c struggle to survive

4 Due to the **resistance** of some bacteria to treatment with antibiotics, people can become very sick from simple infections.
   a increase in cost
   b change
   c ability to fight against something

5 The increase in the numbers of people with the disease is due to the **emergence** of new types of the virus.
   a change or growth
   b being reduced or stopped
   c becoming known or starting to exist

6 The rise of diseases that cannot be treated with drugs is extremely **problematic**.
   a expensive and time consuming
   b dangerous to health
   c full of difficulties that need to be dealt with

7 Hospitals are introducing more rigorous rules on hygiene to **counter** the recent increase in bacterial infections on the wards.
   a defend against
   b investigate
   c keep track of

8 The company has promised to **phase out** the use of dangerous chemicals in its operations.
   a protect against   b end gradually   c warn about

WHILE READING

3 Read the article on page 164. Which statement best expresses the main idea of the whole article?

   a Bacteria will always find a way to get around antibiotics.
   b Antibiotics in the food chain have led to the spread of drug-resistant bacteria.
   c The misuse of antibiotics is a primary factor in the rise of drug-resistant bacteria.
   d Since our strongest antibiotics are powerless against the latest strain of bacteria, we should expect more outbreaks of dangerous diseases.

READING FOR MAIN IDEAS

Recognizing discourse organization

Essays are usually organized to meet general goals. An essay may
   • describe a process
   • compare and/or contrast two or more things
   • describe the causes or consequences of things
   • explain how something works
   • describe a system of classification
   • relate a series of events

Recognizing these discourse structures can help you predict and comprehend the content of a text. The introduction will often give clues as to how the essay will be organized (e.g. *there are three kinds of* ...). There may also be words that signpost different types of organization (e.g. *At the beginning* ... . *then, X is a consequence of Y; In contrast to X, Y* ...).

SKILLS

4 Which discourse structure from the Explanation box best describes the article?

UNDERSTANDING DISCOURSE

SUPERBUGS

1 They are so small that you need a microscope to see them, but so powerful that experts predict they could kill ten million people per year worldwide by the year 2050. They are superbugs – drug-resistant bacteria that have emerged since antibiotics **revolutionized** medicine in the early twentieth century. Indeed, the rise of these superbugs and the use of antibiotics are closely intertwined.

2 All organisms change over time; this is a basic principle of evolution. Smaller organisms, such as bacteria, are able to evolve more quickly, adapting as circumstances require. In the face of antibiotics, bacteria have adapted with deadly efficiency. When a patient takes antibiotics to fight off a bacterial infection, the goal is to kill the bacteria causing the infection. Often, however, although most of the bacteria are killed, a few of the strongest bacteria survive. Thus, only these drug-resistant bacteria are able to reproduce. This sets up a cycle in which increasingly powerful antibiotics are needed to **counter** bacterial infections, eventually resulting in the development of superbugs – bacteria able to resist even the most powerful drugs.

3 Scientists believe that a large part of this cycle is preventable. Few would dispute that patients who are genuinely ill should take antibiotics, but one recent study suggested that almost 50% of all antibiotic use is inappropriate or unnecessary. Some patients are prescribed antibiotics for ailments that would eventually clear up on their own, or for viral infections, against which antibiotics have no effect. In addition, some patients do not finish their course of medication, allowing bacteria to bounce back, but stronger. All of these factors contribute to the rise and spread of superbugs. Although many doctors find it difficult to refuse when patients request medication, in this instance, what may be safe and effective for the individual can be harmful to society as a whole.

4 Another major factor that promotes the spread of drug **resistance** is the use of antibiotics for livestock. In Europe, many countries have long since enacted laws to limit or ban antibiotic use in livestock. However, in the United States, 80% of antibiotic use is for animals. In part, the drugs are used to prevent the spread of infection among animals, especially those that live in crowded conditions. However, farmers also use antibiotics because these drugs help animals to gain weight quickly. Unfortunately, such non-therapeutic use of antibiotics is **problematic** because it kills off the beneficial bacteria that normally live in the animals' digestive tract, leaving drug-resistant strains of bacteria to **thrive**.

5 The widespread use of antibiotics for the past 70 years in both the animal and human populations, and the resulting increase in drug-resistant bacteria, have fuelled an ongoing search for more powerful drugs. In the early days of antibiotic research, scientists were successful in finding new classes of drugs, capable of fighting the drug-resistant bacteria that continually appeared. Drug discovery tapered off to almost nothing in the 1990s and 2000s, creating a global panic regarding the future treatment of infection. Investment has led to recent discoveries of new classes of antibiotics in the soil and inside the human nose, which offer some hope, but it will take years for viable drugs to be developed. In the meantime, very few weapons are currently available against the deadliest bacteria. Late in 2015, researchers reported the **emergence** of a strain of bacteria able to resist even the most powerful medications, those only used as a last resort.

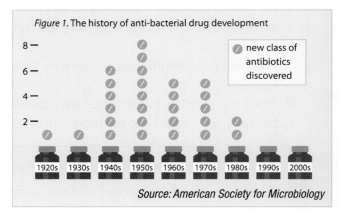

Figure 1. The history of anti-bacterial drug development

Source: American Society for Microbiology

6 What can be done to preserve antibiotics for future generations? Scientists maintain that as individuals, we can make a difference with simple steps, such as regular hand washing. It is also important that patients understand that antibiotics are not always the right course of treatment. They should not be taken for viral infections or even for mild bacterial infections. Finally, it is crucial to take antibiotics out of the food chain. Fortunately, consumers are pushing for this, so we are likely to see changes in this practice in the near future. The fast food giant McDonald's, which sells millions of kilograms of chicken every year, is **phasing out** its use of chicken treated with antibiotics. If both individuals and corporations around the world continue to take steps like these, perhaps superbugs can be stopped. The alternative presents a **grim** picture for future generations.

5 Read paragraphs 1–4 of the article again. Complete the cause and effect chain of drug resistance below.

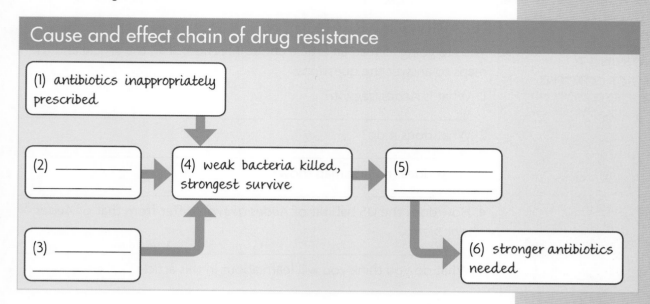

Cause and effect chain of drug resistance

(1) antibiotics inappropriately prescribed

(2) _____

(3) _____

(4) weak bacteria killed, strongest survive

(5) _____

(6) stronger antibiotics needed

READING BETWEEN THE LINES

6 Find the phrases (1–5) in the article. Work out the meaning from the context. Match the phrases with their definitions (a–e).

1 closely intertwined (para 1)
2 in the face of (para 2)
3 on their own (para 3)
4 taper off (para 5)
5 as a last resort (para 5)

a without help
b linked, related
c gradually happen less often
d when every alternative option has failed
e when threatened with

7 Work with a partner. Write a sentence for each phrase in Exercise 6, using the phrase in context correctly. Share your sentences with the class.

DISCUSSION

8 Work with a partner. Discuss the questions.

1 Look at Figure 1 in the article. What does it show? What do you think will happen in the future?
2 Some farmers argue that antibiotics prevent their animals from getting sick and ensure that the meat they produce is safe for humans. Do you think this is a good reason to give these drugs to healthy animals? Why / Why not?

READING 2

PREPARING TO READ

SCANNING TO PREDICT CONTENT

1 You are going to read an article about infection. Scan the article and the maps to answer the questions.

1 What is *Aedes aegypti*?

_____

2 What does it do?

_____

3 What does the first map show?

_____

4 How does the US habitat of *Aedes aegypti* differ from that of *Aedes albopictus*?

_____

5 What do you think you will learn about in this article?

_____

UNDERSTANDING KEY VOCABULARY

2 Read the sentences. Write the correct form of the words in bold (1–8) next to their definitions below (a–h).

1 The new housing development's **proximity** to the airport is problematic because of the noise at night.

2 There is still a risk of **transmission** of the virus through infected water.

3 The illness is widespread rather than being **confined to** any one group in society.

4 It is not possible to **eradicate** some diseases, but it is possible to control them.

5 Not finishing your course of antibiotics **facilitates** the growth of superbugs.

6 Early **detection** of cancer can substantially improve the chances of recovery.

7 There has been a **surge** in complaints about dangerous chemicals in the drinking water since farm animals started mysteriously dying.

8 Many rural populations depend on **domesticated** animals for food and labour.

a _____ (n) identification; diagnosis; discovery

b _____ (n) nearness

c _____ (n) a sudden, large increase

d _____ (v) to make something possible or easier

e _____ (n) the process of passing something from one person or place to another

f _____ (phr) existing in only a particular area or group of people

g _____ (adj) (for animals) under human control

h _____ (v) to get rid of something completely

PLUS

THE GLOBALIZATION OF INFECTION

1 Recent headlines have been filled with alarming news of the spread of pathogens[1] that cause diseases like SARS, MERS, swine flu, dengue fever, chikungunya and the Zika virus. Are these pathogens really on the increase, or have **detection** and reporting methods simply improved? In fact, several studies suggest that the **surge** in these infectious diseases is quite real. Researchers propose a number of reasons for these developments.

2 Probably the most obvious reason is how closely connected the world has become. Human populations regularly travel long distances as immigrants, business traveller, or tourists, carrying diseases with them. For example, it is thought that the Zika virus may have travelled from French Polynesia to Brazil in the blood of infected international athletes. People are not the only world travellers; insects, primarily mosquitoes, can also hop on a boat or a plane and migrate thousands of miles. Scientists refer to the hosts that carry pathogens as *vectors*. When they bite, vectors transfer infected blood to a new victim, spreading the pathogen in both human and animal populations. As these vectors move around the world, and if they can survive and reproduce in their new environment, the range of the disease grows.

3 The pathogens themselves are also highly adaptable. Most pathogens are found in a specific vector. For example, chikungunya is carried by a particular type of mosquito, *Aedes aegypti*, in Africa and Asia, where the disease originated. As the virus travelled across the Pacific, however, it mutated[2] to a new form, which thrives in a different vector, the Asian tiger mosquito, *Aedes albopictus*, allowing the disease to spread beyond the habitat of the original host mosquito.

4 Many infectious diseases originated in warm climates, where insects like mosquitoes live and thrive. As climate change leads to higher temperatures around the world, mosquitoes are now able to survive in areas that were once too cold for them. Figure 1 shows the range of *Aedes albopictus* and *Aedes aegypti*, both major vectors of tropical diseases, in the United States as of 2016. *Aedes aegypti*, once **confined to** tropical Africa, is expected to expand its range even farther with global warming. Both vectors are starting to achieve global reach, including the Middle East, north Africa and south Asia.

5 The increasingly urban nature of the world's population also **facilitates** the **transmission** of disease. In large, crowded cities in developing countries, many people do not have regular household waste collections or access to clean drinking water. A household without running water is likely to catch and save rainwater in open containers – the perfect breeding ground[3] for mosquitoes – as are piles of rubbish and, above all, old tyres.

6 Another aspect of urbanization contributing to the spread of pathogens is our **proximity** to both wild and **domesticated** animals. Many dangerous pathogens have the ability to mutate and jump from one species to another, including to humans. Avian flu is a prime example of such, as is Ebola, which scientists believe originated among gorillas and chimpanzees. As various species experience the destruction of their habitats as a result of deforestation and urbanization, many are forced to live closer to human settlements, increasing the opportunity for the transmission of diseases from animals to humans. Domesticated animal populations are being squeezed as well. They are confined to increasingly crowded spaces, creating conditions that facilitate the transmission of disease.

7 Some pathogens, such as the ones that cause Ebola, are deadly, with no known cure. Others may not be as dangerous, but still have an enormous economic impact in terms of lost productivity and the resources needed to fight them and provide healthcare for their victims. Some of these infectious diseases, once a local menace, now pose a global threat, and it will require a global effort to **eradicate** them.

[1]**pathogen** (n) a small organism that can cause disease
[2]**mutate** (v) to change genetically
[3]**breeding ground** (n) a place where organisms reproduce

Figure 1. The spread of *Aedes albopictus* and *Aedes aegypti* into the United States, as of 2016

Aedes aegypti

Aedes albopictus

Source: CDC

WHILE READING

3 Read the article. Which statements do you think the writer of the article would agree with?

    a Infectious diseases are a concern for people all over the world.
    b Scientists will soon find ways to prevent and treat these diseases.
    c Slowing global warming is the key to eradicating these diseases.
    d Most of these diseases are not likely to pose a threat to the United States in the near future.

4 Read the article again. Circle the factors that contribute to the spread of infectious diseases as discussed in the article. Find four other factors that were discussed in the article and add them to the list.

    a climate change
    b mutation of pathogens
    c lack of access to healthcare
    d drug resistance
    e migration of vectors
    f floods

    1 _____
    2 _____
    3 _____
    4 _____

5 Use the phrases from the boxes to label the cause and effect chains that start with urbanization.

> people collect water   disease spreads more easily
> overcrowded cities   mosquitoes breed freely
> people live in areas without running water

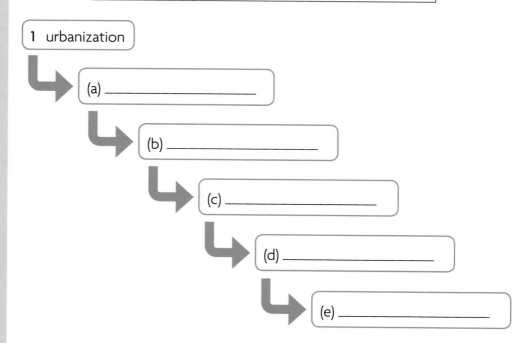

1 urbanization

(a) _____

(b) _____

(c) _____

(d) _____

(e) _____

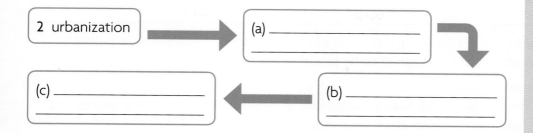

READING BETWEEN THE LINES

6 Work with a partner. Complete the tasks.

MAKING INFERENCES

1 The article states: 'In large, crowded cities in developing countries, many people do not have regular household waste collections or access to clean drinking water.' This implies that some people are receiving these services, but others are not. Who do you think is receiving services and who is not? Why?

2 Review paragraph 2 of the article. Complete the cause and effect chain showing how the range of a disease can grow.

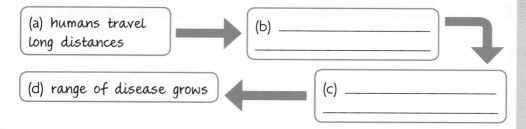

DISCUSSION

7 Work with a partner. Use ideas from Reading 1 and Reading 2 to answer the following questions.

SYNTHESIZING

1 What do you know about each disease discussed in these articles?

2 Antibiotics are for bacterial infections. Antiviral drugs are for viruses. Sometimes, however, antibiotics are used as part of a larger treatment plan for viral diseases. What effect might this have on the increase in superbugs?

3 Both articles end by saying a global effort will be required to combat the spread of pathogens. What do you think can be done?

VERBS AND VERB PHRASES FOR CAUSATION

GRAMMAR

It is important to understand the differences in meaning among verbs and verb phrases that express aspects of causation in order to write with precision.

Direct causation
As climate change **leads to** higher temperatures around the world, mosquitoes are now able to survive in areas that were once too cold for them.

Part of a cause
All of these factors **contribute to** the rise and spread of superbugs.

Makes effect easier to achieve
The increasingly urban nature of the world's population also **facilitates** the transmission of disease.

Passive causation
In addition, some patients do not finish their course of medication, **allowing** bacteria to bounce back, but stronger.

direct causation	part of a cause	makes effect easier to achieve	passive causation
cause be a cause of lead to result in be a/the result of create trigger produce bring about drive	be a factor in contribute to affect impact influence have an effect on have a role in	help facilitate promote fuel encourage foster enable	let* allow permit

* Notice that, unlike other passive causation verbs, *let* is not followed by *to*:
Global travel **lets** pathogens **spread** more easily.

PLUS

1 Complete the sentences with the correct form of one of the verbs or verb phrases from the table above. More than one answer is possible.

  1 Increasing urbanization and international travel are likely to have _____ the emergence and spread of dengue fever in Saudi Arabia.

  2 Scientists have only recently begun to understand how climate change _____ the spread of vectors that carry infectious diseases.

  3 Health officials are targeting containers of standing water that _____ mosquitoes to reproduce and spread disease.

4 A bacterial infection _____ an automatic defensive response in which the body attempts to kill off the invading pathogens.

5 Antibiotics often destroy only a percentage of the bacteria that cause infection, _____ the strongest to survive and even thrive.

2 Write two sentences about global health using expressions from the table in the Explanation box on page 170.

1 _____
_____

2 _____
_____

WORD FAMILIES

3 Complete the word families related to global health and medicine. Use a dictionary to help you.

noun	verb	adjective	
access	(1)_____	(2)_____	
bacteria		(3)_____	
(4)_____	(5)_____	infectious	
(6)mutant; _____	mutate	mutant	
prevention	(7)_____	(8)_____	(9)_____
(10)_____	(11)_____	resistant	
therapy		(12)_____	
transmission	(13)_____	(14)_____	
virus		(15)_____	

PLUS

4 Complete the paragraph with words from Exercise 3 in the correct form.

The spread of infectious disease is a complex phenomenon. Health officials must deal with both (1)_____ and (2)_____ infections, caused by pathogens that can be (3)_____ from one host to another in different ways. What makes the situation even more challenging is that these pathogens can (4)_____ over time, allowing them to become (5)_____ to medicines. Once this occurs, these drugs are no longer (6)_____ and scientists need to find new ways to treat the infections. Many experts believe that a better option would be to develop a vaccine to (7)_____ these diseases from (8)_____ people in the first place.

CRITICAL THINKING

At the end of this unit, you will write a cause-and-effect essay. Look at this unit's writing task in the box below.

> Many infectious diseases that were once geographically limited are now present globally. Choose one disease and discuss the factors that may have contributed to its development and spread or could do so in the future.

SKILLS

Analyzing causes and effects

In academic writing it is important to be able to provide an analysis of why something happens and of the consequences of events, behaviour or decisions. When you analyze the relationship between events, behaviour and decisions, don't confuse causes with similar relationships, such as:

1 **correlation:** two changes occurring at the same time. For example, there might be an increase in crime at the same time as an increase in the population of homeless people in the same area. This does not mean that the homeless people are responsible for the crime.

2 **sequence:** one thing happening after another. For example, an athlete grows a beard and then his team start winning more games. The new beard appeared first, but it is not a factor in the team's success.

In some cases, you can be certain of a causal relationship. For example, if you heat a gas, it will expand. This is clearly a causal relationship so you can use a strong signal of direct causation. In other cases, the causal relationship is less clear – for example, the relationship between poverty and health problems. In such cases, you should use a weaker signal of causation.

 REMEMBER

1 Work with a partner. List the factors you have read about in this unit that have contributed to the globalization of infection.

_____   _____

_____   _____

_____   _____

_____   _____

_____   _____

UNDERSTAND

2 You are going to write a case history of an infectious disease. Read the case histories for three infectious diseases that have created global concern in recent years on pages 173–174. Then work with a partner and discuss the ways in which all the diseases are similar and how they differ.

A Chikungunya

- first documented cases in Tanzania in the 1950s
- spread through Africa and south-east Asia
- first case in western hemisphere in 2013
- about three million infections per year
- rarely lethal – 1 death per 1,000 infections
- symptoms include joint pain, headaches, fatigue, and may last for months or even years
- vectors: *Aedes aegypti* and more recently, *Aedes albopictus*
- crowded conditions needed to sustain transmission among humans
- virus
- no vaccine
- no specific treatment

B Dengue fever

- frequent epidemics dating back to seventeenth century
- spread with migration of *Aedes aegypti*, which accompanied slave trade
- one-third of global population now at risk
- 50–100 million infections annually
- 22,000 deaths annually
- vectors: *Aedes aegypti* and more recently, *Aedes albopictus*
- crowded conditions needed to sustain transmission among humans
- symptoms include rash, fever, headaches and joint pain
- virus
- vaccine in development
- no specific treatment

C Zika virus

- first identified in monkeys in 1947 in Uganda
- first human infection in 1952
- spread through Africa and Asia in 1950s–1980s
- crossed Pacific and arrived in western hemisphere in 2015
- many of those infected have no symptoms, so it is difficult to estimate the rate of infection
- four million annual infections are projected
- most cases are mild; can cause birth defects if mother is infected
- vectors: primarily *Aedes aegypti*
- crowded conditions needed to sustain transmission among humans
- vaccine in development
- no specific treatment

3 Work with a partner. Find sources of information to look at for your case history – this could be in a library or online. For each source, answer the questions and decide whether the source is trustworthy.

1 Who is the author?
2 What are his or her credentials?
3 When was the content written?
4 Is it a personal webpage or does it belong to an organization?
5 What extension does the website use: .co, .edu, .org, .gov? The extension can give you some idea of the purpose of the website.
6 Explain to your partner why you think this is / is not a trustworthy source.

4 Do research using the sources you identified in Exercise 3. Write a case history for another infectious disease in box D.

> **D** _____
>
> ⦁ _____
> ⦁ _____
> ⦁ _____
> ⦁ _____
> ⦁ _____
> ⦁ _____
> ⦁ _____
> ⦁ _____
> ⦁ _____
> ⦁ _____

 EVALUATE

5 Review your list of factors from Exercise 1. Write the three factors that have contributed most to their development and spread of each disease, or will do so in the future.

factors	chikungunya	dengue fever	Zika virus	_____
factor 1				
factor 2				
factor 3				

6 Work with a partner. Read the facts about chikungunya and dengue fever below. Then list some possible consequences of the spread of these diseases. Think of one consequence for each fact for each group. Make sure the relationships between events are causal and not correlational or simply sequential. For causal relationships, consider the strength of the causality.

Facts about chikunguya and dengue fever:
* Most people who contract these diseases remain ill for 1–2 weeks. They cannot work or attend school during that period.
* Although there is no known cure, many patients seek a doctor's care for relief of the symptoms.
* Some patients, especially young children, require hospitalization.
* A small percentage of cases are fatal.

Consequences:
For individuals and families:

_____
_____
_____
_____

For nations and regions:

_____
_____
_____
_____

7 Review the cause and effect chain you completed on page 168. Develop two or three cause and effect chains for the disease you researched in Exercise 4 you are writing about. These will become the basis of your body paragraphs in the writing task.

CREATE

CAUSE AND EFFECT: LOGICAL CONNECTORS

There are many different ways to express causes and effects using logical connectors.

To connect a cause noun phrase and an effect clause in a single sentence

as a result of [cause]   *because of* [cause]
due to [cause]   *thanks to* [cause]

Survival rates have increased **as a result of** more research into the cause of the disease.

Thanks to increased awareness of the symptoms, diagnoses are being made more quickly.

To connect a cause clause and an effect clause in a single sentence

because [cause]   *since* [cause]

There are fewer doctors **since** funding for training has been reduced.

To connect cause and effect in two sentences

as a result [effect]   *as a consequence* [effect]
consequently [effect]   *therefore* [effect]
so [effect]

Antibiotics have been misused. **As a result**, numbers of antibiotic-resistant bacteria have increased.

People's health is generally better. **Therefore**, life expectancies in many countries have increased.

Some verbs, nouns and connectors look and sound similar, so they are easy to confuse. Take care when using these logical connectors.

Because / because of

Because the earth is getting warmer, the habitat of some mosquitoes is growing.
Some experts believe superbugs have emerged **because of** the misuse of antibiotics.

As a consequence / is a consequence of

Some of the bacteria survive. **As a consequence**, the bacteria become drug resistant.
Often, drug resistance **is a consequence of** the misuse of antibiotics.

As a result / results in / results from

Some of the bacteria survive; **as a result**, the bacteria become drug resistant.
Long-term illness **results in** a loss of productivity for families and entire nations.
Birth defects may **result from** a mother's exposure to the virus during pregnancy.

1 Review the table in Critical thinking, Exercise 5 on page 174. Write three sentences about factors in the globalization of infection. Use logical connectors.

1 _____

2 _____

3 _____

2 Review Critical thinking, Exercise 6. Write two sentences describing the consequences of the spread of infectious diseases. Use logical connectors.

1 _____

2 _____

ACADEMIC WRITING SKILLS

WRITING ABOUT CAUSES AND EFFECTS

Academic writing often includes explanations for why something happens or the consequences of events, behaviour or decisions. The first involves an analysis of causes, whereas the second requires an analysis of effects.

- A cause analysis addresses causal factors in a situation or decision.
- An effect analysis addresses the consequences of an event or situation.

These analyses may be chains; in other words, one cause may lead to an effect that causes another effect. The distinction between causes and effects is not always clear cut, as the effect of one situation can become the cause of another, and so on.

More complex pieces of writing may include both types of analysis.

1 Work with a partner and complete the tasks.

1 Review the list of the effects of climate change on the Arctic and the cause and effect chain on page 178. Number the items in the list in the order they appear in the chain. Write an X if the item does not appear in the chain.

- Glaciers are melting: getting weaker and smaller. _____
- There is an increase in shipping and other commercial activities. _____
- Floating ice, an important habitat for polar animals, is disappearing. _____
- Arctic areas are more accessible to humans. _____
- Sea ice is melting. _____
- Strong Arctic storms are more frequent. _____
- Arctic animals, such as polar bears, have become endangered. _____
- The ocean is getting warmer. _____
- Storms are breaking up weak areas of glaciers. _____

higher ocean temp ➡ glcrs melting/weak ➡ storms break up glcrs

more shipping ⬅ more access ⬅

2 Read the paragraph below describing the cause-and-effect relationships in the chain in Exercise 1. Circle the words and phrases used to describe cause and effect. Is it a cause analysis or an effect analysis?

Higher ocean temperatures have had a dramatic impact in the Arctic, and not everyone thinks this is negative. The warmer climate has weakened the glaciers, making them vulnerable to increasingly frequent storms, which are also fuelled by the warmer water. As a consequence, Arctic areas, almost impossible to navigate in the past, are suddenly more accessible to shipping and commercial operations.

3 Write about one of the cause and effect chains you created in Critical thinking, Exercise 7 on page 175. Write a short paragraph describing the cause-and-effect relationships in the chain. Use the words, phrases and grammatical structures of cause and effect that you have learned in this unit. Then compare your work with a partner.

_____
_____
_____
_____
_____
_____
_____
_____
_____
_____
_____

WRITING TASK

Many infectious diseases that were once geographically limited are now present globally. Choose one disease and discuss the factors that may have contributed to its development and spread or could do so in the future.

PLAN

1 For each of your cause and effect chains from Critical thinking, Exercise 7 on page 175 write a topic sentence that introduces and unites the material in that chain. (Review Academic writing skills, Exercises 2 and 3 on page 178.)

_____

_____

_____

_____

_____

_____

2 Think about the introductory paragraph. Complete the tasks.

1 What background information could you include? Review the case history you wrote in Critical thinking, Exercise 4 on page 174, and highlight possible points to include.

2 What claim will you make about the spread of this disease?

_____

3 Write a thesis statement that expresses the claim.

_____

_____

_____

3 Think about your conclusion. Complete the tasks.

1 How will you begin your conclusion? Make sure you remind your readers of the importance of your claim, but do not repeat your thesis statement.

_____

_____

2 What do you want your readers to think about as they finish your essay?
   a future possibilities
   b wider consequences
   c other: _____

4 Refer to the Task checklist on page 180 as you prepare your essay.

WRITE A FIRST DRAFT

5 Write your essay. Use your essay plan to help you structure your ideas. Write 450–500 words.

REVISE

6 Use the Task checklist to review your essay for content and structure.

TASK CHECKLIST	✔
Have you introduced and provided background on the infectious disease?	
Have you stated your claim clearly in your thesis statement?	
Have you developed and explained the cause and effect chains in the spread of the disease?	
Does each body paragraph provide evidence to support your claim? Where necessary, is this evidence properly sourced?	
Does each paragraph have a topic sentence that unifies all of the material in the paragraph?	
Is there a concluding paragraph that refers to your claim and leaves the reader with something to think about?	

EDIT

7 Use the Language checklist to edit your essay for language errors.

LANGUAGE CHECKLIST	✔
When discussing causation, did you use the verbs and verb phrases you learned about in this unit?	
Did you use the correct form of global health words?	
Did you use logical connectors correctly?	

8 Make any necessary changes to your essay.

OBJECTIVES REVIEW

1 Check your learning objectives for this unit. Write *3*, *2* or *1* for each objective.

3 = very well   2 = well   1 = not so well

I can ...

watch and understand a video about the growing concerns over antibiotics. _____

recognize discourse organization. _____

analyze causes and effects. _____

use verbs and verb phrases for causation. _____

use logical connectors with causes and effects. _____

write about causes and effects. _____

write a cause and effect essay. _____

2 Go to the *Unlock* Online Workbook for more practice with this unit's learning objectives.

UNLOCK ONLINE

WORDLIST

access (n, v) ⊙	grim (adj)	proximity (n) ⊙
accessible (adj) ⊙	infect (v) ⊙	resist (v) ⊙
bacteria (n) ⊙	infection (n)	resistance (n) ⊙
bacterial (adj) ⊙	infectious (adj)	resistant (adj)
confined to (phr)	mutant (adj, n)	revolutionize (v)
counter (v) ⊙	mutate (v)	surge (v)
detection (n) ⊙	mutation (n)	therapy (n) ⊙
domesticated (adj)	phase out (phr v)	therapeutic (adj)
drive (n) ⊙	prevent (v) ⊙	thrive (v)
emergence (n) ⊙	preventable (adj)	transmission (n) ⊙
enable (v)	preventative (adj)	transmit (v)
eradicate (v)	prevention (n)	transmittable (adj)
facilitate (v) ⊙	problematic (adj) ⊙	viral (adj)
fuel (v) ⊙	promote (v) ⊙	virus (n)

⊙ = high-frequency words in the Cambridge Academic Corpus

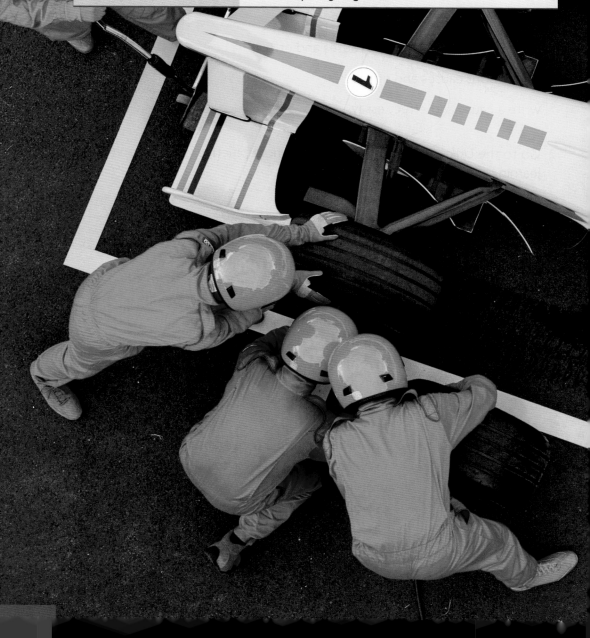

LEARNING OBJECTIVES	IN THIS UNIT YOU WILL ...
Watch and listen	watch and understand a video about an elite aerobatics display team.
Reading skill	use context clues to understand terminology and fixed expressions.
Critical thinking	understand audience and purpose.
Grammar	make concessions and refute counter-arguments.
Academic writing skill	anticipate counter-arguments.
Writing task	write a report giving recommendations.

COLLABORATION

UNL⌀CK YOUR KNOWLEDGE

Work with a partner. Discuss the questions.

1 What sport can you see in the picture? Do you think of this as a team sport or an individual sport? Why?

2 Which is more productive — when members of a group compete or collaborate? Explain your answers.

3 Do you agree or disagree with the following statement? Give reasons for your answer.

   A team's goals are more important than the goals of its individual members.

4 What factors do you think lead to a successful team?

PLUS

WATCH AND LISTEN

PREPARING TO WATCH

ACTIVATING YOUR KNOWLEDGE

1 Think about the qualities of successful teams you know. Then choose three words from the box for each type of team in the table. Compare your ideas with a partner.

> discipline   trust   training   experience   skill   knowledge
> motivation   attention to detail   competitiveness
> patience   good communication   courage

	1	2	3
a team of chefs			
a sales team			
a gymnastics team			

USING YOUR KNOWLEDGE TO PREDICT CONTENT

2 You are going to watch a video about an aerobatics team for the RAF (Royal Air Force). Before you watch, discuss the questions with your partner.

1 What different roles do you think there are on an aerobatics team? Why is each of those roles important?

2 In what ways would flying a jet in an aerobatics team be different from flying a passenger plane? What would be the physical and mental challenges?

3 What do you think the aerobatics team do during the time that they are not putting on displays?

GLOSSARY

elite (adj) belonging to the most skilful or best-trained group of people who do a particular job in a society

hone (v) to make a skill, technique, etc. perfect by practising

personnel (n) the people who are employed in a company, organization, or one of the armed forces

squadron (n) a unit of people who work together in the air force

pulling G (v phr) being affected by a strong force on the body due to the combination a rapid increase in speed and the constant force of gravity

inflate (v) to make something increase in size by filling it with air

WHILE WATCHING

3 ▶ Watch the video. Number the main ideas in the order you hear them.

_____ During the winter the engineers do important tasks.

_____ Keeping the Red Arrows flying is very expensive.

_____ Red One is the team leader.

_____ There are over 120 personnel in the Red Arrows team.

_____ The pilots' jobs are very dangerous.

_____ In the winter, the team practises hard for the summer.

_____ The clothing worn by the pilots can save their lives.

_____ This year the design of the jets is changing.

4 ▶ Watch again. Answer the questions.

1 What roles are there in the Red Arrows team?

_____

2 What qualities does Red One admire in his team?

_____

3 Why is the change to the tailfin design important?

_____

4 What makes the winter training for pilots more difficult?

_____

5 What do the circus engineers do?

_____

6 What effect does wearing G-trousers have on the pilots?

_____

7 What happened in 2011? _____

8 How do some people feel about the running costs of the Red Arrows?

_____

5 ▶ Watch again. Discuss the questions with a partner.

1 Why do you think the Red Arrows are changing the design of the planes?

2 Why does Drew Paxton call the engineers the 'lifeblood' of the squadron?

3 What might happen if the pilots did not wear G-trousers?

4 Why do you think the reporter says the Red Arrows are 'ambassadors for Britain'?

DISCUSSION

6 Work in a small group. Discuss the questions.

1 What is your opinion of the Red Arrows team? Do you think what they do is valuable? Why / Why not?

2 What other teams can you think of that need to work together as closely as the Red Arrows? Why do they need to work that way?

3 Would you like to be part of a team where other people's lives depended on your actions? Why / Why not?

READING

PREPARING TO READ

PREVIEWING

1 You are going to read an article about the value of talented individuals within teams. Work with a partner. Read the first sentence of each paragraph of the article on pages 187–188. Then discuss the questions.

1 What broader lessons do you think we can learn from sports teams?
2 What do you think the connection between chickens and sport might be?
3 Does a team of talented players guarantee success? Why / Why not?

UNDERSTANDING
KEY VOCABULARY

2 Read the definitions. Use the correct form of the words in bold to complete the sentences below.

> **accomplish** (v) to do something successfully
> **amass** (v) to collect a large amount of something
> **coordinate** (v) to make separate things or people work well together
> **detract from** (phr v) to make something worse
> **differentiate** (v) to show or find the difference between one thing and others
> **enhance** (v) to improve the quality of something
> **isolate** (v) to separate something from other connected things
> **peak** (v) to reach the highest or strongest point of value or skill

1 The exercise room and excellent cafeteria _____ the company's image amongst new graduates.
2 We cannot work independently. We will need to _____ our efforts if we want this project to be a success.
3 The unemployment rate _____ in 2010 and has been falling since then.
4 We have _____ a lot in the last five years, but we still have more work to do in order to reach our goals.
5 The team has _____ an impressive number of trophies and medals.
6 We need to find a way to _____ our products from all the other similar products on the market.
7 The player's disruptive behaviour _____ the fans' enjoyment of the game.
8 Analysts have been able to _____ the most important factors in a team's success.

WHILE READING

3 Read the article. Underline the sentences that you think express the main ideas.

4 Complete the summary of the article. Then compare your ideas with a partner.

> Some sports teams are a lot like chickens. Too many high-level individual performers (1)_____ from the (2)_____ of the group. This is most likely to happen in sports such as football and (3)_____ , in which team members need to (4)_____ their actions. Star athletes, like star chickens, may be more likely to (5)_____ their own goals than work for the group's best interests.

5 Scan the article to find the terms below. Explain them in your own words.

   a task interdependence _____

   b the Ringelmann effect _____

THE VALUE OF TALENT

1 Much of the work in today's world is **accomplished** in teams: in business, in scientific research, in government, on film sets and, of course, in sports. Most people believe that the best way to build a great team is to assemble a group of the best, most talented individuals. Facebook's Mark Zuckerberg, commenting on the value of talent, is quoted as saying that one great engineer is worth a hundred average ones. And Zuckerberg is certainly somebody who knows how to build an A-team.

2 Animal scientist William Muir wondered if he could build such an A-team – with chickens. He looked for the most productive egg producers and bred them for six generations. This was his test group. For comparison, he did the same thing with a selection of average egg producers. This was his control group. To his surprise, six generations later, he found that the egg production of the test group was lower than that of the control group. He discovered that the super-producers in the test group used an enormous amount of energy constantly re-establishing a pecking order – competing for the top spot. As a result, they had little energy left for egg production.

3 Of course, chickens are not a team, but this kind of group interaction and its effect on production piqued the interest of researchers who study teams and teamwork. The owners of sports teams spend millions of dollars to attract top talent. Companies spend millions to hire top business people. They want to know if their money is well spent.

4 A recent series of studies examined the role of talent in the sports world. They focused on three different sports: World Cup football, professional basketball and professional baseball. The results were mixed. For football and basketball, the studies revealed that adding talented players to a team is indeed a good strategy, but only up to a point.

Performance **peaked** when about 70% of the players were considered top talent; above that level, the team's performance began to decline. Interestingly, this trend was not evident in baseball, where additional individual talent continued to **enhance** the team's performance (Figures 1 and 2).

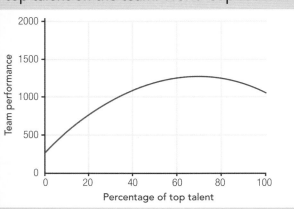

Figure 1. Team performance as a function of top talent on the team: World Cup football

Source: Swaab et al., 2014

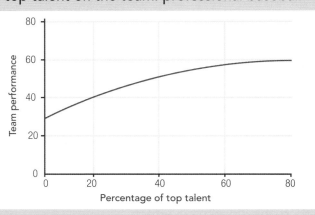

Figure 2. Team performance as a function of top talent on the team: professional baseball

Source: Swaab et al., 2014

5 In looking for an explanation for the different results for different sports, the researchers **isolated** one important factor – the extent to which a good performance by a team requires its members to **coordinate** their actions. This *task interdependence* **differentiates** baseball from basketball and football. In baseball, the performance of individual players is less dependent on teammates than in football and basketball. The researchers concluded that when, during the course of play, task interdependence is high, team performance will suffer when there is too much talent in the group. When task interdependence is lower, on the other hand, individual talent will have a positive effect on team performance.

6 One explanation for this phenomenon is not so far from the pecking order situation among chickens. If a basketball star is pursuing his own personal goals – for example, trying to **amass** a high personal point total – he may be less generous as a team player. He may take a shot himself when it would be better to pass the ball

to a teammate, **detracting from** the team's overall performance. Young children learning to play team sports are often told, 'There is no *I* in *TEAM*.' Stars apparently do not follow this basic principle of sportsmanship.

7 Another possibility is that when there is a lot of talent on a team, some players may begin to make less effort. This is referred to as the *Ringelmann effect.* Maximilien Ringelmann, a French agricultural engineer, conducted an experiment in 1913 in which he asked two, three, four and up to twenty-eight people to participate in a game of tug-of-war. He measured how much force each person used to pull the rope. He found that whenever he added a person to the team, everyone else pulled with less force.

8 Assembling the ideal team – for sports, business, science, or entertainment – is more complicated than simply hiring the best talent. An A-team may require a balance – not just A players, but a few generous B players as well.

READING BETWEEN THE LINES

Using context clues to understand terminology

Working out the meaning of unfamiliar words is a form of critical thinking. Formal writing often contains topic-specific terminology and expressions as well as higher level vocabulary that may be unfamiliar. Elements of context can help you determine the meaning of unfamiliar terms. Here are some context clues to look for.

Cultural or world knowledge

Before the games, athletes carry the Olympic **torch** to cities around the host country.

Everyone is familiar with the tradition of athletes carrying the symbol of the Games, the Olympic flame, so you can guess the meaning of *torch*.

Components of multi-word expressions or parts of words

Recent trade figures are evidence of the **interdependence** of the two countries.

You already know the meaning of the two parts, *inter + dependence*, so you can guess the meaning of the term.

Contrast

The committee rejected the job candidate. He did not seem very energetic, and they were looking for somebody more **dynamic**.

So, somebody who is dynamic is the opposite of somebody with low energy.

Examples

Tycoons, such as Microsoft's Bill Gates, are becoming increasingly rich and powerful.

If you are familiar with the person named Bill Gates, you can guess the meaning of *tycoon*.

Logical inference

Scientists **bred** chickens for six generations to examine their behaviour over time.

If you consider what scientists could do to chickens for six generations with the purpose of understanding their behaviour, you can guess the meaning of *bred*.

---

6 Work with a partner. Discuss the questions. Use context clues to work out the meaning of these terms from the article.

1 **A-team** (para 1): _____
   What does the term mean? Is it limited to sports?

2 **pecking order** (para 2): _____
   Chickens peck one another to show dominance. How could this relate to teams in other contexts, such as business?

3 **tug-of-war** (para 7): _____
   Read the paragraph and describe what you think happens in this game. Do an image search to check. How might this term be used in other contexts?

WORKING OUT MEANING FROM CONTEXT

DISCUSSION

7 Work in small groups. Describe an experience that you have had working in a group, such as a music group, a class or volunteer project or some other context. Answer the questions below.

1 Was it a positive or negative experience?
2 What factors do you think contributed to the group's success or lack of success?

READING 2

PREPARING TO READ

1 You are going to read an article about group intelligence. Look at the statements below. Do you think they are true (*T*) or false (*F*)?

_____ 1 The intelligence of a group is equal to the intelligence of its members added together.

_____ 2 People who have similar interests and backgrounds work together better than people who are very different.

_____ 3 You can tell a lot about how well people are communicating by just looking at their facial expressions.

_____ 4 Communication works best when people believe that others will respect what they say.

_____ 5 In a meeting, it is a waste of time for people to talk to each other instead of listening to the leader.

_____ 6 People can communicate just as effectively using technology (IM, email, teleconferencing) as they can face-to-face.

2 Read the sentences. Write the correct form of the words in bold (1–8) next to their definitions below (a–h).

1 The winner held his fists high in the air, a **gesture** that made it very clear how excited he was.

2 If you want to be well prepared for the sales presentation, you should work in a quiet place that has no **distractions** – not even a window or a television.

3 Collaborative teamwork **underlies** many of the most successful start-up companies.

4 My manager always encourages us to **voice** our opinions, even if she disagrees with them.

5 The recent controversy **stems from** an ongoing disagreement about which company owns the rights to the new software.

6 One of the **fundamental** principles of successful collaboration is the need for a shared sense of purpose.

7 Lots of people tell Leila about their problems at work because she always listens and shows such **sensitivity** to their feelings.

8 This study focuses **exclusively** on the behaviour of basketball players. Football players' behaviour was investigated in a separate study.

a _____ (adj) basic; being the thing on which other things depend

b _____ (adv) only; limited to a specific thing, person or group

c _____ (v) to be the cause of or a strong influence on something

d _____ (n) a movement of the body or a body part to express an idea or feeling

e _____ (n) something that prevents somebody from giving full attention to something else

f _____ (n) the ability to understand how other people feel

g _____ (phr v) to develop as the result of something

h _____ (v) to say what you think about something

WHILE READING

3 Read the article on page 192 and check your predictions from Exercise 1.

4 Read the article again. Underline the sentences that best express the main ideas of the article. Underline no more than six sentences.

5 Write a summary of the article using your annotations to guide you.

_____

_____

_____

_____

_____

6 Read another student's paragraph and offer each other advice for improvement.

THE PERFECT WORK TEAM

1   For years, psychologists have known how to measure the intelligence of individuals, yet only recently have they begun to investigate the issue of group intelligence. This notion **stems from** the observation that some groups seem to work well across tasks, even tasks that are not very similar. Early investigations suggest that group intelligence is not the sum of the intelligence of the individuals in it. So what is the secret to their success?

2   Researchers at Google and MIT have both tackled this question and they believe they finally have a handle on what makes some teams successful. In the Google study, researchers amassed thousands of data points on hundreds of groups and combed through them to find patterns. Are the members of effective groups friends outside of work? Do groups whose members have similar personalities or backgrounds work together best? Does gender make a difference? They floated many theories, but despite their best efforts, found no patterns to support them. In fact, who was in the group apparently did not seem to make a difference; instead, the difference between more and less effective groups seemed to lie in the interaction among the members.

3   The MIT group had already been gathering data on group interaction using digital 'badges' that participants in the study agreed to wear. These badges provided a wealth of information, including how long people spoke and to whom, what kinds of **gestures** they made, where they were looking during interaction, and their facial expressions. As in the Google study, this research group concluded that the key to an effective team is how members interact.

4   Among the findings, the most consistent and significant is that, in effective groups, members spoke for a roughly equal amount of time – not at every meeting or interaction, but across the course of a project. A second consistent finding was that members displayed empathy, an understanding of how it might feel to walk in somebody else's shoes. This social **sensitivity** is measured by a relatively new test, called 'Reading the Mind in the Eyes'. The test assesses individual differences in two key factors, social awareness and emotion recognition, by asking individuals to guess emotions based on only a picture of a person's eyes. A high level of these two features create what one of the researchers in the Google study calls psychological safety; members of the group feel comfortable **voicing** their opinions and making suggestions without fear of a negative response from other members of the group, and they believe that others will listen to them and value what they say. When these conditions are present, the group as a whole tends to be effective.

5   There were additional findings that support these general ones. For example, in effective groups, members face one another directly when they speak and they use energetic and enthusiastic gestures. They also communicate directly with one another, not just through the leader or manager of the group. In fact, the MIT study found that side conversations between individual members during meetings, far from being a **distraction**, actually increased the group's productivity. All the findings underline the importance of having face-to-face meetings instead of phone calls or teleconferences or communicating by email. The positive behaviours uncovered in these studies occur primarily or **exclusively** in face-to-face interaction. The MIT team estimates that 35% of a team's performance can be explained just by the number of their face-to-face exchanges.

6   One might argue that most of these findings are obvious, and needless to say, good managers have probably always understood these principles. Our social and professional lives, however, are not always structured in ways that facilitate the kind of interaction that apparently **underlies** effective group performance. Understanding group intelligence can help businesses and other organizations make the **fundamental** changes necessary to improve group performance.

7 Read the article again. Complete the table with results from the MIT study about the characteristics of effective groups and their members.

major findings	1 Equal speaking time across the course of the project
	2
additional findings	3
	4 Use energetic and enthusiastic gestures
	5
	6

8 Scan the article to find the terms. Explain each of them in your own words.

a group intelligence: _____

_____

b psychological safety: _____

_____

READING BETWEEN THE LINES

Using context clues to understand fixed expressions

You can use some of the techniques described on page 189 to determine the meaning of idioms and other fixed expressions.

With idioms, sometimes understanding each word can help you understand the whole meaning, but often the meaning is not clearly related to its components. In those cases, you will need to use a more global approach, such as logical inference.

9 Work with a partner. Use context clues to work out the meaning of the expressions. Paragraph numbers are given in brackets.

1 have a handle on (para 2): _____

_____

2 walk in somebody else's shoes (para 4): _____

_____

3 needless to say (para 6): _____

_____

DISCUSSION

10 Work in small groups. Answer questions below to do a version of the test mentioned in Reading 2. Then use ideas from Reading 1 and Reading 2 to answer question 4.

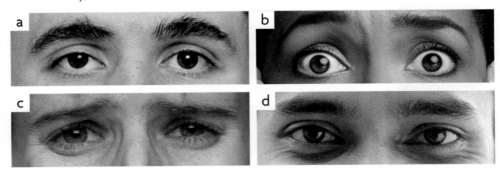

1 Choose a word that you think best describes how the person is feeling in each photo. Discuss the reasons for your choices.

2 Explain how an ability to judge the expressions accurately could affect team performance in some of the teams you have read about in this unit.

3 What would the perfect work team look like for these situations? Think about the type of people who might be in the team and how they might behave.

- a team of sales agents
- a team working on a production line
- a team researching a group project

⊙ LANGUAGE DEVELOPMENT

LANGUAGE FOR HEDGING

In formal writing, writers need to take care when they make a claim to ensure that it is not too strong or overly general. They may use special language to limit their claims and to make sure the claims are accurate. Hedging protects writers from challenges that their work is untrue or misleading. Writers also use hedged language to make it clear that they understand that other viewpoints exist and have credibility. At the same time, too much hedging can make a claim vague and empty. It is important to strike a balance between these extremes.

Bold claim

When task interdependence is low, individual talent **will** have a positive effect on team performance.

Hedged claims

Early investigations **suggest that** group intelligence is not the sum of the intelligence of the individuals in it.

Some groups **seem to** work well across tasks, even tasks that are not very similar.

An A-team **may** require a balance – not just A players, but a few generous B players as well.

Hedging devices

There are many ways to hedge or soften a claim.

Quantifiers and approximators
most/some/many
fairly/somewhat
often/usually
more or less

Adverbs and adverb phrases
for the most part
primarily
apparently
relatively
perhaps
typically
mainly
generally

Modal verbs
can/could/may

Lexical verbs and phrases
tends
suggests
seems
appears
is likely to

Introductory phrases
There is evidence that …
It appears/seems that …
It has been suggested that …
This indicates that …
It may be the case that …
It is (often) thought that …
It is widely believed/assumed that …

---

1 Rewrite the bold claims to make them more modest. Compare your sentences with a partner.

1 Human error is the cause of traffic fatalities.

_____

2 Lack of sleep leads to both emotional and physical problems.

_____

3 If you know your personality type, you can find the job that is best for you.

_____

4 Tall people make the best basketball players.

_____

5 People who are obese will develop diabetes.

_____

6 We will run out of fossil fuels in about 100 years.

_____

2 Write three hedged statements of your own about building teams for effective collaboration.

1 _____
_____

2 _____
_____

3 _____
_____

WRITING

At the end of this unit, you will write a report. Look at this unit's writing task in the box below.

> Applying the principles you have learned in this unit, present your recommendations for assembling and organizing an effective and satisfied team in a report for a start-up company.

SKILLS

Understanding audience and purpose

Writers write for a range of purposes: to inform, entertain, instruct or persuade. Most of the time, they also write for a specific audience. A report to a group of business professionals will be different from an academic essay for a professor. It is important to keep both purpose and audience in mind whenever you write. Academic essays and professional reports have different formats and features.

	argumentative essay	report
purpose	to persuade	to inform, explain and make recommendations
audience	not specific (except your teacher)	specific
typical features	claim (thesis statement) supporting evidence conclusion	executive summary subheadings bullet points

 UNDERSTAND

1 Read the report opposite. Answer the questions.

　1 What is the purpose of the report?

　2 Who is the audience?

　3 What format and features does the report have?

Executive summary

The high staff turnover and absence rate at the company is likely to be the result of low employee satisfaction. Many employees experience high levels of stress and feel they have little investment in the company. Several recommendations are offered that may increase employee satisfaction and motivation.

Introduction

Recently, the company has experienced considerable staff turnover. Just last month, six employees left the company. In addition, there has been a high absence rate, with most employees calling in sick at least once a month. This has negative implications for the bottom line; profits were down 4% in the first two quarters of this year.

Workplace satisfaction

The following steps were taken to uncover the source of these developments: (1) interviews with departing employees, (2) a survey of current employees and (3) in-depth research on employee satisfaction.

Interviews with former employees
Former employees found their jobs too stressful. Five of them agreed to be interviewed about their reasons for leaving the company. Two reported leaving for economic reasons; they received job offers from competitors at a higher salary. However, all five reported a high level of stress in their jobs. They felt they could not take time off on weekends; they answered texts and emails until late at night. Several said they had not taken a vacation in more than a year. They mentioned that members of their families complained about how little time they spent at home. Two people reported that the stress had affected their health.

Survey of current employees
The survey results of 52 current employees revealed low job satisfaction. Employees are happy with their salaries, but they are not happy with how decisions are made in the company. Many said they do not feel free to voice their opinions and that their managers rarely ask for their input or listen to their suggestions. Several mentioned the poor communication from senior management.

As a result of dissatisfaction in these areas, many said they are no longer motivated to do their best. Thirty percent said they take days off even when they are not ill. More than 20% said they would leave the company if they received another job offer.

Employee satisfaction
Experts on workplace issues suggest that problems like these have several sources. Surprisingly, most are not related to money.

- Appreciation: Employees want to know that their work – and their opinions – are valued.
- Good relationships and communication: In an effective office, employees get along with one another and with their bosses. They communicate regularly, especially when there are problems and they solve them together.
- Career development: Employees are more likely to stay at a company if they feel there is room for them to grow and that the company supports their career development.
- Work–life balance: No matter how much employees love their jobs, they can't work all the time. It is important for them to get away from the office to spend time with family or friends. They will return to the office more relaxed and motivated to work hard.

Recommendations

- Find ways to reward employees when they perform well.
- Establish a clear career path for high-performing employees.
- Improve lines of communication.
  - Have more face-to-face meetings.
  - Establish a space where employees can meet and relax.
- Establish a 'no-communication' policy after certain hours and on weekends so employees can relax when they are away from the office.
- Allow employees to take days off for important personal events.

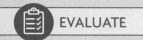
2 Work in a small group. What new information did you learn from the report regarding maintaining effective work teams? Make some notes to use for your own report.

3 You will write a report making recommendations to Cybergogo. Read the description of the company. Then work in small groups and discuss the questions below. Make notes.

Cybergogo is high-tech company that analyzes data and develops mathematical models.

- It is a relatively new company – it began as a start-up[1] three years ago.
- The head of the company is very assertive, has strong opinions and tends to make decisions based on them.
- Almost all the employees are young – under 35 – and have degrees from elite universities. Most of them expect to run their own start-ups soon.
- There is no central office. All employees work at home, from coffee shops or while they are travelling anywhere in the world. Most of their communication is digital.
- The company is bidding for a big job for a major international food service company. They have to prepare a proposal in the next six months.
- The last time Cybergogo bid for a similar job, they did not get the contract, in part because they did not complete the proposal on time.
- One reason for their failure was a lack of agreement on how to complete the project. Two people left the company soon after. One of them was the Chief Technology Officer.
- The new Chief Technology Officer started at the company just two months ago. He has not met most of the staff yet.

[1]**start-up** (n) a small business that has just been started

---

1 What is Cybergogo's primary goal – In other words, how do they hope your report will help them?

_____

_____

2 What are some intermediate goals, that is, things the company needs to accomplish in order to reach that goal?

_____

_____

3 What are the top two or three challenges you think the organization faces?

_____

_____

4 Consider the goals and challenges of the company and answer the questions.

1 What are your recommendations around the way Cybergogo's employees work?

_____

_____

_____

2 What evidence for these recommendations will you include in your report?

_____

_____

_____

3 What are your recommendations for any changes in communication policy at the company?

_____

_____

_____

4 What evidence for these recommendations will you include in your report?

_____

_____

_____

5 What are your recommendations for any changes in recruitment at the company?

_____

_____

_____

6 What evidence for these recommendations will you include in your report?

_____

_____

_____

7 Do you have any other recommendations?

_____

_____

_____

GRAMMAR FOR WRITING

CONCESSION AND REFUTATION

In formal writing, writers often need to acknowledge the validity of counter-arguments. This is called concession. Concession is usually followed by a refutation of the counter-argument. Concession and refutation follow a standard structure:

1 Your argument: Present your thesis statement or one of your supporting arguments.

2 Concession: Acknowledge a counter-argument and any supporting evidence.

3 Refutation: Show why the counter-argument is not valid by providing support for your claim.

(1) Eyewitness reports should not **generally** be relied on as the only form of evidence in a court of law.

(2) It is widely believed that eyewitnesses **can** provide reliable reports and there is no doubt that they **can** provide valuable information.

(3) However, research **suggests** that their reports are not **always entirely** accurate.

Notice that all parts of your claim and the concession contain hedged language (bold text).

Use concession linkers to contrast concessions with refutations.

to connect two clauses in a single sentence

although   *even though*   *whereas*   *while*

Many business interactions are now conducted remotely, which can lead to business efficiency by reducing costs, **although** evidence suggests that face-to-face meetings may be more effective.

to connect ideas in two sentences

however   *nevertheless*   *on the other hand*

Of course, talented individuals bring a lot to a team. **Nevertheless**, research using professional sports teams shows that peak performance is reached when 70% of players were considered to be top talent.

to connect a noun phrase and a clause in a single sentence

despite   *in spite of*

Despite the valuable information that they sometimes provide, research suggests that eyewitness reports should not be relied on to be 100% accurate.

1 Work with a partner. Read the claims 1–3 and counter-arguments. Brainstorm ways to refute the counter-argument.

1 Claim: Sugar makes children behave badly. Counter-argument: Sugar has always been part of people's diets.

2 Claim: Coffee makes you thirsty. Counter-argument: Coffee contains water, so it cannot make you thirsty.

3 Claim: Antibiotics are being overprescribed. Counter-argument: Antibiotics help people get better more quickly.

2 Now write and then refute a concession statement for the claims in Exercise 1. Include:

- hedged language throughout
- a logical connector that links the concession with your claim

ACADEMIC WRITING SKILLS

ANTICIPATING COUNTER-ARGUMENTS

In formal writing, writers must anticipate, explore, acknowledge and refute opposing points of view. This generally requires more than a single concession statement. To effectively refute an opposing point of view, it is important to have a full understanding of it. Writers begin by exploring the other point of view and the evidence for it fully (see bold text in example below). Then they refute the argument by providing support for their own claim (see underlined text in example below).

Eyewitness reports should not generally be relied on as the only form of evidence in a court of law. It is widely believed that eyewitnesses can provide reliable reports, and there is no doubt that they can provide valuable information. **These statements are an important building block in many criminal cases.** However, research suggests that eyewitness reports are not always entirely accurate. In fact, <u>an eyewitness report usually reflects a partial and often inaccurate memory of events as they happened</u>. For this reason, we should not depend on them too heavily and other supporting evidence must be found.

1 Expand the statements you wrote in Grammar for writing Exercise 2, Question 2 into a paragraph, using the additional information provided below.

- Coffee makes the mouth feel moist and fills the stomach with liquid.
- Coffee speeds up all of the body's processes, including water leaving the body.
- You need to drink one additional glass of water for every cup of coffee.
- Regular coffee drinkers' bodies adjust to their caffeine intake.
- Any change in your caffeine intake can lead to thirst or dehydration.

2 Work with a partner. Review your partner's paragraph in Exercise 1. Check that all of the features described in the Explanation boxes on pages 200–201 are included, using appropriate language, accurately. Offer your partner advice for improvement.

WRITING TASK

Applying the principles you have learned in this unit, present your recommendations for assembling and organizing an effective and satisfied team in a report for a start-up company.

PLAN

1 Think about the introduction to your report. Answer the questions.

- How will you introduce your topic?
- What background information will you provide?

2 Think about the three main issues for Cybergogo. Each issue should be in a separate paragraph, beginning with a topic sentence that states the issue clearly. Each issue should be supported by evidence of why it is a problem. Note down supporting details from the readings to support your claim.

First body paragraph

Problem/Issue:

_____

_____

Topic sentence:

_____

_____

Evidence:

_____

_____

Second body paragraph

Problem/Issue:

_____

_____

Topic sentence:

_____

_____

Evidence:

_____

_____

Third body paragraph

Problem/Issue:

_____

_____

Topic sentence:

_____

_____

Evidence:

_____

_____

3 Complete the tasks below. If you think your claim is controversial, include a concession. Why might people believe these are valid points of view (e.g. _technology makes communication easier_)?

_____

_____

4 List your recommendations. You should have at least one recommendation for each of the problems/issues you have described. Use bullet points.

_____

_____

5 Write an executive summary of your report and add it to the beginning.

1 State the problem you are trying to solve.
2 State what you believe to be cause of the company's problems. Be general and brief (one or two sentences).
3 State your recommendations in very general terms (e.g. _changes in hiring_).

_____

_____

_____

_____

_____

6 Refer to the Task checklist on page 204 as you prepare your report.

WRITE A FIRST DRAFT

7 Write your report. Use your plan to help you structure your ideas. Write 450–500 words.

REVISE

8 Use the Task checklist to review your report for content and structure.

TASK CHECKLIST	✔
Are the audience for your report and the purpose of your report clear to the reader?	
Have you addressed the organization's goals?	
Have you made a general claim about the organization's problem and what it needs to do?	
Have you addressed challenges that organization faces?	
Have you provided support for what you believe are the causes of these problems?	
Have you acknowledged and countered any alternative points of view?	
Have you made specific recommendations to the organization?	
Have you used bullet points in your recommendations?	
Does your report include an executive summary?	

EDIT

9 Use the Language checklist to edit your essay for language errors.

LANGUAGE CHECKLIST	✔
Have you used hedging language in your claim to avoid taking an absolute position?	
Have you used hedging language elsewhere in your report where appropriate?	
Have you followed the standard structure for concession language, using hedging language where appropriate?	
Have you punctuated your sentences correctly according to the type of hedging and concession you have used?	

10 Make any necessary changes to your report.

OBJECTIVES REVIEW

1 Check your learning objectives for this unit. Write *3*, *2* or *1* for each objective.

3 = very well   2 = well   1 = not so well

I can ...

watch and understand a video about an elite aerobatics display team.   _____

use context clues to understand terminology and fixed expressions.   _____

understand audience and purpose.   _____

concede and refute points.   _____

anticipate counter-arguments.   _____

write a report giving recommendations.   _____

2 Go to the *Unlock* Online Workbook for more practice with this unit's learning objectives.

UNLOCK ONLINE

WORDLIST		
accomplish (v)	fairly (adv) ⊙	sensitivity (n) ⊙
acknowledge (v) ⊙	for the most part (adv phr)	somewhat (adv) ⊙
amass (v)	fundamental (adj) ⊙	stem from (phr v)
apparently (adv) ⊙	gesture (n) ⊙	suggest (v) ⊙
coordinate (v) ⊙	isolate (v) ⊙	tend (v) ⊙
detract from (phr v)	maintain (v) ⊙	typically (adv) ⊙
differentiate (v) ⊙	more or less (phr)	underlie (v) ⊙
distraction (n)	peak (v) ⊙	voice (v) ⊙
enhance (v) ⊙	primarily (adv) ⊙	
exclusively (adv) ⊙	relatively (adv) ⊙	

⊙ = high-frequency words in the Cambridge Academic Corpus

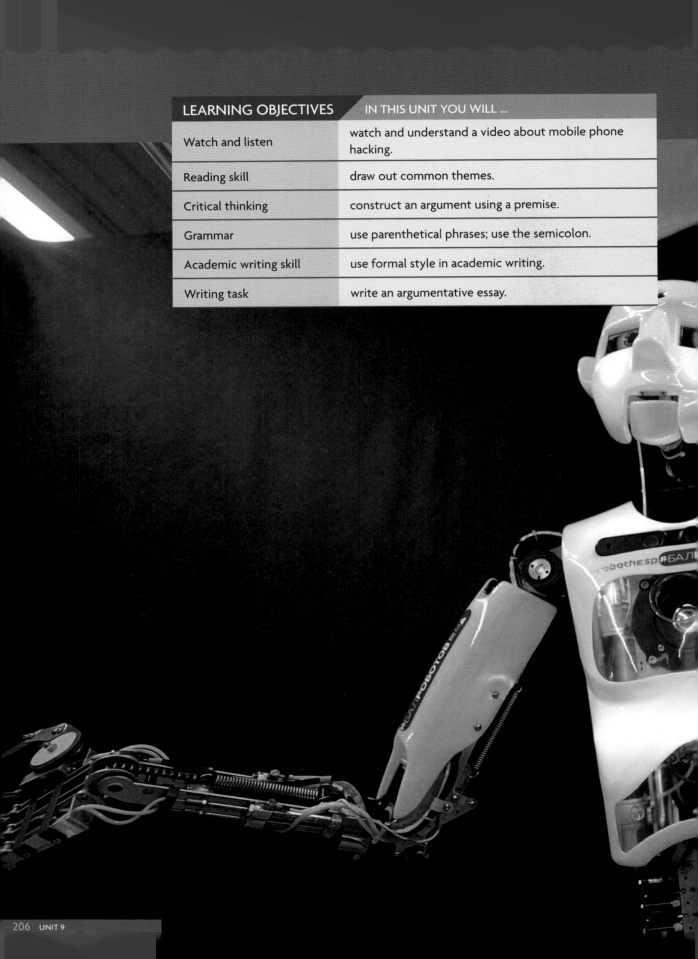

LEARNING OBJECTIVES	IN THIS UNIT YOU WILL ...
Watch and listen	watch and understand a video about mobile phone hacking.
Reading skill	draw out common themes.
Critical thinking	construct an argument using a premise.
Grammar	use parenthetical phrases; use the semicolon.
Academic writing skill	use formal style in academic writing.
Writing task	write an argumentative essay.

UNL⬤CK YOUR KNOWLEDGE

Work with a partner. Discuss the questions.

1 What are some of the technologies that humans are trying to develop at the moment? Think about the areas in the box.

> transport   communications   health   energy

2 Which of these technologies do you think are needed most urgently?
3 What are some technological advances that have taken place in your lifetime?
4 What impact (positive and negative) have these technological advances had on how people live?

PLUS

WATCH AND LISTEN

PREPARING TO WATCH

ACTIVATING YOUR KNOWLEDGE

1 You are going to watch a video about phone hacking. Before you watch, work with a partner. Discuss the questions.

1 Do you ever use public Wi-Fi networks? If yes, in what situations? If not, why not?
2 How do you think hackers attack other people's devices? Do you know of any cases where people have been hacked?
3 Do you use the same password for all of your social media apps? How often do you change your passwords?

PREDICTING CONTENT USING VISUALS

2 Look at the photos and discuss the questions with a partner.

1 What are the differences between the phone in the first photo and the phone in the third photo?
2 In your opinion, which of these phones would be more difficult to hack? Why?
3 The people in the video are conducting an experiment. Can you guess what they are trying to find out?

WHILE WATCHING

UNDERSTANDING MAIN IDEAS

3 ▶ Watch the video and check your predictions from Exercise 2. Which sentence best expresses the main idea of the video?

1 Famous people are often targeted by hackers.
2 Using free Wi-Fi can expose your phone to hackers.
3 Phone hackers can change your social media profile.

UNDERSTANDING DETAIL

4 ▶ Watch the video again. Write details for each main idea.

1 The old mobile phones had two disadvantages.

_____

2 Tom and Oliver are cybersecurity experts.

_____

3 Modern mobile phones transmit data over 3G and Wi-Fi.

_____

4 Hackers have two ways to attack mobile phones over Wi-Fi.

_____

5 Once hackers connect to a phone they can see all the data going in and out.

_____

6 You can protect your personal data in two ways.

_____

WORKING OUT
MEANING FROM
CONTEXT

5 Work with a partner. Read the sentences from the video and work out the meanings of the words in bold from the context. Match the words in bold (1–6) with the correct definitions (a–f) below.

'… with the right equipment, it was quite easy to **eavesdrop**[1] on people's conversations … . Are today's **multitasking**[2] smartphones any safer than those old bricks?'

'Wi-Fi, on the other hand, is very **susceptible**[3] to hackers. There's two primary ways they do this. One of them is setting up what we call a **bait**[4] network.'

'… any data going from that phone, through your network and then out to the internet, is **up for grabs**[5]. […] And what we're seeing is people **harvesting**[6] login details, for social media, for email accounts, and then using that information.'

a available for anyone to take _____
b something that is said or offered in order to attract people or to make them react in a particular way _____
c doing two or more activities at the same time _____
d collecting and storing a large amount of something _____
e to secretly listen to someone _____
f easily harmed by someone or something _____

DISCUSSION

6 Work with a partner. Discuss the questions.

1 Why do you think hackers harvest login details? What do you think they do with the information?
2 Which of the phone security tips mentioned in the video is the most useful to you?
3 Do you think that the younger generation is more reckless with phone security than older people? Why / Why not?

READING

READING 1

PREPARING TO READ

1 You are going to read a popular science blog about augmented reality (AR). Work with a partner. Look at the photos and discuss the questions.

1 What do you think *augmented reality* means?
2 What equipment and devices do you think are used for AR displays?
3 How might AR be useful in everyday situations?

2 Read the words and their definitions. Use the correct form of the words in bold to complete the sentences below.

---

domain (n) a field, area of knowledge, etc. belonging to or controlled by a particular person or group of people

hazard (n) something that is dangerous and likely to cause damage

immersive (adj) seeming to surround the audience, player, etc. so that they feel completely involved

interpretation (n) translation of one language into another

projection (n) an image displayed by a device onto a separate screen or another surface

simultaneous (adj) happening or being done at exactly the same time

superimpose (v) to put an image, words, etc. onto another image or surface

supplement (v) to add something to something else in order to improve it

---

1 Whilst drivers are focused on their devices they may fail to identify _____ on the road ahead.
2 The new virtual reality glasses offer a completely _____ experience.
3 On the new device, you can receive _____ audio and video from two different sources.
4 You can _____ your English classes with apps for learning English.
5 Social networking is no longer the _____ of the young; many over-sixties are regular users of Facebook and Twitter.
6 The lecturer used a _____ of human anatomy to explain the digestive system to the students.
7 The new app allows you to _____ images on print, and print on images.
8 His _____ of the report from the Chinese office was incorrect so the board didn't understand the new project.

AR: CHANGING THE WORLD AROUND US

1 Do you look up at the sky at night and marvel at the universe? Would you like to know more? Nowadays, all you have to do is point your smartphone at the night sky to reveal the names of the stars, constellations and planets. Or, do you love fashion but hate trying on clothes in shops? These days there are mirrors which take the hard work out of shopping by **superimposing** your chosen outfits directly onto a live reflection of your body. These advances are both examples of augmented reality (AR) – technology which enhances our experience of the real world with digital information and graphics. AR has numerous potential applications to improve every area of our daily lives.

What is augmented reality?

2 Unlike virtual reality, which creates an **immersive** 3D environment, augmented reality interacts with and enhances the world that surrounds us. AR devices can **supplement** the environment with interactive 3D **projections**. AR apps for smartphones and other devices use the camera and GPS to overlay real-time video with digital content.

Travel has never been easier

3 Forget carrying around heavy guidebooks. Tourists can now download apps that superimpose facts and information directly on their surroundings. As you walk the streets of a famous city, you can read reviews and recommendations from other travellers overlaid on the places on your route. If you don't know the language, just point your smartphone at a foreign sign and a translation will appear. Experts suggest that future AR apps will allow **simultaneous interpretation** of spoken language too.

The directions are on the road

4 With AR navigation technology – specifically devices for motor vehicles – drivers don't need to take their eyes off the road to look at a screen. With a dashboard-mounted set, directions to your destination can be projected onto your view of the road ahead. In addition to guiding you to your destination, AR GPS apps for drivers can display speed limits and traffic and weather warnings. Future AR navigation apps may even be able to warn drivers about possible **hazards**, such as cyclists or pedestrians crossing the road.

Helping engineers and technicians

5 Imagine being an engineer or a technician working on an oil or gas field. You have been asked to go out and find a leaky pipe or repair a faulty pump. In the past, finding a broken pipe in the field could be problematic. Now, with an AR headset you can clearly see detailed blueprints of the pipes overlaid on your view of the field. What's more, there is no longer any need to memorize maintenance instructions. AR can assist you with that; it not only labels the different components of a mechanism, but can display step-by-step instructions on how to maintain them, as well as warnings about any environmental conditions that may make a repair hazardous.

Medicine

6 Medicine is the field that has seen the greatest uptake of AR applications. AR allows medical professionals to see a patient's internal organs and circulatory system displayed on their skin. One of the most common uses is with IV injections; medical professionals can now use handheld scanners to project a patient's veins onto their skin. This has significantly reduced the number of failed needle insertions, which often occur with children and older patients. AR apps are being developed to allow surgeons to see vital information directly displayed on the patient's organs. AR projections can help medical students gain experience of elements of surgical procedures without any danger to live patients.

7 The future of AR technology is unlimited. Once the **domain** of the gaming and retail industries, AR has revealed its potential to revolutionize our lives. Across tourism and travel, industry and engineering, and even surgery, it is already making our lives easier. Augmented reality technologies are opening our eyes to a world where real and digital universes can coexist in harmony.

WHILE READING

3 Read the blog on page 211 and check your ideas from Exercise 1. Which sentence best expresses the main idea of the blog?

  a AR technology has the potential to change how we see reality.

  b AR technology has revolutionized many industries.

  c AR technology has practical applications in many areas of life.

4 Read a summary of the blog written by a student. Six facts are incorrect. Correct the mistakes.

> AR involves an immersive 3D experience. A common use of AR is visually mapping and providing procedures for complex systems, such as machines and the human body. AR technology allows technicians to view blueprints overlaid on the field and to identify faults with broken machines. Medical professionals can see patients' bones projected onto their skin as a guide. AR also allows student doctors to practise on real bodies. Other applications of AR technology involve providing information about the real-time environment. Travellers can use AR apps to see information about places and to translate spoken words. Using a smartphone screen, AR GPS apps can project directions and traffic information on the windscreen.

Drawing out common themes

When getting to grips with a wider field, it can be useful to read and summarize general interest texts such as the blog on page 211. These texts may be more concerned with providing detail than analysis. Bringing your own ideas to the text about what the common themes are will deepen your understanding of the topic and give you a basis for further research and discussion, in which you can test your ideas.

After you have read the text in detail, read it again, underlining any analysis and annotating any common themes in different parts of the text which have not been explicitly stated. Then write a summary that brings together the main ideas and the common themes.

5 Read the summary in Exercise 4 and underline two sentences in which the student has drawn out common themes.

6 Read the blog again. Follow the procedure in the Explanation box and find more common themes. Discuss your ideas with a partner.

7 Write a summary of the blog. Include main ideas and common themes.

READING BETWEEN THE LINES

8 Underline two speculations in the blog about the future of AR apps. Then work with a partner and discuss the questions.

1 There are now devices which can translate spoken language. What do you think the potential problems with such devices could be?

2 Do you think that drivers will, one day, be able to see warnings of hazards in the road? Why / Why not?

DISTINGUISHING FACT FROM OPINION

DISCUSSION

9 Work with a partner. Discuss the questions.

1 What could be some possible issues with relying on AR displays when driving or travelling?

2 What other fields could take advantage of AR technology? How?

READING 2

PREPARING TO READ

1 You are going to read an essay about using AR technology in education. Read the sentences. Write the correct form of the words in bold next to their definitions below.

UNDERSTANDING KEY VOCABULARY

1 This smart board is an invaluable educational **aid**.
2 The IT technician **inspected** my laptop and found some malware.
3 He is a well-known **advocate** of the use of cloud computing in schools.
4 Early child development involves learning to **manipulate** objects.
5 Publishers try to attract student attention through **engaging** content.
6 There are **numerous** advantages to travelling with a smartphone.
7 We need to **embrace** the use of technology in the classroom.
8 The **novelty** of VR games may soon wear off.

a _____ (v) to enthusiastically accept new ideas or methods
b _____ (n) a person who publicly supports an idea or cause
c _____ (n) a piece of equipment that helps you to do something
d _____ (adj) attracting and maintaining interest
e _____ (v) to examine carefully
f _____ (adj) many, multiple
g _____ (n) the quality of being new or unusual
h _____ (v) to control something using your hands

PLUS

2 Work with a partner. Discuss the questions.

1 How could AR be used to teach science subjects, like Biology, Physics or Chemistry?
2 How could AR be used to teach other subjects, like languages or History?
3 What are the possible disadvantages to using AR in the classroom?

WHILE READING

3 Read the essay and check your predictions from Exercise 2.

4 Read the essay again. Match each main idea (a–g) below to the correct body paragraph (2–7). There are two ideas which are not mentioned in the essay.

a The initial drawbacks of AR will be short lived. _____
b AR has the potential to bring greater equality in education. _____
c Engineering lecturers have been using AR to teach science. _____
d AR allows subjects like Biology to be presented in an engaging way. _____
e The cost of AR technology may prevent rural schools from implementing it. _____
f The educational benefits of AR are supported by research studies. _____
g AR could make numerous school subjects more interactive. _____

5 Read the essay again. Complete the table with details about each idea in the right-hand column. Then compare your notes with a partner.

AR as an aid in education

current applications	
future applications	
reported benefits	
possible drawbacks	

AR in education
– A positive or a negative development?

Using AR to teach science

1 From primary school to higher education, AR apps and devices are now available for use as educational **aids**. The most common devices are handheld and project digital content onto a student's book or on a student's desk – supplementing their course with 3D interactive content. This 3D content has the power to engage students in ways that teachers could previously only dream of. It follows that the use of AR in education can only be a positive development – with huge future potential.

2 One of the greatest benefits of using AR in education so far is that it has brought science to life. Science need no longer be taught using 2D pictures and lifeless models, which may be uninspiring for young learners; with AR, science can become vivid and fully interactive. There are already several AR apps that help students examine the anatomy of different species or models of human organs. Students can view and **manipulate** the 3D objects from all angles, allowing them to learn more independently and effectively than with traditional content.

3 The potential of AR to bring the same life to other subjects is equally promising. For example, in Geography classes, AR might allow students to view amazing natural phenomena without the limitations of time or place. In History lessons, students could explore ancient monuments or engage with historical figures. Whatever the subject, it is AR that can go one step further than previous technologies in bringing the real world to the classroom.

4 It comes as no surprise then that educational researchers assert that one of the major outcomes of using AR in the classroom is an increase in student motivation. Bacca et al. (2014) claim that students who used AR in their classes reported not only better understanding of the subject, but also greater enjoyment in studying. Radu (2014) maintains that educational AR applications lead to better learning performance and long-term memory retention. It is the tactile and interactive nature of AR applications that improves retention and understanding of new subject content.

5 **Advocates** of AR in education also emphasize its usefulness for schools in remote locations, where students do not have easy access to museums or science exhibitions. In the past, only students from elite schools could afford to travel to famous places like the British Museum or the Louvre. Soon – with the assistance of AR technology – students from remote or underprivileged schools around the world may be able to visit these places and **inspect** the artefacts in 3D. In some ways, the AR experience would be even more immersive than a real trip to a museum because, with AR projection, students could touch and manipulate historical objects freely.

6 Despite the **numerous** advantages associated with using AR in schools and universities, not everybody is convinced that it is a positive development. Critics point out the presence of attention tunnelling when using AR in class. This means that the students are so focused on the 3D display that they do not attend to the content of the lesson. However, this reservation is arguably short sighted in that, as with past innovations such as the internet, the **novelty** of AR in the classroom will soon diminish; once students become accustomed to these 3D projections, they will be able to refocus their attention on the subject at hand.

7 It is evident that the adoption of AR technology by educators will be a positive development for all involved. AR applications allow students to learn in an interactive and **engaging** way. It is early days for the use of this technology but its applications in education seem limitless. It is only when we **embrace** such innovations in technology that we can learn of their full potential and develop them further.

6 Find the words in the essay on page 215. Work out the meaning of each word from the context and match the words with their definitions below.

1 uninspiring (para 2)
2 angle (para 2)
3 elite (para 5)
4 underprivileged (para 5)
5 short sighted (para 6)

a _____ belonging to the richest and most powerful group in society
b _____ unable to imagine how things might change in the future
c _____ a physical position from which something can be seen
d _____ without the money, possessions or opportunities that the average person has
e _____ not interesting or exciting in any way

DISCUSSION

SYNTHESIZING

7 Work with a partner. Use ideas from Reading 1 and Reading 2 to answer the following questions.

1 Why do you think AR increases student motivation and retention?
2 Do you agree with critics who claim that the increase in student motivation is due to the novelty of AR technology in the class? Why / Why not?
3 Which of the applications of AR in Reading 1 and Reading 2 do you think are most likely to become commonly used first? Why?
4 Which applications do you think might be unlikely to become widely used? Why?

PLUS

⊙ LANGUAGE DEVELOPMENT

REPORTING EXPERT OPINIONS

VOCABULARY

There are many verbs that can be used to report researchers' or experts' opinions about a problem or to relate the results of a study.

Instead of writing *Researchers say that* ... , you can vary your style by using verbs such as: *maintain, claim, assert, suggest, observe, acknowledge, conclude, state.* The subtle differences in meaning between these verbs will add precision to your writing.

Bacca et al. (2014) **claim** that students who used AR in their classes reported not only better understanding of the subject, but also greater enjoyment in studying.

Radu (2014) **maintains** that educational AR applications lead to better learning performance and long-term memory retention.

To report current scientific thinking and conclusions that are currently relevant, use the present simple on the reporting verb followed by a *that* clause.

Experts **suggest** that future AR apps **will allow** simultaneous interpretation of spoken language. (current thinking)

Experts **suggested** that simultaneous interpretation of spoken language **would be** possible by the early twenty-first century. (historical thinking, now disproven)

1 Match the words in the box to the best definition. Use a dictionary to help you.

> acknowledge   assert   claim   maintain
> observe   suggest   state   conclude

a _____ to continue to insist that something is true

b _____ to say that something is certainly true

c _____ to communicate an idea cautiously because there is no proof

d _____ to say that something is true without absolute proof

e _____ to decide something based on the results of a study, reasoned argument, etc.

f _____ to accept or admit that something is true (often unwillingly)

g _____ to present an idea or a fact clearly in speech or writing

h _____ to notice or identify something during a study

2 Choose the best verb to complete the sentences. Then work with a partner and compare your answers.

1 Even sceptics of the use of AR in the classroom *acknowledge / suggest* that it has various benefits for young learners.
2 The researchers looked at the exam results of one school using AR and *claimed / suggested* that there was no observable improvement in subject knowledge retention.
3 Research *suggests / concludes* that there may be good reason to doubt these findings.
4 The latest government report *states / observes* that more funding will be directed towards the use of new technology in schools.
5 Despite opposition, advocates of the adoption of this new technology by educators *maintain / conclude* that AR increases retention and understanding of the subjects.

3 Report three opinions or research results from Reading 2. Use three different verbs from the box in Exercise 1. Compare your sentences with a partner.

1 _____
  _____
2 _____
  _____
3 _____
  _____

IT CLEFTS

Clefts with *it + be* emphasize a specific piece of information in a sentence. They are particularly useful in writing, where intonation cannot be used to create emphasis.

Students have benefited the most from the introduction of AR technology in science classes. (no emphasis)

It is **students** <u>who</u> have benefited the most from the introduction of AR technology in science classes. (emphasizing students rather than teachers)

Notice how we use defining relative clauses with *that, which, who etc.* after the emphasized information.

It is **the introduction of AR technology** <u>which</u> students have benefited the most from in science classes. (emphasizing AR technology rather than other innovations)

When *it* cleft sentences emphasize adverbial or prepositional phrases, we follow this with a *that* clause with a subject.

It is **in science classes** <u>that</u> students have benefited the most from the introduction of AR technology. (emphasizing science rather than other subjects)

It is **only when we embrace such innovations in technology** <u>that</u> we can learn of their full potential and develop them further.

4 Are the sentences correct (✔) or incorrect (✘)? Correct the mistakes.

1 ☐ It is the internet has revolutionized education in remote areas of the world.

_____

2 ☐ It is in the development of new innovations that invest most of our time and effort.

_____

3 ☐ It is the teacher, not just the technology, that increases student motivation.

_____

4 ☐ In the classroom that the usefulness of the new technologies is really tested.

_____

5 ☐ It is not until we have trialled new technology in the classroom we can draw any conclusions about its usefulness.

_____

PLUS

5 Rewrite the sentences to emphasize the sections in bold. Compare your sentences with a partner.

1 **Parents** have the greatest influence over a child's development.

_____

_____

2 **The 3D projections created by AR** allow learners to visualize complex phenomena.

_____

_____

3 **Rural schools** should be funded to incorporate AR technology in their classrooms.

_____

_____

4 We can **only** improve new technology **when we acknowledge its limitations**.

_____

_____

5 Cloud computing makes **record keeping** easier for teachers.

_____

_____

WRITING

CRITICAL THINKING

At the end of this unit, you will write an argumentative essay. Look at this unit's writing task in the box below.

> Choose an emerging technology that you think will have positive impact on learning outcomes. Present an argument to support your position.

SKILLS

Constructing an argument using a premise

When we evaluate the future impact of something, we need to consider current practices and their underlying aims, as well as all of the needs and expectations of all the people affected. Critical thinkers consider both positive and negative outcomes, whatever their personal opinion.

1 The table below lists some of the features of cloud computing in education. Work in small groups and discuss the possible benefits and drawbacks of each feature. Note your ideas in the table.

ANALYZE

cloud computing		
features	benefits	drawbacks
Students can access e-books and digital materials easily.		
Students can take exams online.		
Students can communicate with other students via a webcam.		
Students can listen to lectures at home.		
School documents and student information are stored in the cloud.		

2 Beyond the features above, think of other possible arguments for and against the use of cloud computing in schools. Write your ideas in the table. Then work in a small group and compare your ideas.

arguments for	arguments against

3 Choose another new technology with features that have potential applications in the classroom. Do some research about how this technology has been used, its benefits, and any potential drawbacks or challenges it poses. Complete the table below.

features	benefits	drawbacks/challenges

 **EVALUATE**

4 Exchange tables with a partner. Give feedback on his or her table.

1 Are these features likely to be used in the classroom? Does their use seem realistic, now or in the future?
2 Are they likely to be beneficial?
3 Are the drawbacks a realistic reflection of problems in the classroom?
4 Can you think of any other benefits or drawbacks?

5 Add any information from your partner's feedback to your table. Based on all of this information, do you think this technology would be a beneficial addition to the classroom? Why / Why not? Write a sentence stating your view. This will be your thesis statement in the writing task.

GRAMMAR FOR WRITING

PARENTHETICAL PHRASES

Writers use parenthetical phrases (such as appositives, non-defining clauses and other structures) to interrupt a sentence and give the reader extra information, explanation, examples or comments. Parenthetical statements can be removed from a sentence and it will still make sense. We can use commas, brackets ( ) and dashes – to indicate parenthetical phrases. Each of the types of punctuation has a different effect on the reader.

Commas are the standard punctuation for a parenthetical phrase.

Unlike virtual reality, **which creates an immersive 3D environment,** augmented reality interacts with and enhances the world that surrounds us.

In other subjects, **such as History and Literature,** students can see a superimposed figure of a famous historical person.

Snap, **the instant messaging app,** has added AR to its smart spectacles.

Brackets make the statement quieter and less intrusive – the writer is telling the reader they might or might not need the information. Brackets often give examples or explanation.

With a lightweight head-mounted set **(smart glasses),** information about each exhibit is displayed automatically as the visitor looks at it.

Dashes make the statement stand out more – the writer wants the reader to notice this information. Dashes are often used for commenting.

With AR navigation technology — **specifically devices for motor vehicles** — drivers don't need to take their eyes off the road ahead to look at a screen.

3D printing — **which is a marvel to behold** — is a relatively recent invention.

1 Read the sentences and add punctuation to the parenthetical phrases. Use the punctuation (commas, brackets or dashes) that you think is the most appropriate.

1 Communication devices smartphones, tablets, etc. aid the learning of foreign languages.

2 Smartphones which are an amazing piece of technology are now affordable to many students.

3 The app industry which is ever growing has expanded into the domain of education.

4 In the past before the internet students had to rely on their school libraries to get information.

5 Mitra an expert in the field of cloud computing and education suggests that all future education will happen outside the classroom.

6 Opponents of the use of new technology specifically smartphone apps maintain that it distracts children from learning.

2 Rewrite the sentences below to include the correct parenthetical phrases from the box. Use the punctuation (commas, brackets or dashes) that you think is the most appropriate.

> whose attitude I find difficult to understand
> especially those who are motivated
> such as tourist information
> the condition in which a person is too focused on one stimulus
> which is beneficial to subject knowledge retention

1 Enabling students to manipulate 3D objects in class is one of the aims of educational technology developers.

_____

_____

2 Many students use mobile devices to learn English outside the classroom.

_____

_____

3 Technophobes will never be convinced that using technology to learn is more engaging than traditional methods.

_____

_____

4 Attention tunnelling may be a potential drawback until the novelty diminishes.

_____

_____

5 AR content can be viewed through a number of different devices.

_____

_____

USING THE SEMICOLON

Use a semicolon (;) to connect independent clauses that contain similar ideas. Using a semicolon helps the reader see the close connection between the ideas in the two clauses.

AR can assist you with that; it not only labels different components of a mechanism, but can display step-by-step instructions on how to fix it.

In the sentence above, the use of the semicolon is correct; both parts are independent clauses.

~~3D printing has been used in schools to facilitate teaching science and design; which is an innovative way to illustrate complex ideas.~~

Here the use of a semicolon is incorrect because the second half is not an independent clause.

Correct run-on sentences by placing a semicolon before the conjunctive adverb.

~~There are various disciplines that can benefit from the adoption of cloud computing however, schools should be cautious about the privacy issues that may emerge with time.~~

There are various disciplines that can benefit from the adoption of cloud computing; **however,** *schools should be cautious about the privacy issues that may emerge with time.*

3 Is the use of a semicolon in each sentence correct (✔) or incorrect (✘)? Correct the mistakes.

1 ☐ Scientists speculate that all future learning will happen in the cloud; which will no longer require students and teachers to meet in one place.

2 ☐ 3D printers can be expensive for some schools, thus; the government that should fund the purchase of 3D printers in all schools.

3 ☐ With AR apps; students can see exotic animals in 3D they can touch a 3D puma or a jaguar projected in front of them.

4 ☐ In my opinion, the use of AR in education is a positive outcome; it enhances students' learning experience and helps with retention.

5 ☐ The use of technology in the classroom will doubtless improve learning outcomes; however, not all students can afford to buy expensive smartphones or tablets.

FORMAL STYLE IN ACADEMIC WRITING

Formal style means that we avoid language that resembles spoken forms and is colloquial or emotional. Formal style appears in academic journals and textbooks. However, in informal texts, such as magazines, blogs and internet articles, it is common to find the forms marked in the table with an asterisk*. The remaining forms in the table below are primarily found in spoken language.

- Avoid contracted forms, such as: *don't, can't, won't, it's, isn't.
- Avoid the personal pronouns, *I, you and we.
- Do not use exclamation marks or language that shows strong emotions, such as marvellous, awful.
- Avoid informal or colloquial vocabulary, such as that shown in the table.

colloquial word forms	gonna, wanna, gotta	~~wanna~~ **wish to / would like to** stress the importance of …
general* nouns	kids, guys, things, stuff	~~Kids in schools~~ **Young learners / Schoolchildren** should have …
quantity*	loads of, lots of, tons of, a bit of	~~Lots of~~ **A significant number of** students use smartphones to …
emphasis*	really, totally	Teachers claim cloud computing is ~~really~~ **extremely / particularly** useful for …
linking	anyway, the thing is, in the end, at the end of the day	~~At the end of the day~~ **Finally / In conclusion** they claim that …
informal phrases	how come, and all that, kind of, have got to, I reckon	They asked ~~how come~~ **why / the reason** ~~that~~ the technology was …

1 Underline the informal language in each sentence. Compare your answers with a partner.

1 One of the things about technology is that it can be difficult to use.
2 I'm gonna outline some of the disadvantages of cloud computing.
3 It's a wonderful educational aid with lots of useful applications and it isn't expensive.
4 It helps kids learn science in a meaningful way.
5 It's a kind of app that helps you learn new vocabulary.
6 How come we don't use it in all schools?
7 I think it's OK and everyone should use it!
8 I can't imagine what life would be like without this technology!

PLUS

SKILLS

2 Work with a partner. Rewrite the sentences in Exercise 1 in a more formal style.

WRITING TASK

▶ Choose an emerging technology that you think will have positive impact on learning outcomes. Present an argument to support your position.

PLAN

1 Review your notes in Critical thinking, Exercises 3–5 on page 222. Complete the outline below with notes on your arguments and add supporting details. Present an opposite point of view to show that you understand different perspectives. Make sure you refute it with a counter-argument.

Paragraph 1:
Feature 1: _____
Supporting details: _____

Paragraph 2:
Feature 2: _____
Supporting details: _____

Paragraph 3:
Feature 3: _____
Supporting details: _____

Present an opposite point of view to show that you understand different perspectives. Make sure you refute it with a counter-argument.

2 Review your table and notes in the Critical thinking section again. Choose one of the drawbacks that is opposite to your opinion to include in your essay.

Paragraph 4:
Opposite point of view

_____

Counter-argument

_____

3 Think about your introduction.

1 Review your thesis statement from Critical thinking, Exercise 5. Make any revisions based on the review of your notes.
2 Your readers may not be familiar with the technology. What information can you add in the introduction to help them understand this technology?

4 Think about your conclusion.

  1 Restate your thesis statement, summarizing the main arguments that support it.

  2 Include a statement or observation that leaves readers with something to think about regarding this technology.

5 Refer to the Task checklist below as you prepare your essay.

WRITE A FIRST DRAFT

6 Write your essay. Use your essay plan to help you structure your ideas. Write 450–500 words.

REVISE

7 Use the Task checklist to review your essay for content and structure.

TASK CHECKLIST	✔
Is your opinion clearly identifiable throughout the essay?	
Do all three arguments support your opinion?	
Have you acknowledged and countered an opposite point of view?	
Have you summarized the three main arguments in the conclusion?	
Does your conclusion leave your readers something to think about?	

EDIT

8 Use the Language checklist to edit your essay for language errors.

LANGUAGE CHECKLIST	✔
Have you used a variety of verbs to report expert opinion?	
Have you used *it* clefts to emphasize the main points?	
Have you used dashes, commas and brackets appropriately to indicate parenthetical phrases?	
Have you used the semicolon to show a close connection between independent clauses?	
Have you used a formal style, avoiding colloquial language and contractions?	

9 Make any necessary changes to your essay.

OBJECTIVES REVIEW

1 Check your learning objectives for this unit. Write *3, 2* or *1* for each objective.

3 = very well   2 = well   1 = not so well

I can ...

watch and understand a video about mobile phone hacking.   _____

draw out common themes.   _____

construct an argument using a premise.   _____

use parenthetical phrases.   _____

use the semicolon.   _____

use formal style in academic writing.   _____

write an argumentative essay.   _____

2 Go to the *Unlock* Online Workbook for more practice with this unit's learning objectives.

 UNLOCK ONLINE

WORDLIST		
advocate (n) ⊙	engaging (adj) ⊙	numerous (adj) ⊙
aid (n) ⊙	hazard (n) ⊙	observe (v) ⊙
assert (v) ⊙	immersive (adj)	projection (n) ⊙
claim (v) ⊙	inspect (v)	simultaneous (adj) ⊙
conclude (v) ⊙	interpretation (n) ⊙	state (v) ⊙
domain (n) ⊙	manipulate (v) ⊙	superimpose (v)
embrace (v) ⊙	novelty (n)	supplement (v) ⊙

⊙ = high-frequency words in the Cambridge Academic Corpus

LEARNING OBJECTIVES — IN THIS UNIT YOU WILL ...

Watch and listen	watch and understand a video about languages in Ireland.
Reading skill	use background knowledge to annotate a text.
Critical thinking	evaluate and synthesize arguments.
Grammar	hedge predictions.
Academic writing skills	avoid overgeneralizations; refute counter-arguments.
Writing task	write a pros and cons essay.

UNL🔒CK YOUR KNOWLEDGE

Work with a partner. Discuss the questions.

1 Which of the languages in the box are global languages? Which ones may become even more important in the future? Why?

> Hindi   Russian   Chinese   Spanish   Arabic

2 What are the benefits of knowing a number of languages?

3 In your opinion, are some languages easier to learn than others? Give examples.

4 What problems would somebody face when learning your language?

 PLUS

PREPARING TO WATCH

ACTIVATING YOUR KNOWLEDGE

1 You are going to watch a video about the Irish language. Before you watch, work with a partner. Discuss the questions.

1 Where is Ireland?
2 What do you know about the history of the relationship between Ireland and England?
3 What do you think it means when *a language dies*?
4 What could have caused a language, like Irish, to become almost extinct?

PREDICTING CONTENT USING VISUALS

2 Look at the photos and discuss the questions with a partner.

1 What kind of area are the people from?
2 What language(s) do you think they speak there? Why?
3 What do think the students are learning?
4 How do you think the students feel about the English language?

GLOSSARY

the Irish Potato Famine (n phr) a period of famine in Ireland between 1845 and 1852 that caused the starvation of approximately one million people and led to mass emigration to the USA and elsewhere

death knell (n phr) a warning of the end of something

WHILE WATCHING

UNDERSTANDING MAIN IDEAS

3 ▶ Watch the video. Are the statements below true (*T*) or false (*F*)? Correct the false statements.

_____ 1 In the nineteenth century, the Irish language nearly died out.

_____

_____ 2 The golfers at Connemara golf course speak only Irish.

_____

_____ 3 The children at the local school think of themselves as English speakers.

_____

4 ▶ Watch the video again and answer the questions.

1 What did the English do to the Irish language in 1831?

_____

2 What else contributed to the fall in the number of Irish speakers in the nineteenth century?

_____

3 What is happening in Irish schools today?

_____

4 What helped preserve the Irish language in Connemara?

_____

5 What do the children do in English?

_____

6 What do the children do in Irish?

_____

5 Work with a partner. Read the two extracts from the video script and discuss the questions.

'At the height of their colonial ambition, they attempted to suppress Irish culture and identity entirely.'

1 What does the presenter mean? What aspects of culture might have been suppressed?

'Imperialist Brit that I am, they're kind enough to speak English to me — which, given the history, is quite an ask.'

2 Why does the presenter say the golfers are kind?

6 Work with a partner. Discuss the questions.

1 What does the presenter mean by *linguistic oppression*?
2 What is the presenter referring to when he says: 'This part of Connemara suffered as much as any'?
3 According to the information in the video, how can Irish survive?
4 What does the presenter mean when he says: 'You wouldn't be able to cope in the world if you didn't speak English'? Do you agree with him?

DISCUSSION

7 Work with a partner. Discuss the questions.

1 What are some of the reasons languages die?
2 Are there any local languages or dialects in your country that are endangered? Why?
3 What can be done to preserve endangered languages?
4 Is there value in trying to preserve an endangered language? What exactly?

READING

READING 1

PREPARING TO READ

1 You are going to read the introduction to a linguistics textbook about loanwords. Read the words and their definitions. Use the correct form of the words in bold to complete the sentences below.

> **be derived from** (phr v) to come from a particular origin
> **commodity** (n) product you can buy or sell
> **commonly** (adj) frequently, usually
> **conquer** (v) to take control of a country or people, or defeat by war
> **dialect** (n) a local, usually spoken, form of a language
> **incorporate** (v) to include something as part of something else
> **it follows that** (phr) used to say if one thing is true, then another thing is true
> **terminology** (n) words and phrases used for a particular subject

1 If he speaks English, _____ he must understand English.
2 _____ such as wheat are shipped all over the world.
3 The words *language* and *dictate* _____ Latin.
4 Many _____ used words in English come from French.
5 It's difficult for me to understand northern _____ .
6 The names of many foreign foods have been _____ into English.
7 England was _____ by the French in 1066.
8 Medical _____ mostly comes from Latin.

2 Look at the menu from a restaurant. The underlined words are loanwords. Write the loanwords next to the correct language of origin.

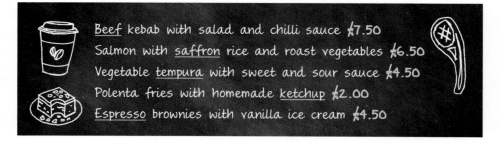

Beef kebab with salad and chilli sauce £7.50
Salmon with saffron rice and roast vegetables £6.50
Vegetable tempura with sweet and sour sauce £4.50
Polenta fries with homemade ketchup £2.00
Espresso brownies with vanilla ice cream £4.50

a _____ Italian   b _____ French   c _____ Chinese
d _____ Arabic   e _____ Japanese

3 Scan the introduction to the textbook and check your answers from Exercise 2.

Loanwords in English

1 Language and its words are never static; they travel across countries and continents. Words that travel – that are **incorporated** into another language – are known as loanwords, and there is probably no language in the world that does not include them. *Café* from French, *kindergarten* from German and *safari* from Arabic are examples of loanwords that are used in modern English.

2 Words from another language can be incorporated into the new language in different ways. Some loanwords – for instance, *café* – retain their original spelling and meaning. Other words like *sugar,* which **is derived from** the Arabic *sukkar,* keep their root meaning but change in their pronunciation or spelling. In some cases, loanwords change their meaning when they are adopted. For example, the word *ketchup* comes from Cantonese, a Chinese **dialect**. It entered the English language in the seventeenth century, when samples of the sauce were brought to the UK from Asia by sailors. Mushroom ketchup, not tomato ketchup as we know it today, soon became a favourite condiment on the dining tables of London. In a more extreme change of meaning, the Japanese term *tycoon* was used in the nineteenth century by English travellers to address the Japanese shogun. Nowadays, it is used in English to talk about somebody powerful in business.

3 Loanwords can enter a language for a variety of reasons. Geographical and political domination have traditionally been the biggest contributing factors. Loanwords go primarily in one direction; the language of the dominant group transfers to the language of the group that has been **conquered**. For example, a great number of loanwords from French entered English during a period of French domination. These include English words for *beef, mutton, liberty, justice* and *government.* In general, members of the dominant group use words from the conquered group only if they encounter things or places for which they have no word, as occurred in the British colonies[1]. English incorporated loanwords that reflected these unfamiliar environments. Certain names of animals, such as *chimpanzee* and *mamba,* are derived from African languages. *Jungle* was adapted from a Hindi word, *jangal. Bungalow* is derived from a Hindi word meaning 'belonging to Bengal' and was used in the seventeenth century to describe a certain type of house in Bengal. Later, it came to mean 'a one-storey house'.

4 Other loanwords in English are related to important historical events. For example, *guerrilla*, Spanish for 'little war', entered English in the nineteenth century during a period of struggle between the Spanish and Napoleon's troops. The German word *blitzkrieg*, meaning 'sudden war', and *kamikaze* from Japanese, became part of the English lexicon in the 1930s and 40s, during World War II. The words *cosmonaut* and *sputnik* came from Russian and entered English during the twentieth century 'Space Race' between the US and the USSR.

5 Commerce and intercultural exchange are another common source of loanwords; even before the age of globalization, many **commodities** entered English through international trade and travel. For instance, *saffron*, *cotton* and *coffee* have Arabic roots; they were sold by Arab traders across Europe and Asia. Fruits like *lemon* and *orange* were also brought to Europe by Arab merchants, and the Arabic roots of these words are evident not only in English, but in Spanish, French and German. The origin of *chocolate* and *tomato* can be traced to the Nahuatl, the language of pre-Colombian inhabitants of Mexico. Both words entered English by way of Spanish.

6 Scientific and academic exchange has been yet another influential source of loanwords. A considerable number of academic words in English have Latin origins. The reason for this is that, for centuries, Latin was the lingua franca[2] of science and law. In modern English, much of our scientific and technical vocabulary, our medical **terminology** and many legal terms come from these roots. For example, *school* and *scholar* are derived from the Latin word *schola*; *dental* and *dentist* have their origins in the Latin for tooth, *densus*.

7 In modern times, globalization, immigration and the rise of low-cost intercontinental travel have led to an unprecedented level of linguistic[3] and cultural exchange. Several Japanese words, such as *sushi, tsunami, tempura* and *anime*, are now **commonly** used in English. We have also witnessed a surge of foreign food names in English – Italian *latte* and *espresso* and Cantonese *chow, wok* and *dim sum* to name just a few.

8 Languages change constantly, in part as a reflection of cultural and socio-political events; **it follows that** the study of loanwords in English can reveal a great deal about the cultural history of its speakers.

[1]**colony**: an area controlled by a more powerful country that is far away
[2]**lingua franca**: a language used for communication by groups who don't speak the same language
[3]**linguistic**: related to language

WHILE READING

4 Read the introduction to the textbook. Complete the outline with
information from Reading 1. Write the main ideas (I–II) and (a–e).

I. Loanwords def. _____
   • e.g. café, kindergarten, safari

II. _____
   • keep spell. and meaning, e.g. _____
   • _____ , e.g. sugar
   • _____ , e.g. ketchup, tycoon

III. Sources of loanwords
   a) _____
      • liberty, justice, government from _____
      • chimpanzee, mamba from _____
      • _____ , _____ from Hindi
   b) _____
      • guerrilla – during _____
      • _____ and _____ during WWII
      • cosmonaut and sputnik during _____
   c) _____
      • _____ sold by Arab traders
      • chocolate, tomato from _____
   d) _____
      • scien., tech., _____ and legal terminology
        from _____
   e) _____
      • unprecedented level of linguistic and cultural exchange
        e.g. _____
      • _____ , e.g.
        Italian latte, espresso. Cantonese chow, wok, dim sum

5 Read the introduction to the textbook again and complete the gaps in the
notes above with details and examples. Compare your notes with a partner.

Using background knowledge to annotate a text

Critical readers are active readers, taking notes and asking questions as they read. To better understand a text, annotate it with your background knowledge about the subject. As you read, relate the ideas to your own experience and knowledge. Note your additional examples and ideas in the margins. This will help you develop questions for further research, synthesize ideas from multiple sources and develop original ideas for your writing.

ANNOTATING

6 Read the introduction to the textbook again and add notes in the margin on the points below next to the relevant paragraphs. Discuss your notes in small groups.

   a Which words mentioned in the text are also loanwords in your language?
   b What other loanwords can you think of in your language?
   c Which cultures and languages has your language taken words from?
   d Do you think these loanwords came into your language for the reasons mentioned in the text? Which ones? Highlight or underline the relevant places in the text.

READING BETWEEN THE LINES

MAKING INFERENCES

7 Work with a partner. Discuss the questions. Then join another pair of students and compare your answers.

   1 Does the modern English meaning of the word *tycoon* have any relationship with its original meaning in Japanese?
   2 Why do you think the incorporation of new words usually goes in one direction in cases of political domination?
   3 What is the relationship between the availability of low-cost flights and the increase in linguistic exchange?
   4 What do you think led to the use of the word *anime* in English?
   5 Why do you think the same Italian words for different types of coffee are used all over the world?

DISCUSSION

8 Work with a partner. Discuss the questions.

   1 Are there any words from your language that are used in English? What are they? How did they enter the English language?
   2 Look back at your notes about loanwords in your language. Are these words spelled and pronounced the same way as in their original language?
   3 Is knowing about word origins beneficial for vocabulary learning? Why / Why not?

PREPARING TO READ

UNDERSTANDING KEY VOCABULARY

1 You are going to read an essay about English loanwords entering other languages. Read the sentences. Write the correct form of the words in bold next to their definitions below.

1 Many people believe that our leaders should take a stronger **stance** on maintaining standards for our language.

2 I fully **endorse** the necessary steps that the government is taking to simplify our spelling rules.

3 The book we read about the history of English **distorted** the facts. What really happened was very different.

4 It is **futile** to try to prevent people from speaking their own language. They will do it no matter what the government does.

5 At one time, people held the **misguided** belief that knowing more than one language had negative consequences.

6 Globalization can result in the **dilution** of local cultures, traditions and values.

7 Your high school English exam is not the **equivalent** of an international exam.

8 The teacher introduced a new rule – that students must speak English at all times. However, it was extremely difficult to **enforce**.

a _____ (v) to make people obey something or do something

b _____ (n) something that has the same value, meaning, etc. as something else

c _____ (v) to publicly support

d _____ (n) a publicly held point of view

e _____ (adj) having no effect or achieving nothing

f _____ (v) to change something so that it is false or wrong

g _____ (adj) based on an incorrect understanding

h _____ (n) the process of making the content of something weaker

PLUS

2 Work with a partner. Discuss the questions.

1 Are there any technology and social media words in your language that come from English? If yes, make a short list.

_____

2 How do you say *tweet* and *selfie* in your language?

3 What language do you use to text friends? What language do you use on social media? Why?

4 Do you ever use English to talk to your friends and family? If so, when and why?

5 Where and how often do people in your country hear and read English?

WHILE READING

3 Read the essay on page 240. Match the paragraphs (1–6) with the correct main idea (a–h). There are two ideas you do not need to use.

a Loanwords are usually adjusted to follow the rules of a new language. _____

b Language purists struggle to keep up with language change. _____

c French and Spanish students struggle with English. _____

d Linguistic purism can increase students' educational burden. _____

e Some people oppose the use of English loanwords in their languages. _____

f Several countries have passed laws against the use of English words in public. _____

g Loanwords are a valuable addition to any language. _____

h Knowing more than one language has a number of advantages in the modern world. _____

4 Read the essay again. Write *T* (true), *F* (false) or *DNS* (does not say) next to the statements below. Then correct the false statements.

_____ 1 People in non-English speaking countries accept the use of English terminology.

_____ 2 French people are not supposed to use the English words *computer* and *email* when they speak French.

_____ 3 Being multilingual improves your long-term memory.

_____ 4 The French Academy enforces French words for *tweet* and *selfie*.

_____ 5 French scientists prefer to use the French word for *cloud computing*.

_____ 6 Loanwords often lose their original pronunciation and spelling.

_____ 7 Removing loanwords from a language has some cultural and historical benefits.

_____ 8 Most people would not be able to identify the loanwords in their language.

LINGUISTIC PURISM AND ENGLISH AS A GLOBAL LANGUAGE

1   In the last decade, we have witnessed a surge of English words from technology and social media being adopted by other languages all over the world. This linguistic phenomenon has split public opinion in some countries with respect to whether they should use the English words or create local **equivalents**. Opponents of the incorporation of English words into their language argue that accepting English terminology may lead to cultural **dilution** and a loss of linguistic and cultural identity; they want to preserve their languages in a pure form, keeping them free of foreign influences. Although this linguistic purism may have emotional appeal, there are several problems with this **stance**.

2   One issue with linguistic purism is that – in a highly competitive global economy – it has the potential to limit young people's opportunities. In many countries – for example, Spain, France and Indonesia – linguistic purism is **endorsed** by national academies. These institutions oppose the use of English words like *computer, email* and *download*. In France, the use of French equivalents in public documents is actively **enforced** by the French Academy. There are numerous other examples of non-English terms that are promoted by these academies instead of internationally recognized English words. Because of this, students in these countries have the added burden of learning this terminology again in English. Using the English words is seen as not supporting the local language and culture. This kind of negative attitude towards using foreign words may discourage young people from studying other languages.

3   Yet, to cope in the modern world, these young people need to speak a global language, so throwing up barriers to language learning puts them at a disadvantage. Being able to navigate the web and social networking sites and interact with co-workers in multiple languages will be of great benefit to them as they enter the workforce. It's no surprise that multilingual employees are so highly sought after by companies and institutions worldwide. The benefits of multilingualism go beyond economic advantages, however. Knowing two or more languages has also been shown to improve cognitive processes and to have a direct impact on an individual's multitasking and decision-making abilities.

4   Not only is the attempt to prevent English words from entering a language **misguided**, it is also **futile**. On social media networks, English words, in an unstoppable flow, are pushing their way into other languages. In science and technology, innovations spread across many fields at a speed that linguistic purists cannot hope to match. It took the French Academy 18 months to come up with a French equivalent for the term *cloud computing* – in the meantime, French scientists and IT experts had already begun using the technology and the accompanying English term. It is likely that many will continue to do so. A similar phenomenon can be seen in popular culture. For example, at the time of writing, words such as *tweet* and *selfie* still don't have accepted French equivalents.

5   Language is dynamic; it is constantly changing, adding new words to fill existing gaps, and losing others that are no longer needed. New loanwords usually change once they enter a language, adapting to the new language's rules. Loanwords often change their pronunciation (for example, *wi-fi* in French) or their spelling when they are incorporated into a new language. They also take on the suffixes and prefixes of the new language. In short, they become an essential part of their new language. As a result, most speakers are unaware that many of the words that they use every day have foreign origins. The existence of loanwords reflects important cultural phenomena and historical events; erasing them would **distort** the language and its cultural heritage.

6   With billions of people currently using social media around the world, we are entering an era of accelerated linguistic and cultural exchange. No doubt linguistic purists will continue to battle against English loanwords, but thankfully, this is not a universal stance. Indeed, people all over the world understand that accepting new words does not diminish their language and culture; rather, the process enriches them. We should see a more liberal attitude towards language change in coming generations.

READING BETWEEN THE LINES

5 Work with a partner. Find the phrases in the essay. Work out the meaning of each phrase from the context and write an explanation. Then join another pair of students and compare your ideas.

1 cultural dilution (para 1):

_____

2 emotional appeal (para 1):

_____

3 throwing up barriers (para 3):

_____

4 highly sought after (para 3):

_____

5 an era of accelerated linguistic and cultural exchange (para 6):

_____

6 Work with a partner. Discuss the questions.

1 The author mentions social media multiple times. What role does the author believe it plays in the linguistic purism movement and the spread of global languages?

_____

2 What is the importance of language in preserving people's national or cultural identity?

_____

3 The author says loanwords enrich a language. What does she mean by this?

_____

DISCUSSION

7 Work in small groups. Use ideas from Reading 1 and Reading 2 to answer the following questions.

1 Are there any words in your language that are untranslatable to English? Which words? Why are they difficult to translate?

2 What do people in your country think about the incorporation of English words into their language?

LATIN PREFIXES IN ACADEMIC ENGLISH

VOCABULARY

Understanding the meaning of some common prefixes can help you with the meaning of new words.

prefix	meaning	examples
inter-	between, among	interaction (n), intervene (v), intercontinental (adj), interpretation (n), interface (n)
pre-	before	preliminary (adj), predict (v), precede (v), presume (v)
post-	after	postgraduate (n, adj), postwar (adj), postdate (v), postpone (v)
co-	together	coexist (v), collaborate (v), cooperation (n), co-worker (n), cofounder (n)
dis-	not, reverse, undo	disproportionate (adj), displace (v), discourage (v), distasteful (adj), disambiguation (n)

1 Write the correct words from the table above next to the definitions.

1 _____ (v) to delay an event until a later date or time
2 _____ (v) to live together in the same place or at the same time
3 _____ (v) to force somebody or something out of its usual position
4 _____ (v) to be or go before something or somebody in time or space
5 _____ (n) a person you work with
6 _____ (adj) too large or too small in comparison to something else
7 _____ (v) to intentionally get involved in a difficult situation in order to improve it
8 _____ (adj) happening before a more major event or action

PLUS

2 Complete the sentences with words from the table above in the correct form. Compare your answers with a partner.

1 Role plays are designed to encourage _____ between language students.
2 The new language learning software has all the functions we need but the _____ is not very user-friendly.
3 She is now the _____ of a very successful tech start-up that helps people learn a second language.
4 Nobody can _____ which words will be incorporated into a language.
5 My parents _____ me from learning Hungarian; it is not a global language.
6 _____ travel has facilitated cultural exchange.

HIGHLIGHTING SUPPORTING EXAMPLES

Use a variety of linking expressions to indicate examples and supporting details.

specifically	*especially*	*as shown by*
in particular	*such as*	*as exemplified by*
that is	*for instance*	*as demonstrated by*
i.e. = that is	*for example*	*as illustrated by*
namely	*e.g. = for example*	

Always use commas (before and) after *for example* and *for instance*.
For example, a great number of loanwords from French entered English during a period of French domination.

Use commas or other appropriate punctuation when the example is not essential to the meaning of the sentence (a parenthetical phrase).
Several Japanese words, **such as sushi, tsunami, tempura and anime,** are now commonly used in English.

Don't use commas when the examples are essential to understand the meaning of sentence.
Loan words **such as selfie and cloud computing** have gained widespread use across many languages.

3 Read the sentences and add punctuation only where it is needed.

1 Spanish for example replaced many local languages in South America.
2 Languages such as Spanish and Portuguese are used in countries that were once colonies.
3 Romance languages such as French, Italian and Spanish are rooted in Latin.
4 French for instance is used as a lingua franca in different African countries.
5 Language purists often oppose the use of global languages in particular English.

4 Rewrite the sentences to add more supporting examples or details. Use linking expressions from the Explanation box. Then compare your sentences with a partner.

1 Languages always change.

_____

2 People will always need a lingua franca to communicate.

_____

3 Words travel with people.

_____

4 Not knowing English can affect your career.

_____

5 English is the language of social media.

_____

6 Many loanwords in English are related to food.

_____

WRITING

CRITICAL THINKING

At the end of this unit, you will write a pros and cons essay. Look at this unit's writing task in the box below.

> In the last century, English has become a global language, the lingua franca of science, technology, business and education. Its global dominance has affected other cultures and languages in various ways. One outcome has been an increase in the use of English as the language of instruction in universities that had previously used the local or national language. Write an essay on the pros and cons of English-medium university education in your country or another country that you know well.

Schoolchildren singing a traditional song in Hawaiian

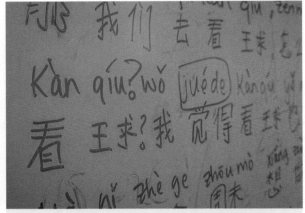

Chinese characters in a classroom and their literal equivalent in English

Evaluating and synthesizing arguments

Anyone can voice an opinion, but academic arguments require support. When you evaluate opinions, ask yourself: are they based on facts? Personal experience? A statement from an expert? Statistics? If you find common claims across different texts, consider the support that each text provides. You can combine them to create a stronger argument when you write your own text. Also consider any counter-arguments each text provides and think about ways you might refute them.

SKILLS

1 Read the opinions about English-medium university instruction. Decide if each person is for or against English-medium instruction. Underline the reasons each person gives for their views.

'Going to an English-medium university really gave me the edge against the competition. I got an offer from an international bank at a great salary right after I graduated. The fact that I am fluent in English and Chinese was a really important asset that I could offer. From this job, I can move anywhere. My English proficiency gives me mobility in the job market that I would never have without it.'

Zhang Liu, China

'Studying in English is a great idea in theory, but the problem is that most students at my university don't know English well enough to understand the material in their classes. Some of them are completely lost. They don't want to ask questions because they are afraid to use their English. I know some students who don't even bother to go to class anymore. The professors know we are struggling so they try to make the material easier, but that really lowers the standard of our education. And some of our professors – they don't speak English that well either, so they just read their lectures. It's so boring. It would be better to study in our native language.'

Anonymous student

'As an engineering student, I prefer to read my courses in English than in Russian. It makes my life much easier and helps me communicate with other students when I travel to other universities on exchange schemes or to conferences. I don't struggle with the terminology; it removes the language barrier. Also, the vast majority of cutting-edge research is published in English.'

Anton, a postgraduate student from Moscow

'By offering all instruction in English, we can attract the best students and professors from all over the world. They all benefit from interacting with one another in English. We can provide the very best education, with up-to-date materials and cutting-edge technology. And, because studying in English is so popular, we can charge substantial tuition. Students will pay for the best educational experience.'

Dr Uzun, president of a private Turkish university

'The introduction of English-medium instruction to our universities has created a two-tiered education system. The top level is for students who have gone to bilingual schools or whose families could pay for extra English lessons. They are the only ones who can pass the English entrance exams. So, the people who have had an advantage all their lives continue to have an advantage at university. The second tier is for students who didn't study in English. Their English is not good enough to pass the university entrance exam. Some are denied admission. Others have to spend an extra year studying English before they can start their studies and even then, they often struggle in their classes. It seems very unfair.'

Sonia, university student

'I was quite pleased when we switched to English as our medium of instruction. I don't think it's a real issue for most of our students; it's part of a global shift. In the last few decades, we have observed an increase in multilingualism around the world. Most students speak two or three languages when they start university anyway. Due to increased migration and travel, many people have to learn additional languages throughout their lives. This trend has a very positive impact on intercultural exchange and cultural relations.'

Dr Khan, a lecturer in Culture and Communication

2 Work with a partner. List all the arguments for and against English-medium instruction (EMI) from Exercise 1 in the first column of the table. Decide whether you agree or disagree with each argument. Compare your answers with another pair.

arguments	agree	disagree	strongest?
For: competitive edge in the job market			

3 In the last column, tick (✔) the boxes of the two strongest arguments. It doesn't matter whether you agree or disagree with the overall position of the arguments. Explain to your partner why you think they are the strongest.

4 Choose a country to research and write about – either your own country or one you know well. Think about the merits of EMI at universities in your chosen country. Based on the table in Exercise 2, do you support or oppose it?

5 Conduct some research on EMI in the country you are going to write about. This could be from academic research or by interviewing people. Make a list of all of the arguments, both for and against EMI.

6 When you have finished your research, discuss your findings with other students.

  1 Having conducted research, do you still have the same opinion? If you have changed your mind, look at the arguments you agreed and disagreed with in the table in Exercise 2 and change anything you now don't agree with.

  2 Make a note of the arguments for and against EMI that you agree with. Write down any evidence that you found that supports each of the arguments you agreed with.

GRAMMAR FOR WRITING

HEDGING PREDICTIONS

Predictions about the future will always require supporting evidence. However, even when you do provide such evidence, it is usually a good idea to avoid making claims which are too bold or overly general. To hedge claims about the future, use these modal verbs and other expressions of probability to hedge your predictions:

tentative certainty	should / may well / be (highly) likely to / be (highly) unlikely to
possibility	could / might / have the potential to

French scientists and IT experts had already begun using the technology and the accompanying English term. It **is likely** that many will continue to do so.
Opponents of the incorporation of English words into their language argue that accepting English terminology **may** lead to cultural dilution and a loss of linguistic and cultural identity.
It **has the potential to** limit young people's opportunities.

Notice that we use *should* to refer to the future to say something is probable because it is right, the norm, logical or expected.
We **should** see a more liberal attitude towards language change in coming generations.

1 Rewrite the definite predictions to make them more modest. Use a variety of hedging expressions from the Explanation box. Compare your answers with a partner.

1 Chinese will be the next global language.

_____

2 Greek will definitely not become a new lingua franca.

_____

3 The global domination of one language will result in the disappearance of many local languages.

_____

4 Students will learn English if the medium of instruction is English.

_____

5 In the future, young people will not want to learn foreign languages other than English.

_____

6 Schools will stop teaching local languages altogether and focus on English only.

_____

ACADEMIC WRITING SKILLS

AVOIDING OVERGENERALIZATIONS

To avoid overgeneralization in academic writing, make sure that your statements are true in all cases. If not, you may need to modify your claims or provide evidence to prove them.

Students don't know enough English to understand the material.
All cutting-edge research is published in English.

These statements are too general. You can modify them by being more specific.
Most of the students don't know enough English to understand the material.
The vast majority of cutting-edge research is published in English.

Remember to use quantity expressions before nouns to avoid overgeneralizations: *some, many, a lot of, not all, a (significant/small) proportion of, a (small/large/significant) number of, few, not a lot, little*
You may also be able to provide a more concrete basis for the less general statement.
Most of the students **at my university** don't know enough English to understand the material.

PLUS

1 Rewrite the sentences to avoid overgeneralizations.

1 The French do not like to speak English.

_____

2 The English are not good at foreign languages.

_____

3 Nobody can learn a new language in a month.

_____

4 Teachers encourage their students to study English outside the classroom.

_____

5 In the colonial era, the English adopted the local words for animals.

_____

6 Globalization is the cause of language extinction.

_____

2 Rewrite the sentences to avoid overgeneralizations. Provide a concrete basis for the less general statement.

1 English instruction in my country is not good.

_____

2 People can't learn a new language if they start studying after the age of 15.

_____

REFUTING COUNTER-ARGUMENTS

When you make an argument, you should anticipate counter-arguments.

1 You can concede or acknowledge anything you think is valid about the counter-argument with expressions such as:
While it is/may be true that …
Although this argument may …
Although this linguistic purism may have emotional appeal, there are several problems with this stance.

2 You can simply concede or acknowledge the existence of the argument with expressions such as:
Although it has been argued that …
Some people claim that …
Although it has been argued that *the use of English loanwords will have a negative impact on French language and culture, there is no evidence to support this.*

3 You can also reject the counter-argument altogether with expressions such as:
It is simply not true that …
It cannot be argued that …
… is wrong
It is simply not true that *linguistic purism has educational benefits.*

When you refute or contest a counter-argument, be sure to provide evidence to support your refutation.

3 Refute the statements below. Compare your sentences with a partner.

1 Most English loanwords come from Spanish.

_____

_____

2 Learning English takes away valuable time from other areas of study.

_____

_____

3 Using English as a medium of instruction makes the system fairer and more equal for everyone.

_____

_____

4 The words sugar, saffron and cotton come from Latin.

_____

_____

5 Using English words will have a negative effect on our culture.

_____

_____

WRITING TASK

In the last century, English has become a global language, the lingua franca of science, technology, business and education. Its global dominance has affected other cultures and languages in various ways. One outcome has been an increase in the use of English as the language of instruction in universities that had previously used the local or national language. Write an essay on the pros and cons of English-medium university education in your country or another country that you know well.

PLAN

1 In a pros and cons essay you must present a balanced view. Review your notes in the Critical thinking section on page 246. Choose the three strongest arguments related to EMI in your country. Write each of them as a topic sentence in the table.

Argument 1

Topic sentence: _____

_____

Possible counter-arguments: _____

_____

Supporting details: _____

_____

Argument 2

Topic sentence: _____

_____

Possible counter-arguments: _____

_____

Supporting details: _____

_____

Argument 3

Topic sentence: _____

_____

Possible counter-arguments: _____

_____

Supporting details: _____

_____

---

2 Note your supporting details in the table above. Include examples where they are appropriate.

3 For each of the arguments, consider the opposing position. Make a note of any possible counter-arguments in the table. You may not need to include this for every claim. Only include it if there is a relevant counter-argument to that view.

4 Write one or two sentences presenting some background to the issue from the Writing task box in your own words for your introduction.

_____

_____

5 State your position in support of or against EMI in your country in a thesis statement. This does not need to be a strong statement if you don't have a strong view. You may have mixed feelings about the issue. If so, you can include some hedging in your thesis statement.

_____

_____

6 Write one or two key sentences for your conclusion. Evaluate the situation or make a tentative prediction about the future.

_____

_____

WRITE A FIRST DRAFT

7 Refer to the Task checklist on page 252 as you plan your essay.

8 Write your essay. Use your essay plan to help you structure your ideas. Write 450–500 words.

REVISE

9 Use the Task checklist to review your report for content and structure

TASK CHECKLIST	✔
Does the introduction describe the situation and present the issue?	
Does the essay have a thesis statement that makes your position clear?	
Have your presented three arguments supporting and/or opposing EMI?	
Have you provided evidence to support your arguments, including examples?	
Have you included and, where appropriate, refuted counter-arguments?	
Does your conclusion restate your position?	
Does your conclusion contain an evaluative comment or a prediction for the future?	

EDIT

10 Use the Language checklist to edit your essay for language errors.

LANGUAGE CHECKLIST	✔
Have you used a variety of linking expressions to highlight examples?	
Have you used correct punctuation when introducing examples?	
Have you made predictions about the future using hedging expressions?	
Have you used appropriate language to acknowledge and refute counter-arguments?	
Have you checked that your sentences do not contain overgeneralizations?	

11 Make any necessary changes to your essay.

OBJECTIVES REVIEW

1 Check your learning objectives for this unit. Write *3, 2* or *1* for each objective.

   3 = very well   2 = well   1 = not so well

   I can ...

   watch and understand a video about languages in Ireland.   _____

   use background knowledge to annotate a text.   _____

   evaluate and synthesize arguments.   _____

   hedge predictions.   _____

   avoid overgeneralizations.   _____

   refute counter-arguments.   _____

   write a pros and cons essay.   _____

2 Go to the *Unlock* Online Workbook for more practice with this unit's learning objectives.

WORDLIST

be derived from (phr v)	displace (v)	it follows that (phr)
coexist (v)	disproportionate (adj)	misguided (adj)
cofounder (n)	distasteful (adj)	namely (adv) ⦿
coincide (v) ⦿	distort (v)	postdate (v)
collaborate (v)	endorse (v)	postgraduate (adj)
commodity (n) ⦿	enforce (v) ⦿	postpone (v)
commonly (adj) ⦿	equivalent (n) ⦿	postwar (adj) ⦿
conquer (v)	futile (adj)	precede (v)
cooperation (n) ⦿	incorporate (v) ⦿	preliminary (adj) ⦿
dialect (n) ⦿	interact (v) ⦿	presume (v)
dilution (n) ⦿	interaction (n) ⦿	stance (n) ⦿
disambiguation (n)	intercontinental (adj)	terminology (n) ⦿
discourage (v)	interface (n) ⦿	

⦿ = high-frequency words in the Cambridge Academic Corpus

GLOSSARY

⊙ = high-frequency words in the Cambridge Academic Corpus

Vocabulary	Pronunciation	Part of speech	Definition
UNIT 1			
adaptive ⊙	/əˈdæptɪv/	(adj)	having the ability to change when conditions change
affluent	/ˈæfluənt/	(adj)	having a lot of money or owning a lot of things
anonymous ⊙	/əˈnɒnɪməs/	(adj)	having no unusual or interesting features
compatible ⊙	/kəmˈpætəbəl/	(adj)	able to work successfully with something else
demolition	/ˌdeməˈlɪʃən/	(n)	the act of destroying something, such as a building
energy-efficient	/ˈenədʒiːˌfɪʃənt/	(adj)	using little electricity, gas, etc.
fast-growing	/ˌfɑːstˈɡrəʊɪŋ/	(adj)	used to describe activities, organizations, etc. that are getting bigger very quickly
irreversible	/ˌɪrɪˈvɜːsəbəl/	(adj)	not possible to change; impossible to return to a previous condition
longevity ⊙	/lɒnˈdʒevəti/	(n)	how long something lasts
long-term ⊙	/ˌlɒŋˈtɜːm/	(adj)	continuing a long time into the future
memorabilia	/ˌmemərəˈbɪliə/	(n)	a collection of items connected to a person or event
one-way	/ˌwʌnˈweɪ/	(adj)	travelling or allowing travel in only one direction
opt for	/ˈɒpt ˌfɔː/	(v)	to choose something, especially of one thing or possibility instead of others
out-of-date	/ˌaʊt əv ˈdeɪt/	(adj)	if clothes, colours, styles, etc. are out of date, they are old and not fashionable
practice ⊙	/ˈpræktɪs/	(n)	something that is usually or regularly done
prompt	/prɒmpt/	(v)	to make someone decide to do something
renovation	/ˌrenəˈveɪʃən/	(n)	the repair of a building to bring it into good condition
retrieve	/rɪˈtriːv/	(v)	to find and bring something back
scenario ⊙	/sɪˈnɑːriəʊ/	(n)	a description of a current or future situation
state-of-the-art	/ˌsteɪtəvðiːˈɑːt/	(adj)	very modern and using the most recent ideas and methods
vibrant	/ˈvaɪbrənt/	(adj)	lively and energetic
vulnerable ⊙	/ˈvʌlnərəbəl/	(adj)	not well protected; able to be harmed
well-known ⊙	/ˌwel ˈnəʊn/	(adj)	known or recognized by many people
UNIT 2			
anxiety ⊙	/æŋˈzaɪəti/	(n)	an uncomfortable feeling of nervousness or worry about something that is happening or might happen in the future
arouse	/əˈraʊz/	(v)	to make a person remember or feel a particular thing

Vocabulary	Pronunciation	Part of speech	Definition
associate 💿	/əˈsəʊsɪeɪt/	(v)	to connect somebody or something in your mind with somebody or something else
controversy 💿	/ˈkɒntrəvɜːsi / kənˈtrɒvəsi/	(n)	a lot of disagreement or argument about something, usually because it affects or is important to many people
convey 💿	/kənˈveɪ/	(v)	to express an idea so that it is understood by other people
criteria 💿	/kraɪˈtɪəriə/	(n)	standards used for judging something
curiosity	/kjʊəriˈɒsɪti/	(n)	an eager wish to know or learn about something
distinctive 💿	/dɪˈstɪŋktɪv/	(adj)	easy to recognize because it is different from other things
evocative	/ɪˈvɒkətɪv/	(adj)	making a person remember or feel a particular thing
evoke	/ɪˈvəʊk/	(v)	to make somebody remember something or feel an emotion
foremost	/ˈfɔːməʊst/	(adj)	best known or most important
generate 💿	/ˈdʒenəreɪt/	(v)	to cause something to exist
inspire	/ɪnˈspaɪə/	(v)	to make somebody have a particular strong feeling or reaction
opposition to	/ɒpəˈzɪʃən ˌtə/	(n)	disagreement with
outrage	/ˈaʊtreɪdʒ/	(n)	a feeling of anger and shock
provoke	/prəˈvəʊk/	(v)	to cause a reaction, especially a negative one
refine 💿	/rɪˈfaɪn/	(v)	to improve something by making small changes
reinforce 💿	/ˌriːɪnˈfɔːs/	(v)	to give support to something; to make stronger
resemble 💿	/rɪˈzembəl/	(v)	to look like or be like something
retain 💿	/rɪˈteɪn/	(v)	to keep; to continue having
stir up	/ˈstɜː ˌʌp/	(phr v)	to cause an unpleasant emotion or problem to begin or grow
strategic 💿	/strəˈtiːdʒɪk/	(adj)	helping to achieve a plan
subsequent 💿	/ˈsʌbsɪkwənt/	(adj)	next; happening after something else
suspicion	/səˈspɪʃən/	(n)	a belief or idea that something may be true
sustainable 💿	/səˈsteɪnəbəl/	(adj)	causing little or no damage to the environment and therefore able to continue for a long time

UNIT 3

abhorrent	/əˈbɒrənt/	(adj)	morally wrong; evil
abuse 💿	/əˈbjuːs/	(n)	the use of something in a way that is harmful or morally wrong; cruel, violent, or unfair treatment of someone; rude and offensive words said to another person
abusive	/əˈbjuːsɪv/	(adj)	rude and offensive; causing another person mental or physical harm
accountable	/əˈkaʊntəbəl/	(adj)	Somebody who is accountable is completely responsible for what they do and must be able to give a satisfactory reason for it.

Vocabulary	Pronunciation	Part of speech	Definition
anonymity	/ˌænɒnˈɪməti/	(n)	the situation in which somebody's name is not given or known
assemble	/əˈsembəl/	(v)	to bring people together in a single group
combat ◉	/ˈkɒmbæt/	(v)	to try to stop something unpleasant or harmful from happening or increasing
confront ◉	/kənˈfrʌnt/	(v)	to face, meet, or deal with a difficult situation or person
disturbing	/dɪˈstɜːbɪŋ/	(adj)	upsetting; causing worry
eliminate ◉	/iˈlɪmɪneɪt/	(v)	to remove; to get rid of completely
exhibit	/ɪgˈzɪbɪt/	(v)	to show something by your public behaviour, appearance, etc.
hostile ◉	/ˈhɒstaɪl/	(adj)	unfriendly; showing strong dislike
humiliation	/hjuːˌmɪliˈeɪʃən/	(n)	shame and loss of self-respect
insulting	/ɪnˈsʌltɪŋ/	(adj)	rude or offensive
malicious	/məˈlɪʃəs/	(adj)	intended to harm or upset other people
negative ◉	/ˈnegətɪv/	(adj)	not expecting good things, or likely to consider only the bad side of a situation
offensive	/əˈfensɪv/	(adj)	causing offence
precedent ◉	/ˈpresɪdənt/	(n)	an action or decision that becomes an example for future actions or decisions
prosecute	/ˈprɒsɪkjuːt/	(v)	to officially accuse somebody of committing a crime in a law court
regulate ◉	/ˈregjəleɪt/	(v)	to control an activity using rules or laws
resolve ◉	/rɪˈzɒlv/	(v)	to solve or end a problem or difficulty
run into	/ˈrʌn ˌɪntuː/	(phr v)	to experience something unexpectedly
threatening	/ˈθretənɪŋ/	(adj)	expressing a threat of something unpleasant or violent
withdraw	/wɪðˈdrɔː/	(v)	to stop participating

UNIT 4

accumulate	/əˈkjuːmjəleɪt/	(v)	to collect a large number of things over a long period of time
aspiring	/əˈspaɪərɪŋ/	(adj)	wishing to become successful
attainable	/əˈteɪnəbəl/	(adj)	possible to achieve
break even	/ˈbreɪk ˌiːvən/	(idiom)	to have no profit or loss at the end of a business activity
brick-and-mortar	/ˌbrɪk ən ˈmɔːtə/	(adj)	existing as a physical building, especially a shop, rather than doing business only on the internet
component ◉	/kəmˈpəʊnənt/	(n)	one of the parts of something
fluctuating	/ˈflʌktʃueɪtɪŋ/	(adj)	to change frequently from one level to another
follow suit	/ˈfɒləʊ ˌsuːt/	(idiom)	to do the same thing as someone else
generate revenue	/ˌdʒenəreɪt ˈrevənjuː/	(v phr)	to create a flow of money into a business by selling a product/service

Vocabulary	Pronunciation	Part of speech	Definition
incentive ⊙	/ɪnˈsentɪv/	(n)	something that encourages a person to do something
make a profit	/ˌmeɪk ə ˈprɒfɪt/	(v phr)	to create more revenue than the outgoings of a business
marketing tool	/ˈmɑːkɪtɪŋ ˌtuːl/	(n)	something that helps a business to inform customers about a product/service
on a large / small scale	/ɒn ə ˈlɑːdʒ/ˈsmɔːl ˌskeɪl/	(adv)	If we do something on a large/small scale, the activity is large/small in size.
ongoing ⊙	/ˈɒnˌɡəʊɪŋ/	(adj)	continuing to exist or develop, or happening at the present moment
outweigh	/ˌaʊtˈweɪ/	(v)	to be greater or more important than something else
pioneer	/ˌpaɪəˈnɪə/	(n)	a person who is one of the first people to do something
proposition ⊙	/ˌprɒpəˈzɪʃən/	(n)	a proposal or suggestion, especially in business
retention ⊙	/rɪˈtenʃən/	(n)	the ability of a company to keep its customers, employees, etc.
revenue ⊙	/ˈrevənjuː/	(n)	the money that a business receives regularly
shrewdly	/ˈʃruːdli/	(adv)	in a way that is based on a clear understanding and good judgment of a situation, resulting in an advantage
start-up costs	/ˈstɑːtʌp ˌkɒsts/	(n)	the amount of money needed to start an organization, a business, a piece of work, etc.
track record	/ˈtræk ˌrekɔːd/	(n)	all the achievements or failures that somebody or something has had in the past
transition ⊙	/trænˈzɪʃən/	(n)	a change from one form or type to another
utility bills	/juːˈtɪləti ˌbɪlz/	(n pl)	bills to be paid for services used by the public, such as an electricity, water or gas supply

UNIT 5

Vocabulary	Pronunciation	Part of speech	Definition
arrive at	/əˈraɪv ˌæt/	(phr v)	to reach an agreement, decision, etc.
attribute to	/əˈtrɪbjuːt ˌtə/	(phr v)	to say that something is caused by something else
cognition ⊙	/kɒɡˈnɪʃən/	(n)	the use of conscious mental processes
conduct a study	/kənˈdʌkt ə ˌstʌdi/	(v phr)	to do academic research, such as an experiment
conformity	/kənˈfɔːməti/	(n)	behaviour that follows the usual standards that are expected by a group or society
constrain	/kənˈstreɪn/	(v)	to limit something
contend	/kənˈtend/	(v)	to claim
contradictory ⊙	/ˌkɒntrəˈdɪktəri/	(adj)	If two or more ideas, pieces of advice, etc. are contradictory, they are very different or opposite to each other.
control group	/kənˈtrəʊl ˌɡruːp/	(n)	participants in an experiment who do not receive experimental treatment
emulate	/ˈemjəleɪt/	(v)	to try to do something as well as somebody else does it by copying their approach

Vocabulary	Pronunciation	Part of speech	Definition
establish a causal link	/ɪˈstæblɪʃ ə ˌkɔːzəl lɪŋk/	(v phr)	to show a cause-and-effect connection
experimental group	/ɪksperɪˈmentəl ˌgruːp/	(n)	participants in an experiment who receive experimental treatment
genius	/ˈdʒiːniəs/	(n)	someone with great and rare natural ability
implications ⊙	/ˌɪmplɪˈkeɪʃənz/	(n)	conclusions suggested by the results of an academic study
intervention ⊙	/ˌɪntəˈvenʃən/	(n)	action taken to deal with a problem
label ⊙	/ˈleɪbəl/	(v)	to assign a (usually negative) characteristic to somebody or something
norm ⊙	/nɔːm/	(n)	accepted standard or way of doing something
reproduce ⊙	/ˌriːprəˈdʒuːs/	(v)	to do or make again
research subjects	/rɪˈsɜːtʃ ˌsʌbdʒɪkts/	(n)	all the participants in an experiment
stimulation ⊙	/ˌstɪmjəˈleɪʃən/	(n)	an action that causes somebody to become active, interested or enthusiastic
suppress ⊙	/səˈpres/	(v)	to prevent something from being expressed or known
trait ⊙	/treɪt/	(n)	a particular characteristic that can produce a particular type of behaviour
trauma ⊙	/ˈtrɔːmə/	(n)	severe emotional shock or physical injury that affects you for a long time

UNIT 6

Vocabulary	Pronunciation	Part of speech	Definition
ambiguity ⊙	/ˌæmbɪˈgjuːəti/	(n)	the state of being unclear or having more than one possible meaning
assert ⊙	/əˈsɜːt/	(v)	to say that something is certainly true
assertive ⊙	/əˈsɜːtɪv/	(adj)	forceful; bold and confident
chronic ⊙	/ˈkrɒnɪk/	(adj)	lasting for a long time, especially of a disease something bad
comprise ⊙	/kəmˈpraɪz/	(v)	to have things or people as parts or members; to consist of
dispute ⊙	/dɪˈspjuːt/	(v)	to disagree with an idea, a fact, etc.
earning power	/ˈɜːnɪŋ ˌpaʊə/	(n)	the ability of a person to earn money or of a company to make a profit
entry level	/ˈentri ˌlevəl/	(n, adj)	(at or relating to) the lowest level of an organization, type of work
expertise ⊙	/ˌekspɜːˈtiːz/	(n)	a high level of knowledge or skill
founder ⊙	/ˈfaʊndə/	(n)	somebody who establishes an organization
illustration ⊙	/ˌɪləˈstreɪʃən/	(n)	an example that explains something
job market	/ˈdʒɒb ˌmɑːkɪt/	(n)	the number of jobs that are available in a particular place or for a particular type of work
labour ⊙	/ˈleɪbə/	(n)	workers, especially people who do practical work with their hands
labour force	/ˈleɪbə ˌfɔːs/	(n)	all the people in a particular country who are of the right age to work, or all the people who work for a particular company
mismatch	/ˌmɪsˈmætʃ/	(n)	things that do not work well together

Vocabulary	Pronunciation	Part of speech	Definition
multiple ⊙	/'mʌltɪpəl/	(adj)	very many of the same type, or of different types
persistent ⊙	/pə'sɪstənt/	(adj)	(of a problem) lasting for a long time, difficult to resolve
placement rate	/'pleɪsmənt ˌreɪt/	(n)	the percentage of graduating students who obtain employment within a determined timeframe after receiving their degree or certificate
pose ⊙	/pəʊz/	(v)	to cause something, especially a problem or difficulty
prospective ⊙	/prə'spektɪv/	(adj)	wanted or expected to do a particular thing in the future
training scheme	/'treɪnɪŋ ˌskiːm/	(n)	an officially organized plan or system to teach the skills you need to do a particular job or activity
work-life balance	/ˌwɜːk 'laɪf 'bæləns/	(n phr)	the amount of time you spend doing your job compared with the amount of time you spend with your family and doing things you enjoy

UNIT 7

Vocabulary	Pronunciation	Part of speech	Definition
access ⊙	/'ækses/	(n)	the method or possibility of getting near to a place or person
access ⊙	/'ækses/	(v)	to use a service or get into a place or file of data
accessible ⊙	/ək'sesəbəl/	(adj)	easy to get, reach or understand
bacteria ⊙	/bæk'tɪəriə/	(n pl)	a type of very small organism that lives in air, earth, water, plants, and animals, often one that causes disease
bacterial ⊙	/bæk'tɪəriəl/	(adj)	caused by or relating to a type of very small organism that lives in air, earth, water, plants, and animals, often one that causes disease
confined to	/kən'faɪnd ˌtə/	(phr)	to exist only in a particular area or group of people
counter ⊙	/'kaʊntə/	(v)	to defend yourself against something
detection ⊙	/dɪ'tekʃən/	(n)	identification; diagnosis; discovery
domesticated	/də'mestɪkeɪtɪd/	(adj)	(for animals) under human control
drive ⊙	/draɪv/	(n)	a planned effort to achieve something
emergence ⊙	/ɪ'mɜːdʒəns/	(n)	the fact of something becoming known or starting to exist
enable	/ɪ'neɪbəl/	(v)	to make someone able to do something, or to make something possible
eradicate	/ɪ'rædɪkeɪt/	(v)	to get rid of something completely
facilitate ⊙	/fə'sɪlɪteɪt/	(v)	to make something possible or easier
fuel ⊙	/fjʊəl/	(v)	something that fuels a situation makes it stronger, worse, etc.
grim	/grɪm/	(adj)	worrying, without hope
infect ⊙	/ɪn'fekt/	(v)	to pass a disease to a person, animal, or plant

Vocabulary	Pronunciation	Part of speech	Definition
infection	/ɪnˈfekʃən/	(n)	a disease in a part of your body that is caused by bacteria or a virus
infectious	/ɪnˈfekʃəs/	(adj)	(of a disease) able to be passed from one person, animal, or plant to another
mutant	/ˈmjuːtənt/	(adj)	showing changes as a result of mutation
mutant	/ˈmjuːtənt/	(n)	an organism that is different from others of its type because of a permanent change in its genes
mutate	/mjuːˈteɪt/	(v)	to develop new physical characteristics because of a permanent change in the genes
mutation	/mjuːˈteɪʃən/	(n)	the way in which genes change and produce permanent differences; a permanent change in an organism, or the changed organism itself
phase out	/ˌfeɪz ˈaʊt/	(phr v)	to stop using something gradually or in stages
prevent ⊙	/prɪˈvent/	(v)	to stop something from happening or someone from doing something
preventable	/prɪˈventəbəl/	(adj)	able to be prevented
preventative	/prɪˈventətɪv/	(adj)	intended to stop something before it happens
prevention	/prɪˈvenʃən/	(n)	the act of stopping something from happening in the future by taking action now
problematic ⊙	/ˌprɒbləˈmætɪk/	(adj)	full of difficulties that need to be dealt with
promote ⊙	/prəˈməʊt/	(v)	to encourage people to like, buy, use, do or support something
proximity ⊙	/prɒkˈsɪməti/	(n)	the state of being nearby
resist ⊙	/rɪˈzɪst/	(v)	to fight against something or someone that is attacking you
resistance ⊙	/rɪˈzɪstəns/	(n)	(Biology, Medicine) the ability of harmful bacteria to fight against drugs designed to destroy them
resistant ⊙	/rɪˈzɪstənt/	(adj)	not harmed or affected by something
revolutionize	/ˌrevəˈluːʃənaɪz/	(v)	to completely change something
surge	/sɜːdʒ/	(v)	a sudden, large increase
therapy ⊙	/ˈθerəpi/	(n)	a treatment that helps someone feel better, grow stronger, etc., especially after an illness
therapeutic	/θerəˈpjuːtɪk/	(adj)	causing someone to be more healthy
thrive	/θraɪv/	(v)	to live and develop successfully
transmission ⊙	/trænzˈmɪʃən/	(v)	the process of passing something from one person or place to another
transmit	/trænzˈmɪt/	(v)	to pass something from one person or place to another
transmittable	/trænzˈmɪtəbəl/	(adj)	able to be passed or sent from one person, thing, or place to another
viral	/ˈvaɪərəl/	(adj)	caused by a virus
virus	/ˈvaɪərəs/	(n)	an extremely small piece of organic material that causes disease in humans, animals and plants

Vocabulary	Pronunciation	Part of speech	Definition
UNIT 8			
accomplish	/əˈkʌmplɪʃ/	(v)	to do something successfully
amass	/əˈmæs/	(v)	to get a large amount of something, by collecting it over a long period
apparently 𝗼	/əˈpærəntli/	(adv)	used to say you have read or been told something although you are not certain it is true
coordinate 𝗼	/kəʊˈɔːdɪneɪt/	(v)	to make separate things or people work well together
detract from	/dɪˈtrækt ˌfrəm/	(phr v)	to make something worse
differentiate 𝗼	/ˌdɪfəˈrenʃieɪt/	(v)	to show or find the difference between one thing and others
distraction	/dɪˈstrækʃən/	(n)	something that prevents somebody from giving full attention to something else
enhance 𝗼	/ɪnˈhɑːns/	(v)	to improve the quality of something
exclusively 𝗼	/ɪkˈskluːsɪvli/	(adv)	only; limited to a specific thing, person or group
fairly 𝗼	/ˈfeəli/	(adv)	more than average, but less than very
for the most part	/fɔːr də ˈməʊst ˌpɑːt/	(adv phr)	mostly
fundamental 𝗼	/ˌfʌndəˈmentəl/	(adj)	basic, being the thing on which other things depend
gesture 𝗼	/ˈdʒestʃə/	(n)	a movement of the body or a body part to express an idea or feeling
isolate 𝗼	/ˈaɪsəleɪt/	(v)	to separate something from other connected things
more or less	/ˈmɔːr ə ˌles/	(phr)	mostly
peak 𝗼	/piːk/	(v)	to reach the highest or strongest point of value or skill
primarily 𝗼	/praɪˈmerɪli/	(adv)	mostly
relatively 𝗼	/ˈrelətɪvli/	(adv)	quite good, bad, etc. in comparison with other similar things or with what you expect
sensitivity 𝗼	/ˌsensɪˈtɪvəti/	(n)	the ability to understand how other people feel
somewhat 𝗼	/ˈsʌmwɒt/	(adv)	to some degree
stem from	/ˈstem ˌfrɒm/	(phr v)	to develop as the result of something
tend 𝗼	/tend/	(v)	to be likely to behave in a particular way or have a particular characteristic
typically 𝗼	/ˈtɪpɪkəli/	(adv)	used when you are giving an average or usual example of a particular thing
underlie 𝗼	/ˌʌndəˈlaɪ/	(v)	to be the cause of or a strong influence on something
voice 𝗼	/vɔɪs/	(v)	to say what you think about something

Vocabulary	Pronunciation	Part of speech	Definition
UNIT 9			
acknowledge ⊙	/ək'nɒlɪdʒ/	(v)	to accept or admit that something is true (often unwillingly)
advocate ⊙	/'ædvəkət/	(n)	a person who publicly supports an idea or cause
aid ⊙	/eɪd/	(n)	a piece of equipment that helps you to do something
assert ⊙	/ə'sɜːt/	(v)	to say that something is certainly true
claim ⊙	/kleɪm/	(v)	to say that something is true without sufficient proof
conclude ⊙	/kən'kluːd/	(v)	to decide something based on the results of a study, reasoned argument, etc.
domain ⊙	/də'meɪn/	(n)	a field, area of knowledge, etc. belonging to or controlled by a particular person or group of people
embrace ⊙	/ɪm'breɪs/	(v)	to enthusiastically accept new ideas or methods
engaging ⊙	/ɪn'geɪdʒɪŋ/	(adj)	attracting and maintaining interest
hazard ⊙	/'hæzəd/	(n)	something that is dangerous and likely to cause damage
immersive	/ɪ'mɜːsɪv/	(adj)	seeming to surround the audience, player, etc. so that they feel completely involved
inspect	/ɪn'spekt/	(v)	to examine carefully
interpretation ⊙	/ɪn,tɜːprə'teɪʃən/	(n)	translation of one language into another
maintain ⊙	/meɪn'teɪn/	(v)	to express firmly your belief that something is true
manipulate ⊙	/mə'nɪpjəleɪt/	(v)	to control something using your hands
novelty	/'nɒvəlti/	(n)	the quality of being new or unusual
numerous ⊙	/'njuːmərəs/	(adj)	many, multiple
observe ⊙	/əb'zɜːv/	(v)	to notice or identify something during a study
projection ⊙	/prə'dʒekʃən/	(n)	an image displayed by a device onto a separate screen or another surface
simultaneous ⊙	/,sɪməl'teɪniəs/	(adj)	happening or being done at exactly the same time
state ⊙	/steɪt/	(v)	to present an idea or a fact clearly in speech or writing
suggest ⊙	/sə'dʒest/	(v)	to communicate or show an idea or feeling without stating it directly or giving proof
superimpose	/,suːpərɪm'pəʊz/	(v)	to put an image, words, etc. on top of something else, so that what is in the lower position can still be seen
supplement ⊙	/'sʌplɪmənt/	(v)	to add something to something else in order to improve it

Vocabulary	Pronunciation	Part of speech	Definition
UNIT 10			
be derived from	/biː dɪˈraɪvd ˌfrɒm/	(phr v)	to come from a particular origin
coexist	/kəʊɪgˈzɪst/	(v)	to live together in the same place or at the same time
cofounder	/ˈkəʊfaʊndə/	(n)	someone who establishes an organization with somebody else
coincide ⊙	/kəʊɪnˈsaɪd/	(v)	to happen at or near the same time
collaborate	/kəˈlæbəreɪt/	(v)	to work with someone else for a special purpose
commodity ⊙	/kəˈmɒdəti/	(n)	product you can buy or sell
commonly ⊙	/ˈkɒmənli/	(adj)	frequently, usually
conquer	/ˈkɒŋkə/	(v)	to take control of a country or defeat by war
cooperation ⊙	/kəʊɒpərˈeɪʃən/	(n)	the act of working together with someone or doing what they ask you
dialect ⊙	/ˈdaɪəlekt/	(n)	a local, usually spoken, form of a language
dilution ⊙	/daɪˈluːʃən/	(n)	the process of making the content of something weaker
disambiguation	/dɪsæmˈbɪgjueɪʃən/	(n)	the action of changing something in order to make its meaning absolutely clear
discourage	/dɪˈskʌrɪdʒ/	(v)	to make someone feel less confident, enthusiastic, and positive about something, or less willing to do something
displace	/dɪˈspleɪs/	(v)	to force somebody or something out of its usual position
disproportionate	/dɪsprəˈpɔːʃənət/	(adj)	not the right amount in relation to something else
distasteful	/dɪsˈteɪstfəl/	(adj)	unpleasant or unacceptable
distort	/dɪˈstɔːt/	(v)	to change something so that it is false or wrong
endorse	/ɪnˈdɔːs/	(v)	to publicly support
enforce ⊙	/ɪnˈfɔːs/	(v)	to make people obey something or do something
equivalent ⊙	/ɪˈkwɪvələnt/	(n)	something that has the same value, meaning, etc. as something else
futile	/ˈfjuːtaɪl/	(adj)	having no effect or achieving nothing
incorporate ⊙	/ɪnˈkɔːpəreɪt/	(v)	to include something as part of something else
interact ⊙	/ɪntəˈrækt/	(v)	to communicate with or react to
interaction	/ɪntəˈrækʃən/	(n)	an occasion when two or more people or things communicate with or react to each other
intercontinental	/ɪntəkɒntɪˈnentəl/	(adj)	between continents
interface ⊙	/ˈɪntəfeɪs/	(n)	a connection between two pieces of electronic equipment, or between a person and a computer

Vocabulary	Pronunciation	Part of speech	Definition
it follows that	/ɪt ˈfɒləʊz ˌðæt/	(phr)	used to say: if one thing is true, then another thing is true
misguided	/ˌmɪsˈgaɪdɪd/	(adj)	based on an incorrect understanding
namely ⊙	/ˈneɪmli/	(adv)	used when you want to give more detail or be more exact about something you have just said
postdate	/pəʊstˈdeɪt/	(v)	to happen after a particular time or event
postgraduate	/pəʊstˈgrædʒuət/	(adj)	relating to education undertaken after achieving a first degree
postpone	/pəʊstˈpəʊn/	(v)	to delay an event until a later date or time
postwar ⊙	/ˈpəʊstwɔː/	(adj)	happening or existing in the period after a war
precede	/prɪˈsiːd/	(v)	to be or go before something or somebody in time or space
preliminary ⊙	/prɪˈlɪmɪnəri/	(adj)	happening before a more major event or action
presume	/prɪˈzjuːm/	(v)	to believe something to be true because it is very likely, although you are not certain
stance ⊙	/stɑːns/	(n)	a publicly held point of view
terminology ⊙	/ˌtɜːmɪˈnɒlədʒi/	(n)	words and phrases used for a particular subject

VIDEO SCRIPTS

UNIT 1

▶ Preserving CDs at the Library of Congress

Reporter: The CD is now a collector's item, replaced by digital downloads. But those who built up music libraries in the eighties and nineties may wonder 'How long will those discs work?' – something Fenella France and her team are hoping to figure out.

Fenella France: You can see this one, it looks pretty good.

Reporter: Right.

France: And then this one …

Reporter: Oh my! France is the Chief of Preservation Research and Testing at the Library of Congress.

France: So we've kind of lost the entire reflective layer off of this one.

Reporter: Same CD?

France: Same CD.

Reporter: Produced at the same time.

Reporter: She and her colleagues are studying CDs like this one so they can better understand how to keep them safe for posterity. It turns out not all of the biggest challenges in preserving history involve documents that are centuries old. One would think 'Oh, I need to worry about the parchment or the paper degrading.' Not the things from 20 years ago.

France: That's correct, and that's a challenge, I think. We've always focused on traditional material, so to speak.

Reporter: How long a CD will last is not as simple as how old it is. Different manufacturers use different methods with vastly different results when it comes to durability.

France: We'd like to be able to say 'These particular discs or this specific time, these are the absolute ones at risk.' We don't know how people have stored or used them over time, so all of those factors – the use, the handling, the environment – all come into play in terms of the longevity.

Reporter: Which is where the idea of accelerated ageing comes in. The CDs are actually cooked in these chambers, and by manipulating the humidity and the temperature, the discs can be aged a certain number of years. The only thing that's different is how you've artificially aged them.

France: They were aged under the same conditions. One survived, one did not. So that's the challenge we have, that you never quite know how it's going to affect your CD.

Reporter: And if you want to preserve your CD collection at home, here's a few tips.

France: Probably don't put any nice fancy labels onto the top of CDs.

Reporter: And fair warning, you want to avoid those Sharpies.

France: There are some pens that they say don't cause any damage. There's a little piece in the centre of the disc, and if you need to, just write on that centre region.

Reporter: As for preserving the library's collection, France and her team plan to test the CDs every three to five years to make sure as little as possible is lost to history.

UNIT 2

▶ The role of Helvetica font in graphic design

Man: So, this is what I'm talking about. This is, uh, *Life* magazine, 1953. One ad after another in here – it just kind of shows every single visual bad habit that was, like, endemic in those days. You've got, uh, you know, zany hand lettering everywhere. Exclamation points, exclamation points, exclamation points! Cursive wedding invitation typography down here reading, 'Almost everyone appreciates the best'. Uh, this was everywhere in the fifties. This is how everything looked in the fifties. You cut to, um – this is after Helvetica was in full swing – same product. No people, no smiling fakery. Just a beautiful, big glass of ice-cold Coke. The slogan underneath: 'It's the real thing. Period. Coke. Period'. In Helvetica. Period. Any questions? Of course not. Drink Coke. Period. Simple.

Leslie Savan: Governments and corporations love Helvetica because, on one hand, it makes them seem neutral and efficient; but also, it's the smoothness of the letters makes them seem almost human. That is a quality they all want to convey because, of course, they have the image they're always fighting – that they are authoritarian, they're bureaucratic, you lose yourself in them, they're oppressive. So instead, by using Helvetica, they can come off seeming more accessible, transparent and accountable.

UNIT 3

▶ The Safer Internet campaign

Reporter: Charlotte Thomas was 11 years old when she was first bullied online; now she's 22. The bullying hasn't stopped.

Charlotte Thomas: There's a lot of people online who will post nasty things and they're happy enough to do it behind a screen but they'd never have the courage to say it to someone's face. So the internet makes it very easy for people to do that, especially because you can make fake accounts as well so people might know… not know that it's actually you who's doing that so it is too easy for people to bully others online, I think.

Reporter: The Safer Internet campaign, in its seventh year, wants to change that.

Kevin Gourlay: The children today is to ... they can ... they can try and counter this by, erm, understanding the profiles on social media, understand who their friends are. When something untoward happens if somebody was to say something nasty to you on a ... on a chat room or a social media site you can record it these days.

Reporter: This year it's focusing on images and videos, rather than written messages.

Thomas: The main bully in particular, she posted an unflattering photo of me at my desk on her Facebook and put it as her profile picture and despite asking her personally, asking her teacher to get involved, and asking Facebook to get involved, that photo is still on that girl's profile.

Speaker 1: It's changing the way we see ourselves.

Reporter: The Safer Internet Day is supported by more than a thousand organizations including Sky, which owns Sky News. Recently Sky Academy ran a workshop for young people at its west London studios.

Student 1: You're just cautious with what you say, because sometimes people don't think about what they type and they just send it and it could offend someone, but if you think about what you're saying you can stop yourself from saying something else.

Reporter: And the campaign has backing from politicians too.

Nicola Sturgeon: For me the policies, I think, have to be rooted in education. I think we've got to use schools to try to raise awareness of the dangers of the internet but also give young people the skills that they need to deal with those dangers and we're talking to young people just now with the view to updating our Safe Internet Action Plan for young people because the internet is a great thing, it's a really really powerful er ... tool and everybody should be able to enjoy it safely.

Reporter: The way we live online is constantly changing; the last few years have seen a surge in images and video. Staying safe online needs to keep up to date too.

UNIT 4

▶ Small Business Saturday

Narrator: Visit any UK high street or market place and you will find an array of specialist shops, from fishmongers to craft boutiques, coffee shops to fashion stalls.

Small businesses are at the heart of Britain's economy. There are 5.2 million small businesses in the UK, employing over 12 million people. A third of all purchases in the private sector are made at small firms. Today, on Small Business Saturday, the retailers are bustling with customers, encouraged to go out and explore their unique offerings.

The event takes place on the first Saturday in December every year. Last year over three-quarters of a billion pounds were taken at the tills on Small Business Saturday alone.

David Young, an adviser to the government on business and enterprise, says there has never been a better time to start your own small business.

David Young: We live in a country where over 19 out of 20 firms employ fewer than 10; we have far more people working for themselves now than we've ever had in our past before, and if you look ahead, it's going to be a small firm's world.

Narrator: But many small business owners feel that times for them are challenging.

Eve recently started her business for just £50 and is struggling to keep afloat.

Eve: The money I have last week I pay because they gave me the opportunity to open the shop without, erm deposit, just paying, every week I have to pay £200 that's for the week, you start, then you pay, so every week, Friday, I have to pay £200.

Narrator: Business rates – the taxes that business owners pay on their premises – are a major cost that many would like to see reduced for smaller businesses. Jamie runs the family greengrocer's. His dad sold the family home to start the business ten years ago.

Jamie: We could do with a little bit more than just a basic relief rate from the, erm, business rates really, 'cause I mean, em, we pay a lot for business rates but we don't actually get much for it. We sweep up ourselves, we have to clear up, we have to get rid of our own waste, there's no help towards that. Effectively, all we're paying for is the road to be swept.

Narrator: Kate, who has a craft shop, pays £7,000 a year in business rates on top of her rent. The tax is calculated according to the size of her shop.

Kate: It's a huge chunk; it's over half of what our rent is, to be here, so we do get a small discount on the rates because it's worked out on square footage, but we're quite a big premises for a small business so we don't get as much discount as, say, some smaller stores would do, but it works out at just around seven, seven and half thousand pounds a year.

Narrator: Business experts agree that there are ways to make life easier for small UK firms.

Expert: The majority of businesses in the UK are small, and to start to be able to become medium–large businesses they need help at the bottom level. So ways to find this help in terms of access to finance, but also ways to cut the regulatory burden as well, are critical.

Narrator: Small Business Saturday has been a great success today here in Claygate. But such events are just part of what is needed to keep the heart of Britain's economy beating in the years ahead.

UNIT 5

▶ Lego artist Nathan Sawaya

Narrator: Modelling bricks, such as Lego, are an irresistible toy for many children. But just what is it that makes the brightly coloured blocks so popular? Psychologists say their appeal lies in the ease with which a child can get started on building models from their imaginations. A box of Lego is a chaos of endless possibilities. It doesn't take any particular physical skill to get started and a child can build, change their ideas, undo and rebuild.

And Lego is not just a creative medium for children. New York artist Nathan Sawaya's work has been shown in galleries around the world. His models prove that ultimately, Lego is a three dimensional paint-box, only limited by your vision and imagination.

Nathan: Well, my name is Nathan Sawaya I am a brick artist. Er we're in my art studio, here in New York City.

Well my art studio, err … holds about 1.5 million bricks at any given time and then as I'm working on pieces I just pull from inventory. Err, some of the larger projects I did a billboard in, err … in Hollywood that used, err, over 500,000 individual pieces.

Err, I did, er, a *Tyrannosaurus Rex* skeleton; it measures 20 feet long so that's one of the largest pieces I've ever done. That's currently on tour in Australia.

So just depends, you know, a life-size human form is going to use about 20,000–30,000 bricks per project.

I used to practise corporate law here in New York City and I would spend 80 hours a week in a boardroom negotiating contracts and I found that at the end of the day I would need some sort of creative release. Sometimes it was painting, sometimes it was drawing and sometimes it was sculpting and I found I enjoyed sculpting with Lego bricks, err, and so, err, I eventually would leave the law firm to create art full time out of Lego. I opened the art studio here in New York and, err, left the law firm all behind to become a full-time artist.

Well the process is fairly straightforward. Err, gravity forces me to work up, err, so, er, as I build, err, I do put a little bit of glue and then, err, add the brick. There you go! Well I've got a lot going on lately, erm … I've been receiving several commissions from all over the world which keeps it interesting. I think one of the great parts of my job is that I … every morning I check my email

and I get requests from all sorts of people. Some I take on, some I don't but it keeps it very interesting.

Well the works sell for $10,000–20,000 generally. Some of the larger pieces have sold for more than that. The largest, err … I did sell a piece for six figures. Just amazing.

UNIT 6

▶ Vocational training

Nick Sinetti: I don't really dig the second shift, but you've got to start somewhere.

Reporter: Despite the worst job market in decades, listen to what 20-year-old Nick Sinetti found right out of high school. How many offers did you get?

Sinetti: Um, three, I think.

Reporter: Three offers?

Sinetti: Right.

Reporter: He graduated in 2009 as a certified welder from a career and technical education high school, or what used to be called vocational education. He now works for Air Products in Allentown, Pennsylvania. Of the 7,500 employees that you have here in the United States, how many are, what you would say, are the skilled workers?

John McGlade: 4,000.

Reporter: John McGlade is president and CEO of Air Products. His global company designs and builds high-tech hydrogen equipment and devices. How worried are you that you won't find enough skilled workers in the future?

McGlade: I'm worried. I've been worried.

Reporter: McGlade says he hires about 550 US workers a year. Three hundred and sixty are technically skilled positions that require two years of college or advanced certification. These positions can often go unfilled for 12 months.

McGlade: You need people who are electronics experts, who are instrument technicians, who are mechanics that can work on today's modern equipment.

Reporter: But, this year, funding for vocational education was cut by $140 million, and President Obama is proposing a 20% cut next year. What is your, sort of, biggest fear if there isn't this continued support for vo-tech education?

McGlade: Without the support and without the continued development of the skilled workforce, um, we're not going to be able to fill the jobs.

Reporter: Lehigh Career and Technical Institute would be impacted as well; five per cent of its budget comes from federal grants.

Teacher: 24 divided by 1.5E, you've got to tell us—

Reporter: The school trains about 3,000 students from across the Lehigh Valley. According to the National Association of Career and Technical Schools, these students can earn about $26 an hour more than similar students in non-technical fields.

McGlade: There's going to be more and more of those skilled jobs available that are going to be well paying and be a sustainable career for years and years to come.

Reporter: A career path that McGlade estimates will need 10 million more skilled workers over the next decade.

UNIT 7

▶ Growing concerns over antibiotic usage and resistance

Commentator: Matthew Hawksley from Cambridgeshire developed an MRSA infection after being treated in hospital for injuries resulting from a diving accident. Antibiotics saved his life.

Matthew Hawksley: There was cause for major concern as to whether I'd survive and that, and I was pumped full of antibiotics to help, um, help me counter the MRSA. It seems to have done a good job because I'm still here.

Commentator: But, due to increases in the use of the drugs across medicine and agriculture, bacteria have evolved ways to defend themselves.

Scientist: And what experiment you gonna do, Amelia?

Commentator: One of the British scientists who put the report together says that warnings about antibiotic resistance have been ignored for too long.

Scientist: There's been very much a sense of, err, you know, crying wolf over this: you know, academics, microbiologists, doctors have been saying this is going to happen for over ten years and really no one's taken any notice of this. And certainly academic discovery and research in finding new treatments or what could be the basis for new treatments has been hampered by a lack of funding.

Commentator: In September, the UK published its five-year strategy to slow the spread of antibiotic resistance. It hopes to ensure antibiotics are not overused to treat both humans and animals, to create a sustainable supply of effective new drugs and treatments through research and development, and to change public attitudes from being seen as a 'cure-all' to a 'last resort' medicine – through education and training.

At this laboratory in Norwich, scientists are wrestling with the problem of just how to handle the threat of antibiotic resistance. And they're going back to nature in search of answers.

Scientist 2: Plants have a distinct disadvantage as they can't move out of the way of predators – and they have no end of pred ... predators: large animals, small animals, insects, bacteria ... so they produce a whole array of chemicals to defend themselves. Can we use those chemicals and harness them for our own usage as clinical antibiotics? That's the hypothesis that we're trying to investigate.

Commentator: The message from scientists is clear – people have seen antibiotics as the answer to everything for too long. The challenge now is to find a new solution and fast.

UNIT 8

▶ Behind the scenes look at the RAF Red Arrows

Narrator: At the Royal Air Force base in Scampton, UK – these are the unique Hawk jets of the Red Arrows – an elite team of RAF pilots, engineers and vital support staff.

It takes over 120 people to bring together the Red Arrows' spectacular aerobatic displays. Our report catches up with the team during their preparations for the summer months.

Reporter: In the skies above Lincolnshire the Red Arrows soar and swoop, honing the precision moves they've become so famous for – the man out front: Red One.

Red One: It's an absolute dream job to get, and to sit in the front of, er, such a capable team. Not just the pilots, but all of the personnel that work on the Red Arrows – highly trained, highly skilled and really motivated to do a good job.

Commentator: Now the nine aircraft he leads are being given a makeover. This is the first time the new-look tailfin has been seen, the first permanent change to the design since the Red Arrows were formed in 1964, but it'll be months before being displayed to the public.

Journalist: It's now during the winter months that the hard work is done with up to five training sorties flown each day to make sure that every single performance is perfect come the summer. When it's as windy as this it's even tougher for the pilots.

Commentator: It is also the time for vital engineering work. Corporal Drew Paxton is one of the exclusive circus engineers, picked to travel to displays in the seat behind the pilot.

Drew Paxton: The engineers as a whole on the squadron are the lifeline, the lifeblood of the squadron and if we don't have them then we can't do anything.

Commentator: Everything must be checked meticulously including the potentially lifesaving kit worn by the pilots.

Pilot 2: Err, the G-trousers, once I start pulling G, will start to inflate. Err, my muscles in my legs have to tense against them. Now when they tense against it, erm, the blood doesn't pool in my legs and it will stay in my torso. So now that makes it easier for me to work to keep the blood pumping to my head.

Commentator: But there will always be danger. In 2011 two pilots from the aerobatic team died in separate incidents: getting everything right is crucial. It means a debrief after every flight.

Red One: You've got to do something about your technique.

Commentator: It costs £9,000,000 a year to keep the fast jets flying, too high a cost for some, but this summer they will perform 80 times, ambassadors for Britain as they speed towards a further 50 years of unmatched aerobatics.

UNIT 9

▶ Phone Hacking

Presenter: Mobile phones have changed enormously over the last 25 years. It's really funny to think that this was a social trophy, particularly because the early models only delivered 30 minutes' talk time. And because they were analogue, with the right equipment, it was quite easy to eavesdrop on people's conversations. But we all know about the recent phone hacking scandals. Are today's multitasking smartphones any safer than those old bricks? Tom and Oliver are cybersecurity experts. They specialize in securing the phones of celebrities. And they know the smartphone's weak spot isn't so much voicemail as when it's surfing the net. While I'm out and about and using my mobile, or my iPad, or whatever ... how could I be putting myself at risk?

Oliver: Your phone will transmit data in two ways. One of them is over 3G network – and generally it's very secure. Wi-Fi, on the other hand, is very susceptible to hackers. There's two primary ways they do this. One of them is setting up what we call a bait network. We're sat in a café here; they may set up a fake Wi-Fi network and call it the same as the café we're sat in. The other way is to monitor what phones in the area are looking for. Phones are constantly looking for networks they've previously connected to. So if you've got a Wi-Fi network called Maggie's Home when you're at home, potentially a hacker could see that request for it, and imitate that network to attract your phone to connect.

Presenter: Using specialist equipment, Tom can easily detect those Wi-Fi request signals. In just seconds, he's collected a huge list, from every person's phone in this shopping centre. So, for instance, here, you've got

number 11: now that's obviously someone who lives at number 11. If you were to set up a fake network called number 11, then that means that that phone would connect to it.

Tom: Yeah, once you've got control of that connection, then any data going from that phone, through your network and then out to the internet, is, uh, up for grabs. So you can see that data, and you can manipulate that data and perform attacks on that data.

Oliver: And what we're seeing is people harvesting login details, for social media, for email accounts, and then using that information. Uh, and often, people use the same username and passwords for several different accounts. So once you've got one, for something on a social media site, that could potentially result in some security risks.

Presenter: The first thing I'm going to do is to reunite you with your mobile phones. I've got something of a confession to make here, because we have just spent the last couple of hours trying to hack into your mobile phones – and we did very well. Harry, we've seen all of your Instagram pictures. Electra, we know exactly what you've been up to. But just to show you, Charlie, could you just look at your Facebook profile?

Charlie: *Bang Goes the Theory* is my new favourite show. And I have a profile picture change.

Presenter: Is that your normal picture?

Charlie: No.

Presenter: That was relatively easy to do, wasn't it?

Oliver: Yeah, it was. A real hacker would take that information away, spend a day analyzing it, and even after months, they can still log in as you, using the packets of data that they've captured during that time that you were using that infected Wi-Fi network.

Presenter: How do they make sure that they do keep their personal data personal?

Oliver: Ultimately, connecting to a free Wi-Fi network leaves you at risk – because you don't really know who is on the other end of that network.

Presenter: And our final tip – make sure that you use a different password for every website. Just in case you do accidentally log on to a hacker's network.

UNIT 10

▶ Irish

Teacher: [Speaking in Irish]

Presenter: The English ruled Ireland for centuries. At the height of their colonial ambitions, they attempted to suppress Irish culture and identity entirely. An 1831 act forbade the teaching of Irish in schools. This coincided with *an Gorta Mór*, the Irish potato famine of the mid-nineteenth century that killed over a million of the population. It was very nearly the death knell of the Irish language. Thankfully, all that has changed now. The schools that were the site of linguistic oppression in Ireland are now the place of the language's revival. Nowadays, at the Connemara Golf Course every one of the golfers speaks Irish.

Golfers: [Speaking in Irish]

Presenter: As well as negotiating the perilous task of keeping their language alive, they are also dealing with what must be one of the world's hardest courses. The holes are literally on different islands.

Golfers: [Speaking in Irish]

Presenter: This is a heck of a place to have a golf course, isn't it? You must just blink your eyes on it on long June days when you play until ten at night—

Golfer: We do—

Presenter: Imperialist Brit that I am, they're kind enough to speak English to me – which, given the history, is quite an ask. This part of Connemara suffered as much as any, but its utter remoteness helped preserve the language. Oh dear, I think I've lost my moment now. I won't waste any more balls.

These children and their children will always need a global language.

So you just change between the two very happily?

Girl: Yeah.

Presenter: But you think of yourself as an Irish speaker first?

Girl: Yeah.

Presenter: Is that true of everybody?

Schoolchildren: Yeah.

Presenter: Goodness. If you text each other, do you do it in Irish, or in English?

Schoolchildren: English.

Presenter: Ah … that's interesting. So things like the internet or whatever – are you on Facebook and things like that?

Schoolchildren: Yeah.

Presenter: And do you do that in English?

Schoolchildren: Yeah.

Presenter: Ah. So do you think of English as the language of the internet, but Irish the language of the playground and talking and friendship and things when you're with people?

Schoolchildren: Yeah.

Presenter: You couldn't imagine yourselves only speaking Irish?

Schoolchildren: No.

Presenter: You wouldn't be able to cope in the world if you didn't speak English, is that … ? Yeah.

Schoolchildren: Yeah.

Presenter: Thank goodness you do speak English or we would be having an embarrassing time. Well thank you very much. Mustn't disturb any more of your lessons. Thank you. Was that, *go raibh maith*, no … Thank you?

Schoolchildren: *Go raibh maith agat.*

Presenter: *Go raibh maith agat* … See, I can't get the pronunciation right. Thank you very much.

ACKNOWLEDGEMENTS

The authors and publishers acknowledge the following sources of copyright material and are grateful for the permissions granted. While every effort has been made, it has not always been possible to identify the sources of all the material used, or to trace all copyright holders. If any omissions are brought to our notice, we will be happy to include the appropriate acknowledgements on reprinting and in the next update to the digital edition, as applicable.

Key: B = Below, L = Left, R = Right, T = Top.

Text

Graphs on p. 138 from Bureau of Labor Statistics; Graph on p. 140 adapted from Manpower Group '2016/2017 Talent Shortage Survey.' Copyright © Manpower Group. Reproduced with kind permission; Graphs on p. 145 adapted from *Education at a Glance 2016: OECD Indicators*, OECD Publishing, Paris. DOI: http://dx.doi.org/10.1787/eag-2016-en. Copyright © 2016 OECD. Reproduced with kind permission; Chart on p. 151 adapted from 'U.S. skills gaps.' Copyright © Adecco. Reproduced with kind permission; Table on p. 151 adapted from Bureau of Labor Statistics; Graph on p. 151 adapted from 'The Role of Higher Education in Career Development: Employer Perceptions.' Copyright © 2012 The Chronicle of Higher Education. Reproduced with kind permission; Figure on p. 164 adapted from 'Clinical Microbiology Reviews: Challenges of Antibacterial Discovery' by Lynn L. Silver. Copyright © 2011 American Society for Microbiology. Reproduced with permission; Graphs on p. 188 adapted from 'The Too-Much-Talent Effect: Team Interdependence Determines When More Talent Is Too Much or Not Enough' by Roderick I. Swaab, Michael Schaerer, Eric M. Anicich, Richard Ronay, and Adam D. Galinsky. Copyright © SAGE Publications Ltd.

Photos

All images are sourced from Getty Images.

pp. 14–15: Kerem Uzel/Bloomberg; p. 20: adam smigielski/E+; p. 24 (T): Christophe Boisvieux/Corbis Documentary; p. 24 (B): Glen_Pearson/iStock/Getty Images Plus; p. 31: Barry Herman/Arcaid Images; pp. 38–39: Alexander Spatari/Moment; p. 55: Luke Stanton/Moment; pp. 62–63: Bill Hinton Photography/Moment Open; p. 68: Matthew Horwood/Getty Images News; p. 70: Squaredpixels/E+; p. 73: Blackregis/iStock/Getty Images Plus; pp. 86–87: Maica/E+; p. 91: Anton Novoderezhkin/TASS; p. 92: AFP; p. 100: Jupiterimages/Stockbyte; p. 104: Hero Images; pp. 110–111: Jeremy Sutton-Hibbert/Getty Images News; p. 116: Michael Ochs Archives; p. 123: Gary Burchell/DigitalVision; pp. 134–135: Linda Goodhue Photography/Moment; pp. 158–159: Tim Graham/Getty Images News; pp. 182–183: David Madison/Corbis; p. 190: Caiaimage/Sam Edwards/OJO+; p. 194 (photo a): lisa kimberly/Moment; p. 194 (photo b): LuminaStock/iStock/Getty Images Plus; p. 194 (photo c): Cary Wolinsky/Aurora; p. 194 (photo d): Darren Robb/Taxi; pp. 206–207: SERGEI GAPON/AFP; p. 211 (L, R), p. 215: Coneyl Jay/Stone; p. 216: Izabela Habur/iStock/Getty Images Plus; p. 218: Westend61; p. 220: xiajie1980cn/Moment; p. 221 (L): FatCamera/E+; p. 221 (R): kchungtw/iStock/Getty Images Plus; p. 224: Georgijevic/iStock/Getty Images Plus; pp. 230–231: Luis Acosta/AFP/Getty Images; p. 244 (L): Jeff Greenberg/Universal Images Group; p. 244 (R): JHU Sheridan Libraries/Gado/Archive Photos.

Front cover photography by Danuer/iStock/Getty Images Plus

Video Stills

Below stills are sourced from GettyImages.

p. 64, p. 88, p. 160, p. 184: Sky News/Film Image Partner/GettyImages; p. 112 (a): BSPC/Creatas Video/GettyImages; p. 112 (b, d): Barcroft Media – Footage/GettyImages; p. 112 (c): ITN/GettyImages.

The following stills are sourced from other libraries:
p. 16, p. 40, p. 136, p. 208, p. 232: BBC Worldwide Learning;

We are grateful to the following companies for permission to use copyright logos/Images:
p. 44: IKEA; p. 45(T): FedEx; p. 45 (B): World Wildlife Fund; p. 48: NBC; p. 48: Spotify; p. 48: Tropicana; p. 49: BP.

Illustrations

p. 119, p. 133: Oxford Designers & Illustrators.

Videos

Videos supplied by BBC Worldwide Learning and Getty Images.

AFP Footage; Sky News/Film Image Partner; ITN; Press Association; baddoggy/Creatas Video; Barcroft Media – Footage/Barcroft Media Video; BSPC/Creatas Video; Tribune Broadcasting – Anna Burkart; xavierarnau/Creatas Video; Bloomberg Video – Footage/Bloomberg; Slerpy/Creatas Video; footagefactory/Image Bank Film; gorodenkoff/Creatas Video+/Getty Images Plus; serdarcan/Creatas Video+/Getty Images Plus; Tivoli Entertainment LLC/Iconica Video; Hal Bergman/Image Bank Film; vichie81/Creatas Video; Tribune Broadcasting – Kelsey Kind; Easy_Company/Vetta; BBC Worldwide learning.

Corpus

Development of this publication has made use of the Cambridge English Corpus (CEC). The CEC is a multi-billion word computer database of contemporary spoken and written English. It includes British English, American English and other varieties of English. It also includes the Cambridge Learner Corpus, developed in collaboration with the University of Cambridge ESOL Examinations. Cambridge University Press has built up the CEC to provide evidence about language use that helps to produce better language teaching materials.

Cambridge Dictionaries

Cambridge dictionaries are the world's most widely used dictionaries for learners of English. The dictionaries are available in print and online at dictionary.cambridge.org. Copyright © Cambridge University Press, reproduced with permission.

Typeset by emc design ltd.

UNLOCK SECOND EDITION ADVISORY PANEL

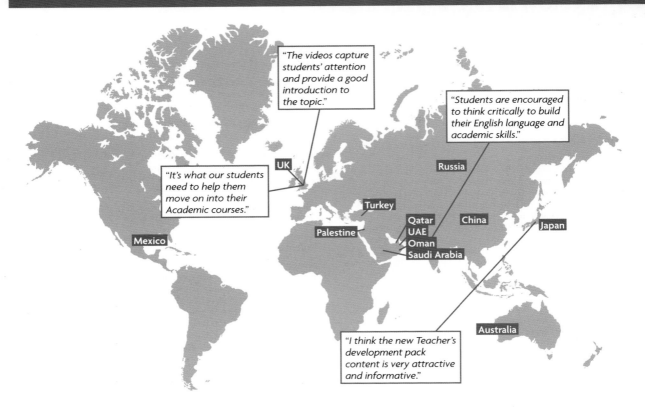

"The videos capture students' attention and provide a good introduction to the topic."

"Students are encouraged to think critically to build their English language and academic skills."

"It's what our students need to help them move on into their Academic courses."

"I think the new Teacher's development pack content is very attractive and informative."

We would like to thank the following ELT professionals all around the world for their support, expertise and input throughout the development of *Unlock* Second Edition:

Adnan Abu Ayyash, Birzeit University, Palestine	Takayuki Hara, Kagoshima University, Japan	Megan Putney, Dhofar University, Oman
Bradley Adrain, University of Queensland, Australia	Esengül Hasdemir, Atilim University, Turkey	Wayne Rimmer, United Kingdom
Sarah Ali, Nottingham Trent International College (NTIC), United Kingdom	Irina Idilova, Moscow Institute of Physics and Technology, Russia	Sana Salam, TED University, Turkey
Ana Maria Astiazaran, Colegio Regis La Salle, Mexico	Meena Inguva, Sultan Qaboos University, Oman	Setenay Şekercioglu, Işık University, Turkey
Asmaa Awad, University of Sharjah, United Arab Emirates	Vasilios Konstantinidis, Prince Sultan University, Kingdom of Saudi Arabia	Robert B. Staehlin, Morioka University, Japan
Jesse Balanyk, Zayed University, United Arab Emirates	Andrew Leichsenring, Tamagawa University, Japan	Yizhi Tang, Xueersi English, TAL Group, China
Lenise Butler, Universidad del Valle de México, Mexico	Alexsandra Minic, Modern College of Business and Science, Oman	Valeria Thomson, Muscat College, Oman
Esin Çağlayan, Izmir University of Economics, Turkey	Daniel Newbury, Fuji University, Japan	Amira Traish, University of Sharjah, United Arab Emirates
Matthew Carey, Qatar University, Qatar	Güliz Özgürel, Yaşar University, Turkey	Poh Leng Wendelkin, INTO London, United Kingdom
Eileen Dickens, Universidad de las Américas, Mexico	Özlem Perks, Istanbul Ticaret University, Turkey	Yoee Yang, The Affiliated High School of SCNU, China
Mireille Bassam Farah, United Arab Emirates	Claudia Piccoli, Harmon Hall, Mexico	Rola Youhia, University of Adelaide College, Australia
Adriana Ghoul, Arab American University, Palestine	Tom Pritchard, University of Edinburgh, United Kingdom	Long Zhao, Xueersi English, TAL Group, China
Burçin Gönülsen, Işık University, Turkey		